The Heart of Black Preaching

The Heart of Black Preaching

Cleophus J. LaRue

Westminster John Knox Press
Louisville, Kentucky

Book design by Sharon Adams
Cover design by Pam Poll
Cover art: The Congregation, *1990, Oil on Canvas, 72″ × 55″,*
by Jonathan Green, Naples, Florida. Collection of Julia J. Norrell

First edition
Published by Westminster John Knox Press
Louisville, Kentucky

This book is printed on acid-free paper that meets the American National
Standards Institute Z39.48 standard. ∞

PRINTED IN THE UNITED STATES OF AMERICA

00 01 02 03 04 05 06 07 08 09 — 10 9 8 7 6 5 4 3 2

Library of Congress Cataloging-in-Publication Data

LaRue, Cleophus James, 1953–
    The heart of black preaching / Cleophus J. LaRue
        p.   cm.
    Includes bibliographical references and index.
    ISBN 0-664-25847-6 (alk. paper)
    1. Afro-American preaching.   2. Sermons, American—Afro-American
    authors.   I. Title.

BV4208.U6.L37 1999
251'.0089'96073—dc21

                                                                99-043131

✳ ✳ ✳ ✳ ✳

In Loving Memory of the Reverends

Henry Clay Dilworth, Jr.

Abraham Lincoln Randon

and

Paschal Sampson Wilkinson, Sr.

"Good and faithful servants"

✳ ✳ ✳ ✳ ✳

CONTENTS

viii ℞ Contents

ACKNOWLEDGMENTS

This book is the product of the many sociocultural experiences that gave shape and substance to my life and preaching ministry. While it is not possible to name all those who were instrumental in bringing it to completion, expressions of gratitude are due the following people:

President **Thomas W. Gillespie** for granting me a yearlong sabbatical and a generous faculty research grant, both of which proved of inestimable value in the completion of this work.

Thomas G. Long, my teacher, mentor, colleague, and friend. He was indispensable to this work from its embryonic stage to its final book form.

Stephanie Egnotovich, my editor at Westminster John Knox, who made this a better book through her expertise and insightful comments.

James F. Kay and **Leonora Tubbs Tisdale,** my colleagues in preaching on the Princeton Seminary faculty. From them I received helpful advice and constant encouragement.

Peter J. Paris and **Geddes W. Hanson,** who mentored me as only African American fathers can do for their own; and Brian K. Blount, colleague and friend. They were generous with their time and most supportive in their comments and counsel.

Richard Weis and **Warren Dennis,** former colleagues at New Brunswick Theological Seminary and early supporters of the completion of this work.

Camille Jones, my able and untiring research assistant; and staff secretary, Judith Attride.

True Light and **Toliver Chapel Baptist Churches,** my former Texas pastorates.

Gardner C. Taylor, S. Howard Woodson, Jr., Gary V. Simpson, and **Frederick Ennette,** my East Coast pastors.

Stephen W. Ramp and **Scott Black Johnston,** Princeton friends and esteemed homileticians in their own right.

Sondra Booze-Bailey, Jerry M. Carter, Donnie Garris, James R. Miller, and **Willie Mae Nanton** for their prayers and friendship.

To my parents, **Tommie and Cleophus LaRue, Sr.;** and my sisters **Linda Ruth Jackson, Arlena Faye Morrow,** and their spouses for their unconditional love and support.

To my daughter, **Coryell,** who has been and remains dearer than life to me.

x   ❧   Acknowledgments

Finally, this book had its beginning in the pews of the Calvary First Baptist Church in Corpus Christi, Texas. It was there I first came to love and appreciate the preached word as it was proclaimed through the ministry of the pastor of my youth, the late Rev. Henry Clay Dilworth, Jr., I thank God for his excellent example and his constant admonitions on "the making of the preacher." This book is dedicated to Rev. Dilworth and also to Abraham Lincoln Randon and Paschal Sampson Wilkinson, Sr.—the three stalwart preachers of my formative years. They were men of great wisdom and courage. I hope this work attests in some small way to the fruits of their labor, but more importantly to the power and saving grace of the One in whose name we preach.

Cleophus J. LaRue
Princeton Theological Seminary
Princeton, New Jersey

Introduction

Many people—preachers, homileticians, and lay folk—praise black preaching. They admire its vitality, relevance, and communicational effectiveness. But what is it about African American preaching that makes it so distinctive and worthy of regard? Some have pointed to the high place of scripture in the African American tradition, others to the black preacher's creative use of language and storytelling, and still others to the free play of emotion and celebration in the preaching event or to communication techniques such as call-and-response.

However, none of these traits is the exclusive property of black preachers. All of them can be found to some degree outside the African American preaching tradition, and none of them fully accounts for the extraordinary character of black preaching. They are important qualities, to be sure, but the reason for the distinctive power of black preaching lies deeper, resting finally in the soul of black Christian experience, that is, in the way that African Americans have come, in the refining fires of history, to understand the character of God and the ways God works through scripture and sermon in their lives today.

In essence, the distinctive power of black preaching is a matter, not merely of special techniques but of extraordinary experiences that have, among other results, forged a unique way of understanding the Bible and applying those insights in very practical ways. The purpose of this book is to show that there is in powerful black preaching a distinctive, biblical hermeneutic that when identified and understood can provide meaningful insights into the preaching that commonly occurs in the traditional black religious experience.

When one considers the historical conditions under which blacks embraced Christianity it is easy to see how their sociocultural experiences would have a profound effect on their understanding of who God is and how God works out God's meaning and purpose in their lives. Consequently, it would seem reasonable to conclude that the distinctive power of black preaching is derived from a way of perceiving God that both affects and is affected by their particular reading of scripture based on their experiences. It is not that blacks have such a vastly different theology or denominational polity from their white counterparts that makes their preaching different. The structure of belief for black Christians is the same orthodox beliefs of white Christians. Blacks have equally drawn upon the rich Christian heritage handed down through the centuries to the Christian church.

Where black preaching differs from traditional understandings of the faith is in its interpretation of the witness of scripture in light of blacks' historical and contemporary experiences. As to a peculiarly black perspective on scripture, Miles Jones has rightly concluded that it is not so much what happened to black people that is important, since something has happened to all people. Rather, "it is how blacks interpret those happenings in light of what has been revealed in and through the Word of God."[1] It is in that vital interpretive encounter between scripture and the struggles of the marginalized that the search for distinctiveness in black preaching should begin.

Chapter 1 will probe the origins of a distinctly black construal of scripture by examining the historical conditions under which blacks embraced the Christian religion and by analyzing the manner in which they used scripture to address their marginalized status.[2] Such an examination will show that the distinctive power of black preaching is tied directly to what blacks believe about God's proactive intervention and involvement in their experiences. As a result of their historical marginalization and struggle, what became most important to blacks in their encounters with Euro-American Christianity was not dogma or abstract theological reflection, but an intimate relationship with a powerful God who demonstrated throughout scripture a propensity to side with the downtrodden.

A central truth blacks quickly came to embrace when they were allowed to read and interpret scripture for themselves is that scripture revealed a God of infinite power who could be trusted to act mightily on their behalf. Historically blacks embraced the Christian God in large numbers only after they were able to make a connection between God's power and their servile situation in life.[3] This direct relationship between black struggle and divine rescue colors the theological perceptions and themes of black preaching in a very decisive manner, particularly in those churches closest to the experience of marginalization.

This particular way of understanding what is important and meaningful about scripture on the basis of a people's sociocultural experiences over time became a way of construing and using all of scripture. A marginalized people's constant seeing in scripture a God who is ever present and ever able has become such an established belief in the life experiences of blacks that it functions at the level of "sacred story."[4] Sacred stories are stories that lie too deep in the consciousness of a people to be directly told. They form consciousness rather than being among the objects of which consciousness is directly aware. What blacks believe the scriptures reveal about the power of God on their behalf operates at this level. It is for them a way of being in the world, a way of looking at life that over a period of time constitutes their reality.

A God who is unquestionably for them is what blacks see when they go to the scriptures. Thus the distinctive power of black preaching is to be found, first and foremost, in that which blacks believe scripture reveals about the sovereign God's involvement in the everyday affairs and circumstances of their marginalized existence. African Americans believe the sovereign God acts in very concrete and practical ways in matters pertaining to their survival, deliverance, advancement, prosperity, and overall well-being.[5]

This belief is foundational to an understanding of the genuineness and authenticity that comes through in the best of black preaching. This way of construing scripture is so ensconced in their sacred story that oftentimes it gets subsumed under the ancillary characteristics of language, emotion, authority, and celebration—characteristics that are in reality the expressive by-products of their gut-level belief in the mighty acts of the sovereign God.

To understand the power of black preaching in this most profound sense it is necessary to identify and describe this deeply embedded biblical hermeneutic that is at the heart of their sacred story and serves as the template that governs their interpretation of scripture. Is it plausible to suggest that the sociocultural experiences of African Americans could cause them to see in scripture a certain pattern that is so markedly different from the way other Christian communities view scripture? Is there not a normative understanding of scripture to which even marginalized blacks must be held accountable?

David Kelsey's claim that individual faith communities interpret scripture in different ways supports my discovery of a distinctly black construal of scripture. In *The Uses of Scripture in Recent Theology*[6] Kelsey argued that all faith communities have some master interpretive lens that guides their interpretation and use of scripture. He contends that our decisions about how to interpret texts are not made on the basis of some normative understanding of scripture, but on a prior decision, based on our social location, in which we try to gather together in one single judgment what Christianity is all about. What we perceive to be the most important aspect of Christianity is the key factor that determines how we construe and use scripture.[7]

Kelsey's point—how a faith community's understanding of the essence of Christianity becomes the lens through which it views all of scripture—supports my claim of a distinctly black biblical hermeneutic at two points. First, it dismisses any notion of a normative understanding of scripture and validates different uses of scripture on the basis of different understandings of the essence of Christianity.

Second, it reinforces my claim that the power of black preaching is not uniquely derivative of style or technique but of how blacks perceive God as a result of their experiences and their interpretation of scripture based on those experiences. The manner in which blacks believe God to be present on their behalf and their absolute certainty that this is what God is about when they interpret scripture is a belief so firmly grounded in black religious life that it indeed becomes the template for how blacks understand all of scripture.

In chapter 2 I show this interpretive lens at work in the preaching of five nineteenth-century African American ministers—John Jasper, Alexander Crummell, Francis Grimké, Daniel Payne, and Elias Morris. Born during slavery, they were roughly contemporaries who preached to a wide array of black and white gatherings in the North and South in post–Civil War America. Though differing in regional, educational, and denominational affiliations, all were shaped by the same sociocultural experience of marginalization and powerlessness that affected the whole of the black race. Thus one finds in their preaching the biblical hermeneutic that is at the heart of powerful black preaching.

The search for this hermeneutic begins in the post–Civil War era since many authorities regard it as the time when African American preaching first came into its most visible expression. In this dynamic postslavery era, African American preaching shed its invisible, guarded status, rose to the challenges of the day, and publicly flourished throughout the nation.[8]

Issues of struggle and survival change through the years for blacks, but this fundamental way of viewing God's involvement in those issues does not. In the interest of demonstrating an ongoing continuity in the manner in which blacks develop their sermons, in chapter 3 I show how this hermeneutic continues to shape and inform black preaching through an analysis of the sermons of six contemporary African American preachers: Jeremiah A. Wright, Jr., Katie G. Cannon, A. Louis Patterson, Jr., Mozella Mitchell, Fred C. Lofton, and Carolyn Ann Knight. Reflecting a cross section of regional and denominational affiliations, they preach regularly to the black masses struggling to survive the challenges of modern day life.

Popular among black and white gatherings alike, they conduct their preaching and teaching ministries in large urban centers where black marginalization and struggle are most apparent, most openly expressed, and most intensely felt.[9] I use these contemporary sermons to describe the characteristics and inner dynamics involved in the crafting of a black sermon. In so doing I hope to bring to conscious formation what seasoned black preachers do by second nature, that is, find out where God or divine initiative is in the text, note the nature of God's involvement in and through the text, make a concrete connection between God's presence and the lives of the listening congregation, and then demonstrate with creativity and keen insight the manner in which God's power is used on behalf of the people of faith.

If, in fact, the power of black preaching lies preeminently in belief and content and not in style or technique, then the homiletical implications of this type of preaching must also center around what blacks believe about God, scripture, and the life situations of those who hear black preaching on a consistent basis. Chapter 4 involves a discussion of several components that must be factored into the preparation process when attempting to preach an effective sermon in the traditional black religious experience. The first component centers on a belief in the God about which blacks preach. One must have a knowledge of and experience with the sovereign God who acts mightily on behalf of the powerless and oppressed. The preaching that flows from this belief is not learned but lived.

An all-powerful God continues to be a precious attribute for a majority of those who constitute the African American faith community, and there is no doubt in their minds that this mighty sovereign is able to save. The God of the black church is conceived by the black religious tradition as being a responsive personal being with unquestioned, and unlimited, absolute power.[10] Marginalized blacks have historically believed that a God who does not care does not count. Thus, a mighty God who takes up the cause of dispossessed African Americans is the major premise that undergirds powerful black preaching. Those who seek to benefit from this kind of preaching must have an unshakable faith in this God of the scriptures.

The second component is the importance of the black sociocultural experience to the preaching event. As is true of other faith communities, the biblical hermeneutic that blacks ascribe to scripture is determined by the ways in which they have experienced God and scripture in their faith community. The African American understanding of God grows out of the unique social situation in which blacks find themselves in America. This assertion must not be understated and is crucial to understanding what prompts, motivates, shapes, and gives life to black preaching. Those who desire to learn how to craft a black sermon cannot be taught some sterile, all-purpose homiletic devoid of any reference to or knowledge of the black sociocultural experience and its ongoing impact on the black situation in life. It is out of this experience that blacks search for, comprehend, and ultimately find meaning in God and in all things religious.

Many of black preaching's most imaginative and creative insights are gained from the preachers' social location on the boundary of the dominant culture, a boundary that provides them with creative perspectives often unavailable to those standing in the center of power.[11] To preach black, then, is to preach out of an awareness of the issues and concerns of life with which blacks struggle and contend daily. The black sermon at its best arises out of the totality of the people's existence—their pain and joy, trouble and ecstasy.[12]

The third component of this kind of preaching is that it is practical and relevant to a broad spectrum of black existence. Because of the harsh and pressing concerns of the sociocultural experience of blacks, the black quest for God has been based on the immediate hopes and aspirations of an oppressed community. Of longstanding there has been a crucial relevancy in black preaching that makes this style of proclamation vibrant, practical, and straightway applicable to a whole range of critical situations. Black preaching reflects the black belief that a personal God is involved in every aspect of human existence in very concrete and tangible ways. There is little or no distinction between the sacred and the secular in black life. Consequently, there are no areas of black life that are off limits to the gospel and no avenues of human experience where black preaching fears to tread. All realms of black life are eventually exposed to the probing searchlight of the gospel.

Black preaching addresses concerns that center on personal piety, care of the soul, and matters pertaining to the inner workings of the institutional church. It also speaks to God's active involvement in matters of social justice and racial corporate concerns. An understanding of how these domains of concrete experience find expression in black preaching can greatly assist preachers in learning how to preach to the many and varied life situations in which blacks find themselves.

In summary, powerful black preaching has at its center a biblical hermeneutic that views God as a powerful sovereign acting mightily on behalf of dispossessed and marginalized people. A belief in this God, an awareness of the sociocultural context of the black experience, and the creation of a sermon that speaks in a relevant and practical manner to the common domains of experience in black life, when taken together, ultimately result in a powerful sermon that resonates in a potent and meaningful way with those in the listening congregation.

This book seeks to provide a clearer understanding of the fundamentals of African American preaching. Though the search is at times elusive, it is nonetheless necessary. Our inability to name the basics of black preaching makes it difficult, if not impossible, to teach systematically the dynamics of this style to those who stand within as well as outside the tradition. Moreover, increasing numbers of African American students, especially those attending predominantly white seminaries, are beginning to insist on homileticians who are sensitive and knowledgeable about the inner dynamics—hermeneutics, context, content, and form—of the African American sermon. While many blacks come to seminary with some experience in preaching, their ability to function competently in this style is based primarily on their imitation of the masters. That is, they copy the sermonic techniques of accomplished preachers whom they have come to admire and respect in their formative, preseminary years.

Imitation of the masters is not necessarily bad, and it is not the sole reserve of blacks. For centuries it was how most priests and ministers learned to preach. But when imitation is all one has to draw on, it produces preachers who, by and large, know what to do but not necessarily why they do it or how to improve it. Also, where rote learning plays a significant role there tends to be an emphasis on style to the neglect of substance. Among African Americans this dilemma is due, in part, to the fact that few black homiletical theories allow them to reflect on their tradition in a critical and creative manner with an eye toward better understanding what they have already learned through imitation and improvisation.

The rewards of discovering, in a more systematic fashion, the foundational features and inner dynamics of black preaching are promising indeed. A more in-depth understanding of this preaching style could be quite fruitful for young seminarians trying to develop the knack for crafting the black sermon; for seasoned pastors who've grown bored with a weekly task that has become trite and mundane; and for preachers who stand outside the tradition, wondering what, if any, features of this style are transferable to their own ways of preaching. This work seeks to identify and describe this well-established hermeneutic at the heart of black preaching and the derivative components that continue to shape and mold this powerful style of proclamation.

1

The Search for Distinctiveness in Black Preaching

What is African American preaching? How do we express the fundamental components of this style of proclamation? Most who have studied black preaching would agree there is no one methodology, style, or expression that constitutes the definitive form of African American preaching. Few, if any, African Americans would claim there is a single style of preaching that is faithful to all it means to be African American and that is appropriate for all its churches. With the inclusion of white religious bodies with significant African American memberships, blacks belong to over two hundred denominations in the United States alone.[1]

In many instances, the only connecting link African Americans have with one another in these multiple denominations is color and race. Thus the term "black preaching" describes a rich and varied tradition, covering a broad configuration of motivations, theological points of view, art forms, structures, and styles of delivery. At first glance, the very breadth, diversity, and complexity of this tradition would seem to hamper the search to identify common methods and dynamics. On closer inspection, however, one can detect an integrative force, a common thread running throughout this style of proclamation that clearly provides its spirit and raison d'être, namely, a distinctive biblical hermeneutic.

CHARACTERISTICS OF BLACK PREACHING

Strong Biblical Content

The search for distinctiveness in black preaching can at times appear to be an endless quest. Some have maintained that what sets the African American sermon apart is its strong biblical content, a product of the high regard African Americans continue to have for the scriptures. In many black churches, biblical preaching, defined as preaching that allows a text from the Bible to serve as the leading force in shaping the content and purpose of the sermon, is the type of preaching considered to be most faithful to traditional understandings of the proclaimed word.

Indeed, it is no secret that the Bible occupies a central place in the religious life of black Americans. More than a mere source for texts, in black preaching the Bible is the single most important source of language, imagery, and story for the sermon. Though biblical literacy in black churches is greatly diminished from earlier years, it has yet to reach the state where the Bible's primacy as a rich resource for black preaching is no longer the case. Depicted in the Bible are the experiences of many black people from slavery to contemporary times. Consequently, knowledge of the Bible, along with the ability to apply Bible verses to every phase of life, are indeed regarded by many African American preachers as crucial ingredients in effective preaching.[2]

Creative Uses of Language

Others have argued that creative uses of language provide African American preaching with its distinguishing feature. To an extent, this is true. Many black preachers seem to possess a genius for the melody of words and the details of scene. Henry Mitchell has noted the enthusiastic response of African American congregations to beautiful language and well-turned phrases.[3] The traditional black church expects and appreciates rhetorical flair and highly poetic language in the preaching of the gospel.

There is little fear in black pulpits of being accused of "pretty preaching." In fact, seasoned pastors from an earlier generation could often be heard admonishing younger ministers not to be afraid "to preach a little." Such encouragements were intended to free the poet in the preacher and allow the presence of God through the power of language to lift the sermon to higher heights. To this end, the employment of literary devices such as antiphonality, repetition, alliteration, syncopation, oral formulas, thematic imagery, voice merging, and sacred time continues to be a compelling concern of the African American preacher.[4] Such rhetorical tools in the hands of a skillful black preacher can evoke a sense of God's awe and mystery in the listening congregation.

Unlike many European and mainline American denominations, where architecture and classical music inspire a sense of the holy, blacks seek to accomplish this act through the display of well-crafted rhetoric. The listening ear becomes the privileged sensual organ as the preacher attempts through careful and precise rhetoric to embody the Word.[5] For this reason, the rhythm, cadence, and sound of words as well as their ability to "paint a picture" in the minds of the hearers are very important in the African

American sermon. The black preacher's careful search for the precise words and phrases are continuing evidence of the importance of rhetoric and the modest circumstances that originally gave it a place of primacy in the black sermon.[6]

Appeal to Emotions

Still others have argued that appeal to the emotions is the distinctive feature in African American preaching. At the turn of the century, W. E. B. DuBois described "the Preacher, the Music, and the Frenzy," as the three distinct, historical characteristics of the black worship experience:

> The frenzy or "Shouting," when the Spirit of the Lord passed by, and, seizing the devotee, made him mad with supernatural joy, was the last essential of Negro religion and the one more devoutly believed in than all the rest.[7]

This unabashed, emotional fervor, of which DuBois wrote nearly a century ago, continues to impact both the preaching of the sermon and the response of the worshiping community. The highly charged nature of the black worship experience is most commonly associated with the antiphonal call-and-response ritual that the preacher and congregation engage in during the sermon. Many black preachers, contemplating the audible participation of those in the pew, intentionally slow their cadences, time their pauses, and chant or semichant their phrases in a most adept and deliberate manner.[8] Their timed delivery is structured to meet the requirements of the old adage:

> *Start slow,*
> *rise high,*
> *strike fire.*
> *Sit down in a storm.*

Such affective (emotional) preaching and the vocal response it evokes from the listeners has traditionally met with stiff resistance among learned African Americans as pyrotechnics of the worst sort. The charge of histrionics notwithstanding, it has never lost its appeal among the commoners of the folk tradition. Criticized by African American intellectuals in the first half of the century as lacking logical organization and requiring little preparation, affective preaching and participant proclamation enjoyed a resurgence of interest even among intellectuals in the 1960s and 1970s.[9]

Ministerial Authority

Still others who have studied African American preaching have sought to account for its distinctiveness through the presence and power of the preacher. Typically, African American congregations view their preachers as special representatives of God, or, even more, as manifestations of the divine presence and thus worthy of great reverence and admiration. Black congregations tend to bestow great authority upon their preachers, and their preachers, in turn, feel a certain freedom to say and do what they wish while preaching the gospel. Some claim that much of the creative genius heard in black preaching is directly attributable to this longstanding freedom and pulpit autonomy.

This authority, however, does not arise automatically but must be earned by the preacher through earnest and effective preaching as well as through meaningful association with the "folks" over a period of time. When the preacher becomes confident of this authority, he or she then enjoys a certain license in the preaching event that allows the preacher to engage in a creative, thought-provoking exchange between the text, the congregation, and the preacher. The preacher, sensing unrestricted access, soars to unparalleled heights in his or her effort "to make it plain," that is, to preach the gospel in such a way that the hearers both understand and identify the good news as a word fittingly spoken to them.

This notion of authority originated prior to the transtlantic slave trade in Africa where the priests and medicine men, because of the importance ascribed to their offices, were accorded a high degree of admiration and respect. The responsibilities of those priests and medicine men were transferred in some measure to the slave preachers in the new world.[10]

Additional Characteristics

While strong biblical content, the creative uses of language, emotion, and ministerial authority are the characteristics commonly associated with black preaching, in recent years contemporary scholars have sought to describe additional broadly based characteristics at a more systematic level of reflection. Henry Mitchell argued for distinctiveness in the emotive/celebrative encounter between preacher and pew that has historically characterized the black religious experience. Thus he tended to emphasize the celebrative aspects of black preaching and an appropriate homiletic for creating such an atmosphere in the worship setting.[11] James Earl Massey, in *The Responsible Pulpit*, viewed the African American sermon as functional, festive, communal, radical, and climactic. When these five traits were present, Massey believed a distinctive black preaching style was usually noticeable.[12]

Gerald L. Davis, in *I Got the Word in Me and I Can Sing It, You Know*, explained the genius of black preaching through the expressive devices and techniques of the "performed" African American sermon. He focused on oral formulas, metrical patterns, and organizing principles of folk narrative methodologies. As a folklorist primarily interested in the structural complexities of language, Davis was more concerned with the sermon as "finished product" than with the hermeneutical dynamics involved in its initial creation and organization.[13]

William B. McClain, in *Come Sunday: The Liturgy of Zion*, considered preaching to be central to the authentic black worship experience and sensed the beginnings of a qualitative difference in black preaching's passionate words and vivid imagery for a disillusioned and disinherited people.[14] Evans Crawford, in *The Hum: Call and Response in African American Preaching*, explained the creativity of black preaching through "homiletical musicality," that is, the manner in which the black preacher uses timing, pause, inflection, pace, and other musical qualities of speech in the sermon's delivery to awaken in the hearers a sense of wonder and thanksgiving toward God.[15]

These recent studies, along with the more traditional characteristics of the black sermon, point to valid aspects of black preaching and make valuable contributions to the field. None, however, has sought to understand what is distinctive about this style of preaching at its most fundamental level, namely, the interpretive process that drives the creation and organization of the content of the sermon. Few who have heard black preaching at its best could deny that a creative mixture and mastery of the aforementioned traits characterize African American preaching.

The problem is that highlighting these traits as foundational properties of black preaching is merely describing characteristics of a process already in motion. It is equivalent to pointing out certain features of a train that has already left the station, without being able to cite to interested observers its point of origination, the fuel that drives its engine, or how it came about that the train is made up of cars that readily identify it. While an exhaustive study of the multifaceted complexity of black preaching is beyond the scope of this work, I do intend to describe the fundamental hermeneutical strategy I believe lends itself to distinctiveness in this style of preaching.

SCRIPTURE AND LIFE EXPERIENCES

To get at the heart of black preaching, one has to understand the interconnectedness between scriptural texts and African American life experiences. While it is true that most black theologizing takes place in the pulpit,[16] it is also true that a certain type of experiential brooding occurs in the embryonic stage of the sermon prior to the actual exegesis of the text. This deliberate, subliminal musing is an essential ingredient in the creation of the black sermon. Since scripture is never interpreted in a vacuum, scripture and the life experiences of blacks always stand in a figure/ground relationship to one another. Scripture and experience interact and play off one another, each impacting the other in a complex interweaving that is difficult to trace and even more difficult to unravel. The primary question that enables us to get at this rudimentary understanding of black preaching may be posed in the following manner: How does the exposition of scripture and the life experiences of blacks encounter, inform, and affect one another in the black preaching event? This question allows us to begin our basic hermeneutical search for distinctiveness by inquiring into the two essential departure points for black preaching: (1) the content of black sociocultural experience, and (2) how that content impacts the sense in which God is believed to be present in and through scripture.

The black church was born in slavery. Thus black preaching originated in a context of marginalization and struggle, and it is to this context that it still seeks to be relevant. It is the interaction of marginalized black experience and biblical interpretation that enables blacks to confront biblical texts in a compelling and creative manner.[17] James Evans argues persuasively that this unique African American sociocultural context of marginalization and struggle is central to the manner in which blacks conceptualize what is important about the gospel:

> Since the first Africans set foot on this soil, people of African descent have had a singularly unique experience in the New World. They brought with them an inherent philosophical heritage, including a distinctive religious sensibility; they encountered the most brutal form of slavery in human history; and they were introduced to north Atlantic Christianity. Because there was no precedent for the experience of people of African descent, they created distinctive ways of conceptualizing and speaking about their ultimate concerns.[18]

Without question, African American preachers, as well as their primary listeners, live in a society that has rejected, debased, and discriminated against them and continues to do so.[19] This context inevitably colors their perception of the Christian gospel and redefines their understanding of its essence in a way that only oppressed people can fully comprehend. Thus an understanding of the content of the black sociocultural context is a critical component in the search for distinctiveness in black preaching.

The second essential departure point for African American preaching is the manner in which blacks understand and use scripture to address their sociocultural context. Blacks, like all other groups, approach the scriptures having been shaped by the experiences of their environment. As a direct result of their struggle against oppression, blacks have historically derived from scripture a central truth that there is a God of infinite power who can be trusted to act mightily on their behalf. This understanding comes out of almost four centuries of oppression and struggle.

From their initial embrace of the Christian religion to the present day, blacks tend to believe the scriptures demonstrate God's mighty actions on behalf of marginalized and powerless people. Biblical narratives, with their intriguing plots and colorful characters, have been the primary vehicles for identifying and describing this power. But while narratives may be a primary choice of blacks, it is not their only choice in scripture. There is much black preaching that is neither drawn from narrative in scripture nor takes narrative form in sermon. Blacks are drawn to biblical narratives as well as other genres of scripture because of what the scriptures say about God and God's power. Their life situations determine what blacks find redemptive in the scriptures, as opposed to some genre-specific partiality.

The biblical stories and scriptural passages that have historically found their way into black preaching are those that have clearly demonstrated the mighty acts of God on behalf of people who were in situations of powerlessness consistent with, though not the same as, those of the forcibly displaced Africans in America.[20] Stories, as well as other passages of scripture, that speak of the mighty acts of God on behalf of the marginalized initially attracted blacks to the God of the Christian religion during the days of slavery. Blacks embraced this God by the thousands in the eighteenth and nineteenth centuries after hearing the good news of God's promise of salvation from sin and death, but also after hearing of what God had done for the oppressed in biblical times.[21] God was understood as identifying with their struggle in a most literal manner. Thus, what became important for blacks was the telling and retelling, the hearing and rehearing of biblical stories—stories that told of perseverance, of strength in weakness, and of hope in hopeless situations.[22]

Likewise, stories or passages of scripture that sent an unclear message or seemed to show God tolerating oppression, or not acting in a consistent fashion to obliterate some blight upon the marginalized were seldom preached by blacks (e.g., recalcitrant Egyptian pharaohs in the Old Testament, the Onesimus slave story in the New Testament, as well as other Pauline passages that appeared to condone slavery.)[23] When suspect passages were preached by blacks they were declared, in many instances, to be inconsistent with the overall intention and actions of God. For example, J. W. C. Pennington, a black proabolitionist pastor, insisting that slavery was incompatible with the Christian gospel, made no effort in his preaching to justify or incorporate scriptures that seemed to support slavery. In fact, he was prepared to reject the Bible in its entirety if God's word had no relevant answer for his enslaved black race:

> Is the word of God silent on this subject? I, for one, desire to
> know. My repentance, my faith, my hope, my love, and my

perseverance all, all, I conceal it not, I repeat it, all turn upon
this point. If I am deceived here—if the word of God does sanc-
tion slavery, I want another book, another repentance, another
faith, and another hope.[24]

A God who sanctions slavery violates a fundamental belief in the black
religious experience about God's nature and God's willful acts on behalf of
the marginalized and powerless. Pennington, so deeply convinced that his
God was antislavery, was prepared to repudiate not only certain portions
of scripture but all of Christianity. Such convictions were not uncommon
among those who staked their hopes on a God whom they trusted implicitly to act on their behalf. Stories and other portions of scripture that res-
onated with their experience of oppression and suffering were heartily embraced by blacks as they sought to make meaning of their servile plight
and to know better this God who claimed to have the power to make their
situation better.

Taken together, these two points of departure—the content of the sociocultural context and the sense in which God is believed to be present in
and through scripture—constitute a distinct interpretive key that blacks
find meaningful in the creation and organization of their sermons. This
historical, formative hermeneutic of a God who acts mightily on behalf of
the marginalized and oppressed is the central template blacks bring to
scripture in preparation for preaching. It has been, and remains to this day,
the defining, distinctive factor in African American proclamation.

A COMMUNAL INTERPRETIVE STRATEGY

Blacks persistently view scripture in a certain way, so persistently in fact
that it becomes the template through which they view all scripture. Their
ability to see a certain pattern places them in the company of other peoples of faith who are drawn to certain aspects of scripture and come in time
to view their particular understanding as representative of the whole.
David Kelsey's work on biblical hermeneutics is most helpful in enabling
us to see this critical component in scriptural interpretation, namely, the
dynamics involved in how and why a community of faith comes to view
scripture in a certain way and not another. In *The Uses of Scripture in Recent Theology*, Kelsey makes two very important foundational interpretive
claims. First, he argues that every faith community brings its own particular template or master lens to scriptural interpretation. Second, he claims
that our decisions about how to construe scripture are not based solely on
a close study of biblical texts but on a prior decision in which we imagi-
natively try to grasp the essence of Christianity.

Kelsey establishes his first claim that individual faith communities bring
their own formative hermeneutic to scripture by pointing out the various

patterns theologians claim to be authoritative in scripture. His thesis posits that in actual practice there is no single, standard concept of scripture. According to Kelsey, scripture is not something objective that different theologians simply use differently. In actual practice it is concretely construed in irreducibly different ways.[25] Kelsey claims there are a variety of ways in which theologians understand scripture's function in the actual practice of theology. He argues his thesis through seven case studies of how the various theologians use particular biblical writings. His cases are drawn from the writings of seven Protestant theologians: Karl Barth, Hans-Werner Bartsch, Rudolf Bultmann, L. S. Thornton, Paul Tillich, B. B. Warfield, and G. E. Wright.

The point Kelsey makes through this study is that scripture is construed in a variety of different ways in order to authorize theological proposals. Put another way: Theologians do not appeal to scripture-as-such to help authorize their theological proposals. In the concrete practice of theology, they choose some aspect or, more exactly, some pattern in scripture to which to appeal:

> Not the text as such, but the text-construed-as-a-certain-kind-of-whole is appealed to. What it means, then to call the text "scripture" varies with the kind of "wholeness" ascribed to it in the concrete decision about which pattern is to be appealed to.[26]

Different theologians decide on different aspects or patterns to appeal to in scripture. They then ascribe a certain wholeness to this pattern in scripture and claim it as authoritative for their theological proposals. Each theologian has a particular construal of scripture authorizing specific theological proposals that in turn claim scripture as their authority.

Having demonstrated that theologians understand and use the concept of scripture in different ways, Kelsey takes up the more fundamental matter of how we actually go about deciding which scriptures or patterns in scripture are more meaningful to us than others. In this portion of the argument, Kelsey develops his all important concept of a *discrimen*,[27] by which he means a distinguishing pattern that guides scriptural use in specific faith communities. Kelsey claims that our decisions about how to construe and use scripture are not made solely on the basis of a close study of biblical texts but on the basis of a prior decision in which we try to gather together in a single, synoptic judgment what Christianity is all about. What one takes as the essence of Christianity is the key factor to one's later decision about how to construe and use scripture.

Kelsey does not leave this all important essence-of-Christianity question to mere whim; if Christianity could mean anything to anyone, it could just as well mean nothing to everyone. But neither does Kelsey accept the idea of a universal or immutable norm for theological reflection. Rather, he understands theological reflection as guided by a *discrimen*, a more flexible standard than an absolute norm, allowing some flexibility of range and perspective. He defines the components of a *discrimen* as a configuration of criteria that are in some way organically related to one another as reciprocal coefficients.[28] The coefficients that constitute the *discrimen* that guides the theological reflection for the theologians in Kelsey's study are basically the same: the conjunction of certain uses of scripture and the presence of God. Some understanding of how these two coefficients are related to one another constitutes the *discrimen* that, in turn, guides theological reflection that determines what the essence of Christianity is for us.

While his argument is rather dense and abstract at this point, Kelsey has rightly concluded that when one attends to the specific characteristics of individual theological positions, one sees that each differs from all the others in its judgment about how to characterize the *discrimen*, that is, how to characterize the distinguishing pattern formed out of the conjoining of scripture and God's presence among the faithful. The judgment about the *discrimen* is a complex matter, challenging one to capture it in all its intricacy. This, according to Kelsey, calls for an act of imagination, not recourse to a universal or immutable norm.[29] The *discrimen*, or pattern, that each theologian eventually chooses is his or her own distinctive construal of the *discrimen* that guides his or her critical theological judgments. That is, each faith community has its own particular characterization of the sense in which God and scripture come together to form a meaningful pattern.

The thrust of Kelsey's argument may be summed up in the following manner: First, there is no single normative understanding of scripture to which all must subscribe. Every theologian who tries to determine the sense in which scripture is authoritative for his or her writing engages in an imaginative construal in which he or she tries to grasp through one dominant pattern what Christianity is all about. Different theologians see different patterns in scripture. Second, the manner in which a theologian determines the pattern is not based solely on a close reading of the text but on the experiences of the theologian's specific community of faith. The pattern a theologian eventually settles on as articulating the essence of Christianity is determined by the manner in which he or she believes scripture and God have come together to shape existence in meaningful ways in his or her faith community.

While Kelsey did not specifically cite a black theologian or preacher in his work, I argue that blacks also see a pattern in scripture to which they ascribe wholeness, and that pattern—a sovereign God who acts in concrete and practical ways on behalf of the marginalized and powerless—is the primary component that lends itself to distinctiveness in their preaching. This foundational biblical hermeneutic provides us with a means for understanding the sense in which exposition of scripture and the life situations of blacks come together consistently and creatively in black preaching.

In summary, historically the African American sociocultural context of marginalization and struggle has required the enunciation of a God and a gospel that spoke to their plight in a meaningful, practical, and concrete way. Consequently, the whole of the African American religious interpretive schema has centered on the specifics of their marginalized experience along with the implementation of some adequate hermeneutic to address it. The manner in which African Americans conceive of God as one who acts mightily on their behalf is such a long-established belief in the black religious experience that it functions at the level of sacred story.

Most blacks who become preachers, especially if they have been nurtured from childhood in the black religious experience, do not have to be taught to conceive of God in this manner.[30] A God who acts mightily on their behalf is simply a part of their reality at the deepest levels of their communal experiences. This formative hermeneutic is not imparted to blacks, by and large, through formal theological study, considering that roughly four-fifths of black clergy are without formal training.[31] Rather, it seems to function intuitively in the black preacher's preparation process. African Americans bring this template with them to scripture, and they set out to meet the requirement of demonstrating it in their early musing over the content and structure of their sermons.

Black preachers approach the text with two fundamental questions in mind with respect to the creation and organization of their sermon: (1) How do I demonstrate to God's people this day through the proclamation of the Word the mighty and gracious acts of God on their behalf? and (2) How best shall I join together scripture and their life situations in order to address their plight in a meaningful and practical manner? The first question initiates the search for that portion of scripture that will conform to the template growing out of their sacred story; the second question helps the preacher to focus on a particular aspect of black experience.

From beginning to end, therefore, the black sermon has as its goal the creation of a meaningful connection between an all-powerful God and a marginalized and powerless people. Scriptural explication and application must fulfill this requirement. African American preaching is shaped at the outset by this fundamental aim, and therein lies the crucial component in its distinctiveness. While the process of contextualizing is not unique to African American preaching, the template through which African Americans view scripture so nuances the sermon-building process that the end result can accurately be described as a black sermon—especially when the ancillary characteristics pertaining to style and delivery are added.

DYNAMICS OF A BLACK BIBLICAL HERMENEUTIC

Genres of Scripture

An analysis of several crucial components in this distinct hermeneutic will enable us to see more clearly how it functions in the sermons of the preachers I include in this book. The first dynamic involves the inclusivity of the various genres of scripture. If the hermeneutic of a sovereign God acting mightily on behalf of the oppressed is indeed the common master lens in black preaching, then it should be applicable to all genres of scripture—proverb, narrative, psalm, parable, epistle, and so forth.[32] A biblical hermeneutic that claims to reflect a wide range of black preaching cannot be limited or confined to one specific genre. Thus, in order for my claim of a formative hermeneutic to hold true, black preaching's much beloved biblical narratives, along with a variety of other scriptural forms, must be identifiable in the sermons under investigation.

Domains of Experience

There must be some way of naming and categorizing the tangible, corporeal situations in which the sovereign God's power is sought and demonstrated in the life experiences of blacks. Thus, the second component in our exploration of this hermeneutic concerns itself with what may be characterized as domains of concrete experience. A domain may be defined as a sphere or realm that covers a broad but specified area of black experience and also provides a category for sermonic reflection, creation, and organization. Domains are based on and grow out of long-standing beliefs and experiences in black secular and religious life. An awareness of these broad areas is immensely important for understanding how the biblical hermeneutic works itself into the actual content of the sermon.

The importance of domains of experience for preaching is twofold: (1) They provide a means of categorizing broad areas of black lived experiences; and (2) once identified and understood, they afford an endless resource of ideas for the content of the black sermon. When the preacher speaks of life out of one of these domains of experience, a bonding takes place between preacher and congregation because the listener senses that the preacher understands some meaningful aspect of his or her life. As the preacher probes the depths of the listeners' life experiences a ray of hope is injected into the preaching moment. The listeners sit attentively, hoping that the preacher is, indeed, about to address some perplexing concern of life or simply some situation in life about which they seek a religious understanding.

Once the listeners have some reason to believe that the preacher is going to address a matter of importance to them, they lean forward with anticipation, hoping to hear how the word of God will intersect their concrete situation. Thus an astute grasp of domains of experience gives the preacher an inside edge on where the listeners' interests and attention lie. It also relieves the preacher of feeling as if he or she is taking blind shots in the dark when searching for meaningful intersections between the scriptures and the life situations of the hearers. Domains keep the preacher from stumbling upon areas of meaning in a congregation's life and allow instead for the sermon to be developed at the study table with a careful pairing of life experiences and the Word of God.

Domains of experience take on even greater importance in black preaching when one recalls that the starting point for the traditional black sermon is seldom a specific theological formulation but rather the concrete life experiences of those who make up the listening congregation. The five broad domains of experience that appear often enough in black life and preaching to constitute a paradigm are: personal piety, care of the soul, social justice, corporate concerns, and maintenance of the institutional church.

Personal Piety

The first and most common domain that reflects black experience and provides a framework for the creation and organization of the black sermon is personal piety. Pietism emphasizes "heart religion," the centrality of the Bible for faith and life, the royal priesthood of the laity, and strict morality. The black attraction to personal piety can be traced in this country to the evangelical revivalism that swept America in the late eighteenth and early nineteenth centuries.[33] In this era of religious fervor, the evangelicals' demands for clean hearts and righteous personal lives became the hallmarks of African American religion in the South.

While nineteenth-century evangelicalism was an enormous movement with many nuances and perspectives, it was broadly defined by the following traits:

1. It emphasized the Christian life as essentially a personal relationship with God in Christ.
2. It stressed the importance of the new birth (a profoundly emotional conversion experience) and how it ushered the convert into a new life of holiness, characterized by religious devotion, moral discipline, and missionary zeal.
3. It rejected the appeal to reason in favor of a direct psychological assault upon sin with an equally direct offer of personal salvation.
4. It dissolved the psychological and social distance between preacher and people, often evoking tearful, passionate outbursts.[34]

Its initial egalitarian thrust and its similarities to the old religions of Africa had great appeal to the slaves who first heard it.[35]

The more narrow understanding of personal piety that concerns itself with faith and personal formation is the dimension that has had and continues to have the greatest impact on black religion. A large number of contemporary blacks experience life in this broad domain, which emphasizes prayer, personal discipline, moral conduct, and the maintenance of a right relationship with God.[36] Many blacks are convinced that they have not heard the gospel if it does not address some aspect of life as it is lived in this domain. Even ministers who are known for their active participation on the social justice front preach sermons from time to time that have as their central focus some matter related to personal piety.

Care of the Soul

The second domain of experience (belief and practice) on which black preaching reflects and to which it is directed may be characterized as "care of the soul."[37] Care of the soul describes that area of experience that focuses on the well-being of individuals. It is, however, more than mere comfort for the bereaved, forgiveness for the guilty, and help for the sick and needy; it is preeminently the renewal of life in the image of Christ. Thus it has as its purpose not only the giving of comfort but also the redirection of life.[38] The preaching that grows out of reflection on this domain concerns itself with the healing, sustaining, guiding, and reconciling of persons as they face the changes and challenges of common human experiences, experiences that are exacerbated in black life through systemic and capricious discrimination and prejudice.

Preaching that centers on experiences in need of healing aims to overcome some impairment by restoring people to wholeness and by leading them beyond their previous condition. Sustaining seeks to help persons overcome an overwhelming sense of loss. Guiding helps them determine what they should do when they are faced with a difficult problem wherein they must choose between various courses of thought or action, while reconciliation helps alienated persons establish or renew proper and fruitful relationships with God, family, significant others, friends, and neighbors.[39] The function of sermons created out of reflection on this domain is to salve or heal the wounds and brokenness of life through some form of encouragement, exhortation, consolation, renewal, instruction, or admonishment.

Social Justice

The third domain centers on social justice. Matters pertaining to racism, sexism, ageism, and other forms of discrimination fall within the scope of this particular domain. Social justice is a basic value and desired goal in democratic societies and includes equitable and fair access to institutions, laws, resources, and opportunities without arbitrary limitations based on age, gender, national origin, religion, or sexual orientation. Racial justice, defined as equal treatment of the races, has been the most prominent component of the social justice domain in black experience. Discrimination and prejudice are the twin evils that the black preacher has spoken out against most vociferously since the inception of the black church.

Those who preach out of this domain view God as the source of social justice and are absolutely certain that God's power is on their side in their quest for social reform. They do not seek necessarily to overthrow the societal system per se but rather to reform it so that it conforms once again to fundamental principles of fairness and equality. Their preaching aims at constructive social change.[40] Consequently, God's power is made available in the present order to bring about fair and just treatment in systems and structures that negatively impact all people, including blacks.

Corporate Concerns

The fourth domain focuses on corporate concerns. Preaching that grows out of reflection on this domain recognizes that certain issues and interests in black life arise out of its unique history and cultural experiences in this country. Many African Americans believe that such matters pertain uniquely to blacks and are best addressed by blacks. Inasmuch as this domain has at its center matters that pertain specifically to blacks, it tends more toward exhortations of self-help, uplift, and racial solidarity.

While this domain often concerns matters of social justice for black people, it is not confined to social justice. Its primary distinction is that it speaks to matters that particularly and peculiarly affect black life. Unlike the domain of social justice, which seeks the common good of all, the corporate concerns domain is specifically geared to black interests. Muslim minister Louis Farrakhan and the large number of Christian ministers who supported the historic Million Man March provide examples of the kind of preaching that stems from this domain. Many black Christian preachers who gathered for the march in Washington, D.C., in October 1995 distanced themselves from Farrakhan's black separatist, anti-Semitic rhetoric and narrow religious orientation. At the same time, however, they acknowledged that some interests and concerns relating specifically to black men can best be addressed by other blacks.[41]

Some of the issues concerned social justice matters, for example, equal opportunity, fair employment and hiring practices, and so forth. Others pertained to moral concerns of family life, such as the care and sustenance of black nuclear families, responsible fatherhood, and black men's atonement for past sins and failures toward their women. The issues addressed by those who spoke at the march were believed to have a disproportionate effect on black men and, subsequently, on black life in general in the United States. Accordingly, their solutions were thought to lie within the reasoned reflection and resolve of other blacks.

Many African Americans believe that matters of vital importance in black life are best dealt with by other blacks, for example, issues such as teen-aged pregnancy, exhortations to blacks to lift themselves from the welfare rolls, black-on-black crime, and calls for educational excellence. They are convinced that some things can best be said to blacks by other blacks. More pointedly, there are some things that should only be said to blacks by other blacks. Issues and concerns that fall within this realm have historically been addressed from black pulpits.

The impetus for such preaching grows out of reflection on those experiences in life where blacks feel they must fall back on their own strength and "lift while they climb." This is the corporate concerns domain. God's power is viewed as enabling blacks to do for themselves what they and they alone must do in order to survive and prosper. Such admonishments are best spoken and best heard when sender and receiver are black.

Maintenance of the Institutional Church

The fifth domain, characterized as maintenance of the institutional church, is vastly important to the ecclesiastical life of the faith community as institution. Since it is more concerned with ethos than specific acts, it operates at a higher level of abstraction and is more inclined to be coupled with one or more domains in a sermon. Owing to the historical importance of the black church in the African American community, blacks, by and large, experience church not simply as a place to attend worship but as a way of life. Church is more than a once-a-week encounter; it is an affirming presence that shapes and molds self-understanding, self-worth, behavior, and lifestyle. For this reason, African Americans tend to identify more strongly with a denomination, a specific fellowship, and a specific location than do their counterparts in the majority culture.[42]

With its elaborate, multilayered social configurations and its highly prized bestowal of rank and authority, the black church takes on heightened significance in the lives of those who otherwise enjoy little control, authority, or sense of self-worth in the broader world. In the institutional black church a janitor in the work world could be a steward, elder, or chairman of deacons. Likewise, an unskilled domestic could be a highly respected head of the missionary society, trustee, or mother of the church. This has been one of the remarkable contributions of the black church to black esteem and self-worth.

Since many of the vital, life-altering experiences of parishioners occur within the context of the institutional church, much preaching in black pulpits is directed toward the maintenance of the institution. Sermons in this domain reflect on the work of the people as a gathered fellowship. Thus the teachings of the faith with respect to discipleship, missions, evangelism, Christian education, benevolence, and so forth, usually find expression in this realm. Sermons that speak to the promotion, building, and upkeep of the physical plant are also common. How members are to behave and interact with one another and the requirements for spiritual growth and maturity within the church's many departments and auxiliaries are also addressed. This kind of preaching, however, is more than stewardship preaching or catechetical indoctrination; it is preaching that gives continued life and sustenance to the institutional church, which in turn reaffirms and upholds its participants.

This kind of in-house preaching is best appreciated and understood by those who value the church as an affirming presence in their lives. Even when outsiders hear preaching in this domain, they may not fully comprehend it because it tends to operate at a level of metacommunication, that is, at a level that assumes a wealth of prior knowledge and previous experience on the part of those who have embraced the church as a way of life. God is viewed as supplying the dedicated devotees with the strength and wisdom to carry out their designated responsibilities both within the institution and in the broader world when required. When necessary, God's providential hand also moves to correct those who would demean the institution with unbecoming behavior, personal or private, or with an open disregard for process that threatens to challenge or overthrow established order and continued progress.

In this domain God's power is localized and internalized in the interest of the continued life of the visible fellowship. This domain gives the preacher license to preach to the choir, that is, the preacher is expected to come forth from time to time with a word of in-house admonition and instruction to the faithful.[43]

Domains and Demonstrations of God's Power

These five domains of experience provide us with (1) the means for understanding the common life experiences of blacks and (2) avenues of core beliefs through which the preacher may travel in an effort to connect God's power to the listener's concrete and tangible life situations. They also provide a treasure of sermon ideas and possibilities. When one conceives of God's power through the prism of personal piety, one is more likely to focus on private morality and appropriate individual moral conduct. Issues relating to social justice and/or corporate concerns are not nearly as important as individual "matters of the heart." Preachers who wholly subscribe to the view that God's power is manifested to enable one to live an upright life tend to believe that the people of God should live above the cares and concerns of the secular world. Christians, they claim, have been called out of the world to live lives separate and apart from the present order.

The adherents of this view who take it to excess are usually apolitical and see little to be gained in sociopolitical involvement at any level. They believe political pronouncements from the pulpit in any form, but especially in preaching, "kill the Spirit" in worship and weaken the witness of the church. In the extreme understanding of this paradigm, the gospel transcends politics and race; therefore, the pulpit is not the place to address social justice or corporate concerns issues. For this reason, preaching that grows out of this domain has often drawn heavy criticism for being highly privatized and escapist. Critics charge that it is overly concerned with otherworldly matters and too often neglects present-day concerns.

While care of the soul is closely aligned to personal piety, God's power in this domain is not sought merely to enable one to live an upright life. Rather, God is viewed as empowering one to withstand the stresses and strains of common human experiences. In this domain God is provider, protector, sustainer, and healer of the faithful, and God's power is manifested in a mighty way to help the believer survive from day to day.

The providential care of God, which permeates much of the preaching in this realm, is a prominent theme in black proclamation, for it is an unshakable faith in that providence that sustains the faithful through the ups and downs of life. At its best, preaching that grows out of the care of the soul domain views God's power as strengthening blacks to survive the many hardships and struggles of life. At its worst, it collapses into distant promises of well-being and delayed gratification (e.g., "things will be all right after a while"), causing its adherents to become patient and passive people, totally reliant on a power outside themselves to make things better.

When one believes that God's power is made manifest in the social justice domain, such power is directed toward the broader society and the naming of God's purposive acts in that world. God's power is believed to be at work on systemic and capricious structures of evil and inequality, and God is understood as acting mightily to make things right for all people, including blacks, in the everyday affairs of their lives. The preaching reflective of this domain believes God's power will bring about large scale changes and triumphs in this life as opposed to some distant, otherworldly promise of vindication. The advance that is sought seldom, if ever, concerns itself with issues of individual piety or care of the soul but rather seeks the common good in matters of political, educational, and economic justice. At its best, this kind of preaching seeks a just world for all humankind; thus it focuses on substantive change in the here and now. When carried to excess, it relies too much on human potential, dismisses the eschatological implications of the gospel, and pays mere lip service to the sovereignty of God.

The corporate concerns domain is closely aligned with the social justice domain. It too is concerned with the advancement and well-being of the masses. It has, however, a more narrow focus in the demonstration of power it seeks. Theoretically, it can apply to any group that has its own specific needs and concerns that lie beyond the interests of the dominant culture. In black preaching, however, it takes a more ethnocentric focus in that it sees God at work in matters and life situations that pertain specifically to blacks. At its best it seeks to appeal to what is highest and most laudable in blacks by reminding them of their integrity and worth as a people, their common bond in past struggles and triumphs, and God's willful and mighty acts on their behalf.[44] At its worst it collapses into a sordid xenophobia and reverse racism with unfounded claims of racial superiority and dominance.

The maintenance of the institutional church domain concerns itself with the establishment and implementation of the character and ideals of institutionalized black religion. It is an area of experience and reflection that takes on greater significance because of the systematic exclusion of blacks from meaningful participation in the larger world. Since the institutional church plays such a large part in black life, blacks expect to hear in the proclaimed word how they are to function in this environment, which provides them with so many rich and meaningful experiences. At its best this kind of preaching enlightens, upholds, and reaffirms people in their commitments to the high ideals of an organized religious body. When taken to excess, it idolizes the visible fellowship (local church or denominational judicatory), putting more emphasis on the organizational structure than the larger cause for which it exists. When it becomes church for church's sake, the means become more important than the ends.

These five domains of experience constitute an integral dynamic in our effort to analyze the makeup of the biblical hermeneutic that I claim blacks bring to scripture when they preach. In that these domains represent ideal types, a sermon is seldom purely of one particular domain in the strictest sense of the term. In fact, a given sermon may have some characteristics from one or more of the domains cited. The overall focus of the sermon, the primary situation in life to which it is addressed, and the makeup of the intended audience will ultimately determine the domain that most fittingly characterizes the sermon.

Extended Metaphors

After determining the domain in which God's power is being manifested, we must describe the type of power being revealed by God. Our overarching template is a God who acts mightily on behalf of the marginalized and oppressed.[45] However, a part of God's appeal is that God acts in ways that are mindful of the specific needs of the African American context. Thus our template must be broad enough to include any powerful act of God that is appropriate to a given context. For this reason we do not initially specify the type of action being manifested by God, since the type of action that is sought can only be determined by the particulars of the context. For example, if we were to say that our template is a God who acts mightily as "liberator" or "provider" or "empowerer," that would greatly limit the different types of power that God could bring to a situation, and it would stifle the creativity of the preachers in their effort to address the specifics of any given context.

Black scholars have given consistent witness in their writings to diverse conceptions of God's power. Such themes as liberation, deliverance, empowerment, providence, reconciliation, parenthood, and election are common themes of the manifestations of God's power in the black religious experience.[46] Many of these themes could also function as supporting metaphors of a God who acts mightily. What is needed is some way of incorporating these specific disclosures into our master lens without limiting God's power to any one of them. One way of providing the greater illumination we seek is through the extended metaphor.

Extended metaphors are necessary to give meaning to our fundamental conception of a God who acts mightily, for no one metaphor can adequately describe all the possible dimensions and circumstances under which God acts. Extended metaphors are the more specific metaphors that serve as ways of describing God's mighty acts in a particular context. These additional ways of conceiving of God, for example, as liberator, provider, parent, or empowerer, are common metaphors in the black religious experience and serve as focusing devices that allow the preacher to hone in on some concrete reality that must be addressed in the life situation of the hearers that day.

That God is going to act in a mighty way on behalf of blacks is a given, one that is true for blacks even prior to their initial approach to scripture. Extended metaphors become helpful when the preacher moves into the specifics of the sermon and begins to focus on the particular situation in which God acts. At this point the preacher reaches for an appropriate metaphor rooted in the dominant concept to support the specific claim to God's power that the sermon makes that day. The extended metaphor allows even greater specificity within the dominant concept, yet grows out of it and is meaningfully related to it in some way.

Extended metaphors are helpful because they allow the preacher a wider sphere in which to act. For example, it would greatly limit our understanding of God's power to proclaim that the sole metaphor in black preaching is God as liberator. This restricted understanding of God's power would not fit every dimension of the ways in which God acts powerfully. In one instance it would limit the text, while in another it would force the text to say more than is actually intended. While the God encountered in scripture does indeed act mightily to liberate,[47] at other times God acts powerfully to sustain God's children, equipping them to survive their present sore trials and afflictions.[48]

On other occasions God does not liberate but rather acts mightily as parent or provider for God's children.[49] A God who acts mightily only as liberator is a confining and restrictive metaphor. A God who acts mightily in a host of ways in various situations has much more elasticity and is more inclusive of the various extended metaphors likely to be found in a black sermon. To say that God acts mightily and also to have the power to determine, based on the context, how that power is best exemplified frees the preacher to be more creative.

With these four distinct components of the black biblical hermeneutic in mind—scriptural genres, domains of experience, demonstrations of God's power through domains of experience, and extended metaphors that allow for flexibility in the demonstration of that power—we begin our examination of the sermons of nineteenth- and twentieth-century African American preachers.

2

❦

The Power Motif in Nineteenth-Century African American Sermons

Having argued in the previous chapter for a distinctive biblical hermeneutic in African American preaching, I will now search for that hermeneutic in the published sermons of several nineteenth-century African American ministers. I begin with an examination of preaching from the nineteenth century, since what we know today as black preaching first came into its most visible expression in the post–Civil War period. The watershed nature of this era of upheaval and transition enabled black preaching to shed its invisible, guarded status, to become publicly discernible, and to flourish without the constraints of slavery.[1]

Numerous works focusing on the sociopolitical involvement of black preachers who distinguished themselves in the years before and after the Civil War have recently been published.[2] In this work, however, I examine the actual content and structure of the sermons of five ministers with varied regional, educational, and denominational affiliations. They are: John Jasper, Alexander Crummell, Francis J. Grimké, Daniel Alexander Payne, and Elias Camp Morris. All five were leading figures in black religious life who made significant contributions in their ministerial careers to the elevation of their race. Two lived in the North—Crummell and Grimké—and were members of predominantly white denominations, Episcopal and Presbyterian respectively. Payne, a bishop of the African Methodist Episcopal Church, was born in the South but lived and worked most of his years in the North, while Morris and Jasper were Baptists also born in the South, who spent their entire lives and ministry there. These figures sought to address the plight of their people in meaningful, practical, and immediate ways amid the critical times in which they preached. In spite of the hopeful promises made to blacks in post–Civil War America, the ministers in our study had to proclaim a God who could speak powerfully to the continued hardships of blacks at every level and walk of life.

Because four of the five individuals whose sermons I will examine were either professionally trained or self-educated, one could argue that their preaching was not really representative of the kind of preaching being done by the multitudes of black ministers. Consequently, I will begin by examining a sermon from John Jasper, a preacher who was less privileged in his formal training but who also employed the biblical hermeneutic that I claim is distinctive to black preaching.

John Jasper (1812–1901)

John Jasper is an important representative of the folk tradition. A folk preacher is one who communicates among the commoners through the spoken word that is never set down in writing but rather passed from generation to generation through the oral tradition. Jasper, a folk preacher in the truest sense, never published his sermons and speeches, unlike his more learned colleagues in the North. Distinctly of the old plantation type, he was for fifty years a slave, and a preacher during twenty-five years of his slavery. A quick-witted and untiring worker in a Richmond tobacco factory, Jasper was converted one day while stemming the sot weed's leaves. Over the years he became something of a legend for preaching a sermon, "The Sun Do Move," that embarrassed many black ministers but attracted large crowds of curious people who came to hear him preach it. To enlightened people who heard the sermon, Jasper appeared to be an ignorant, old simpleton, a buffoon of the pulpit, a weakling to be ridiculed.[3] However, his thoroughly unscientific thesis was delivered with such personal magnetism and natural eloquence that, according to Jasper's biographer, after hearing the sermon scoffers would admit, almost without realizing it, that Jasper was right.[4]

More important than Jasper's oratorical skills, however, is the hermeneutic that informed his sermon. Jasper's understanding of the one who had enough power to make the sun move is the key understanding to his entire theological thought process. The point of his entire sermon is to present the Lord God as the deliverer and able defender of God's ancient people. It is this theological truth that shapes the entire sermon. This theme, far more than scientific questions, characterizes Jasper's preaching. The issue of the sun's movement must be understood in the context of one of the most universal themes in black religion: the liberation of the Jews from Egyptian slavery.

The text Jasper selected for this sermon is an Old Testament narrative that tells of Joshua's request to God for an extension of daylight so that he could finish fighting an important battle. Having led the children of Israel into the land of Canaan through the ashes of Jericho and Ai, Joshua won the Gibeonites as allies. Because of their cooperation with the Israelite invaders, however, the Gibeonites were attacked by the five Amoritish kings. The attack was fierce indeed, and the Gibeonites were scared out of their senses. They sent word to Joshua that they were in trouble and pleaded for his assistance. Wishing to protect those who had come to his aid, Joshua engaged the kings in a furious battle.[5]

To guarantee that he would kill all of the enemy, the victorious general appealed to the Lord to keep the sun up until he had accomplished his grisly task. "And the sun stood still, and the moon stayed, until the people had avenged themselves upon their enemies" (Josh. 10:13):

> He prayed and he fought, and the hours got away too [fast] for him, and so he asked the Lord to issue a special order that the sun hold up awhile and that the moon furnish plenty of moonshine down on the lowest part of the fighting grounds. As a fact, Joshua was so drunk with the battle, so thirsty for the blood of the enemies of the Lord, and so wild with the victory that he told the sun to stand still until he could finish his job. What did the sun do? Did he glare down in fiery wrath and say, "What are you talking about my stopping for, Joshua; I ain't never started yet. I've been here all the time, and it would smash up everything if I were to start"? No, he didn't say that. But what does the Bible say? That's what I ask to know. It says that it was at the voice of Joshua that it stopped.[6]

Jasper is not simply taking on the philosophers; he is challenging their right to deny a mighty act of God. God moved in a special way to liberate and defend God's people. Scientific knowledge aside, Jasper maintains that God has the power to perform this feat. There is undeniably a prior understanding of the power of God that moves Jasper to pursue this extended metaphor of God as a liberator. Jasper's understanding of the God of the Bible leads him to the conclusion that if God so chooses, God can make the sun move. Thus Jasper proclaims to his listeners that he will accept no truth other than biblical truth. The template he brings to scripture will allow him to accept no truth other than that which speaks of a mighty God who is sovereign unto God's self:

> Outside of the Bible I know nothing extra about the sun ... But about the courses of the sun, I have got that. I have ranged through the whole blessed book and scored down the last thing the Bible has to say about the movement of the sun.[7]

Jasper makes explicit his intent to rely solely on the word of God for the truth he is about to argue in his sermon. He is aware of the arguments of the scientists and philosophers of his day, claiming the sun to be the center of the solar system.[8] The title of his sermon, "The Sun Do Move," is intended to refute what was regarded by many in Jasper's day as fact. Jasper's understanding of scripture as portraying the mighty acts of God—acts which are faithful and trustworthy—forbids his entertaining any information that disputes that construal except for the purpose of rebuttal:

> I fear I do lie sometimes—I'm so sinful, I find it hard to do right; but my God don't lie and he ain't put no lie in the Book of eternal truth, and if I give you what the Bible says, then I'm bound to tell the truth.[9]

Although the sermon is titled "The Sun Do Move," Jasper's real purpose is to demonstrate the truthfulness and reliability of the power of God. Even though he argues passionately, and for some in his day persuasively, he is not arguing for the sake of scientific contradiction alone. This is not a sermon delivered solely to demonstrate the superiority of religion over science. Rather, it is a sermon about the power of God to act versus the power of humankind to perceive and to believe:

> I ain't caring so much about the sun, though it's mighty convenient to have it, but my trust is in the Word of the Lord. As long as my feet are flat on the solid rock, no man can move me. I'm getting my orders from the God of my salvation.[10]

What Jasper allowed into the sermon must conform with his understanding of scripture as portraying the mighty acts of God. Even scientific finds that had made their way into the popular culture and thus were somewhat familiar to Jasper and commonly accepted by other Christian preachers meet stiff opposition in Jasper's sermon when they appear to contradict the power and purpose of God.

Jasper cites other examples in which he perceives scientific advances attempting to counter the mighty acts of God.[11] He further argues in his sermon that not only was God able to stop the sun for Joshua, but God actually made it back up for King Hezekiah:

> When, therefore, God told the king that He would make the shadow go backward, it must have been just like putting the hands of the clock back, but, mark you, Isaiah expressly said that the sun returned ten degrees. There you are! Ain't that the movement of the sun? Bless my soul. Hezekiah's case beat Joshua's. Joshua stopped the sun, but here the Lord made the sun walk back ten degrees; and yet they say that the sun stands alone still and never moves a peg. It looks to me he moves around mighty briskly and is read to go anyway that the Lord orders him to go.[12]

The key issue in the above-mentioned passage is that the sun was prepared to go in any direction ordered by God. The recited passage from the Hezekiah narrative is but another example, first and foremost, of a most visible demonstration of the might and power of the sovereign God. The challenge to the scientific thought of Jasper's day is secondary to this mighty act of God. At another place in the sermon, Jasper's template allowed an argument for a flat earth:

> I invite you to hear the first verse in the seventh chapter of the book of Revelation. What does John, under the power of the Spirit, say? He says he saw four angels standing on the four corners of the earth, holding the four winds of the earth, and so forth. Allow me to ask if the earth is round, where does it keep its corners? A flat, square thing has corners, but tell me where is the corner of an apple, or a marble, or a cannon ball, or a silver dollar? If there is any one of those philosophers that's been taking so many cracks at my old head about here, he is cordially invited to step forward and square up this vexing business. I here tell you that you can't square a circle, but it looks like these great scholars have learned how to circle the square. If they can do it, let them step to the front and do the trick. But, my brethren, in my poor judgment, they can't do it; it ain't in them to do it. They are on the wrong side of the Bible; that's on the outside of the Bible, and there's where the trouble comes in with them.[13]

Again, it is important to remember that Jasper made such arguments not because he wanted to dispute the scientific community but because they buttressed his understanding of scripture as portraying or revealing the mighty acts of God on behalf of the marginalized and powerless. It is God's power to act in a mighty way on behalf of God's people that must be defended at all costs. All of these examples from Jasper's famous sermon fall under the rubric of a master lens that impacts what he sees in the scriptures. What is allowed into the sermon must not violate the construal of scripture that constitutes the biblical hermeneutic of the mighty acts of God. This template serves as a governing control on what is allowed into the sermon as Jasper amasses one example after another to support such a belief. Moreover, his governing template pushes him into a hypercreative mode as he grapples to square, dismiss, or make relative materials that seem to contradict or counteract this belief.

The four characteristics of this biblical hermeneutic are evident in Jasper's sermons:

1. The interpretive key itself—a God who acts mightily—is clearly the hermeneutic that informs the sermon.
2. The genre of scripture is narrative, including those passages cited to buttress his argument.
3. The extended metaphors of God as liberator and defender are used to illustrate the specific examples of God's power being manifested on behalf of God's marginalized children.
4. The particular domain of experience is care of the soul.

Implicitly and through the use of double entendre, Jasper is saying to his black congregants that they too can count on this special divine aid as they defy conventional wisdom and struggle to survive in a world that seems bent on their destruction. And his words imply that this same power, made manifest in the impossible situations of the faithful in scripture, was available to discouraged and disheartened post–Civil War blacks who heard Jasper preach this sermon. Northern whites urged Jasper to quit preaching against commonly accepted scientific data, arguing that it ultimately hurt the cause of his people, but from Jasper they received a stinging rebuke. Jasper informed his critics that, quite the contrary, in preaching such a sermon he was not trying to harm his people but trying to lift them:

> I told him John Jasper ain't set up to be no scholar, and don't know the philosophers, and ain't trying to hurt his people, but is working day and night to lift them up, but his foot is on the rock of eternal truth. There he stands and there he is going to stand til Gabriel sounds the judgment note. So I said to the gentleman that scolded me up so that I heard him make his remarks, but I ain't heard where he gets his scripture from, and that between him and the word of the Lord I take my stand by the Word of God every time.[14]

Though Jasper based his sermon on the narrative recounting Joshua's plea to God that the sun be stopped to allow him more time to defeat his enemies, what Jasper really attempted to convey to his listeners was the truths about God that obtain for any and all peoples who have found favor in God's sight. Time and again, Jasper proclaims throughout his sermon that he cares nothing about the movement of the sun:

> What I care about the sun? The day comes on when the sun will be called from his race-track, and his light squinted out forever; the moon shall turn to blood, and this earth be consumed with fire. Let them go; that won't scare me nor trouble God's elected people, for the word of the Lord shall endure forever, and on that Solid Rock we stand and shall not be moved.[15]

The word of the Lord that tells of God's power and might to effect God's will shall endure forever, according to Jasper. It is that truth that Jasper sought to convey to his listeners through the preaching of this sermon. God has all power, and God uses that power on behalf of the marginalized and powerless of society in an immediate and practical way. In this instance the powerless are the post–Civil War blacks of Richmond, who need to hear such a mighty word. The power of this master lens continues to be a key factor in sermon creativity and insightfulness in the black preaching tradition.

Alexander Crummell (1819–1898)

We move now to an examination of the sermons of Alexander Crummell. Crummell, though the most highly educated and extensively published of all the preachers I discuss, shows evidence in his sermons of this foundational hermeneutic that I claim is central to black preaching.

Historian Wilson J. Moses describes Alexander Crummell as a disconcerting anomaly. Crummell, knowledgeable in the classics at a time when the average black American was an illiterate slave, was a black man of letters before the Civil War. He studied in England, where he graduated from Queens College, Cambridge, in 1853. An ordained priest of the Episcopal Church, he spent nearly twenty years in Liberia as a missionary, an educator, and a public moralist. Returning to the United States in 1872, he moved to Washington, D.C., where he spent the remaining twenty-five years of his life. There he finally came to be recognized as one of the more prominent African American intellectuals of the nineteenth century.

A pan-African, statesman, and missionary, Crummell was also a pioneering intellectual and philosopher of language, founding the American Negro Academy in 1897 and serving as the intellectual godfather of W. E. B. DuBois.[16] He was the author of three published volumes of sermons and addresses, numerous provocative articles, several hundred unpublished tracts, and a voluminous correspondence.[17] His importance to this book stems from the fact that his life and work spanned almost an entire century of active involvement in race relations, at home and abroad, during a time of great ferment in America's sociopolitical climate. Through his preaching and other public pronouncements, he manifested a lifelong commitment to racial solidarity and self-help as well as an insistence on the necessity and importance of independent African American institutions.[18]

Like many of his contemporaries among black nationalists, Crummell was a "civilizationist," and thus he believed that his Pan-Africanist ideals could best be achieved through civilizationism.[19] It is through his understanding of civilizationism that one can best view Crummell's concept of the power of God. Civilizationists saw the unfolding of civilization as part of the grand design of providence, governed by universal rules, which they believed were best discovered through Western Protestant Christianity. To Crummell, history moved under the power of God with a purpose and a pattern that could be discerned by intuitive minds. Providence moved progressively and led to ever higher forms of civilization, which ultimately were brought to fruition by the triumph of Christianity.

Christianity was the one, true, perfect religion; all others were either steps upward to Christianity at best or at worst—and often—false religions.[20] For Crummell, the simultaneous Christianization and civilization of black Americans under Anglo-American auspices was clear evidence that blacks were on a progressive road to a new stage of civilization. All good in the world, however, came from submission to the power of God as it was manifested in Christian institutions, which must first evolve to a certain standard, namely, for Crummell, modern Protestantism.

Although his Pan-African civilizationist thought went through three distinct stages, Crummell's basic faith in the power and involvement of God in earthly affairs never changed. That Crummell embraced the hermeneutic of a God who acts mightily is evident in sermons and addresses from the beginning of his career to those near the end of his life. A sermon titled *God and the Nation*, preached on July 30, 1854, deals with the relationship of God to a nation and its people.[21] The text is taken from Psalm 33:12 (KJV), "Blessed is the nation whose God is the LORD; and the people whom he hath chosen for his own inheritance." From this sermon, along with others I cite that are structured in similar fashion, one gets a sense of the place and power of God in Crummell's world view: (1) History moves under the power of God with purpose and design; (2) God is sovereign over all nations of the earth, including America; and (3) Whatever a nation or a people ultimately becomes, both corporately and individually, depends upon its character and obedience to almighty God. This sense of God's might and purpose was instilled in Crummell in his youth and followed him throughout his life as he struggled to advance the cause of his people.

On May 14, 1863, midway through his career, Crummell preached a sermon in Trinity Church in Liberia in which he spoke of the providential hand of God in the colonization of Africa:

> All human events have their place in the grand moral economy of God, in which He himself is an ever-present, ever-active agent; they are all elements and instruments in His hand, for the accomplishment of the August objects of His will ... So indeed has it been in all the world's history of colonization. The great, vital, permeating power, propelling, guiding, checking,

ordering it, has been the spirit of God, resting upon, entering into the hearts of men, owning and governing them, albeit ofttimes unknown to themselves ... we see everywhere God's hand in history; we feel that its anointing spirit is the breath of God. In all the movements of society, or the colonization of peoples, we see the clear, distinct, "finger of God," ordering, controlling, directing the footsteps of men, families, and of races.[22]

We can see from this passage that Crummell believes that God is in charge of history. God has the power to effect change and to control the destinies of God's created order. In the days when Crummell believed it was God's will for blacks to unite under one common bond and that the home of that union would be in Mother Africa, he shows God's power as being manifested on behalf of black progress and advancement. While his thinking on nationalism changed, his thoughts on the power of God to effect positive change remained constant.

That Crummell embraced some understanding of this foundational black biblical hermeneutic throughout his professional life is also evident in a sermon he delivered thirty-one years later in St. Luke's Church in Washington, D.C., on December 9, 1894, near the end of his long and distinguished career. The occasion was the fiftieth anniversary of his ordination to the priesthood.[23] The sermon is based on Leviticus 25:10 (KJV), "And ye shall hallow the fiftieth year ... and it shall be a Jubilee unto you." The first part of the sermon consists of a recapitulation of the problems that Crummell faced for fifty years as a minister in the predominantly white Episcopal Church. He refers to some incidents as "shades" because they grew out of the darkness of racism and to others as "light" because of the generous spirits of people who rose above the prejudicial spirit of the times. But all the remembrances to which he refers concern themselves with what Crummell terms "the deadly caste spirit of the age ... bent to the most despised people in the land."[24]

After recounting his years in England, Africa, and finally back in America, Crummell gives an assessment of life based upon his fifty years of ministry in a country torn by racial prejudice and strife. "And now," says Crummell, "you may ask me—what is the conception of life which my experiences have wrought within me?" It is in his answer to this question that one can see the black hermeneutic of a God who acts mightily governing his thought process. His lifetime experiences with race and caste did not make him bitter, cynical, or atheistic; rather they imbued him with a sense of God's power and might. Crummell knew from firsthand experience that the impossible odds he faced as a young black minister bucking the accepted mores of the day could only be overcome by the power of the

Almighty. And from his experiences he identified two truths he had learned; both concern themselves with God's power and proactive stance toward the degraded and despised blacks.

The first truth is that God never leaves Godself without a witness:

> My answer is, first of all, that no age, no Church, no people are ever left, by the Almighty, destitute of grand prophets, devoted priests, and glorious reformers. The great benefactors to whom I have referred lived, in what has been called, the "Martyr Age" of American history, the times when it was a reproach for any man to show devoted interest in the Negro race.[25]

Crummell viewed the people who raised themselves above the caste spirit of the age and came to his aid in every phase of his life as emissaries of almighty God, sent by God to effect God's will in spite of the encumbrances of the racist order of the day. Never in all the history of the world, says Crummell, has the Almighty been wanting of the gallant spirits, ready at any sacrifice, to vindicate the cause of the poor and needy and to "wax valiant in the fight" for the downtrodden and oppressed. Crummell places those who helped him overcome the barriers of race prejudice in the company of the great people of the ages—including apostles, prophets, and martyrs—who, when faced with impossible odds and powerful enemies, were delivered nonetheless by the powerful arm of God.

The second truth Crummell gleaned from fifty years of ministry is that, despite the hardships imposed on him, he remained an abiding optimist. He remained optimistic because he always believed that God was at work on his behalf:

> All along the lines of my own personal life I have seen the gracious intrusions of a most merciful providence. Every disaster has been surmounted and eclipsed by some saving and inspiring interpretation. It is not merely a personal experience. It is a wider truth. It is a fact and a principle which pertains to the large and struggling race to which we belong. There is a Divine, an infinite, an all-powerful hand which moves in all our history; and it moves for good.[26]

Crummell remained an optimist after fifty years of racism and its perilous consequences, for he was convinced that almighty God had been at work to bring good out of those painful circumstances. Even though the incidents he cited in this sermon refer to his personal life, he sees God's fortuitous movement in his life as being representative of a wider truth in the lives of all black people—God is at work in various ways to lift blacks and bless them despite the many hindrances placed in their paths. This understanding of God not only informed a lifetime of preaching, but it permeated the whole of Crummell's life.

Having established that a God who acts mightily is a reasonable concept to extract from Crummell's religious self-understanding, I turn now to a more detailed analysis of a sermon by Crummell in order to show this hermeneutic at work in his pairing of scripture and human situation. While Crummell preached a broad range of sermons reflective of the five domains of black experience, because of his pan-Africanist sentiments he soared to creative heights when preaching out of the corporate concerns domain, that is, on issues specifically of black concern that are best spoken by blacks to other blacks.

One of Crummell's most famous sermons, "The Destined Superiority of the Negro," provides valuable insight into the specifics of the hermeneutic that informed his preaching throughout his ministerial career. Taken from Isaiah 61:7, the portion of the text selected by Crummell reads, "For your shame ye shall have double, and for confusion they shall rejoice in their portion" (kjv),[27] part of a poem from Isaiah 61:1–11. It is a prophetic passage that depicts the new age Israel will one day enjoy when it returns from the Babylonian exile. The entire passage would have been quite familiar to Crummell's black listeners since the first strophe of the poem—a quote used by Jesus at the beginning of his prophetic ministry—was often quoted by black ministers as the touchstone of their own prophetic ministries:[28]

> The Spirit of the Lord God is upon me; because the Lord hath anointed me to preach good tidings unto the meek; he hath sent me to bind up the broken-hearted, to proclaim liberty to the captives, and the opening of the prison to them that are bound ... (Isa. 61:1–3; Luke 4:18–19, kjv)

The second strophe begins the good tidings, for it proclaims that the cities long laid waste will rise again:

> They shall build up the ancient ruins, they shall raise up the former devastations; they shall repair the ruined cities ... (Isa. 61:4–5)

The third strophe of the poem (61:6–7), and the one from which Crummell selects his scripture, is a continuation of the description of the new age:

> But ye shall be called the Priests of the Lord: men shall call you the Ministers of our God: you shall eat the riches of the Gentiles, and in their glory shall ye boast yourselves. For your shame ye shall have double; and for confusion they shall rejoice in their

portion: therefore in their land they shall possess the double: everlasting joy shall be unto them. (Isa.61:6–7, KJV)

Isaiah prophesies that in the new age Zion's unique status shall be recognized, and among the peoples of the world she will perform the priestly functions of instruction and intercession. In return for this service, the nations will serve Israel by performing life's ordinary labor. Roles will be reversed: rich and powerful peoples will minister to Israel, and the despised Israelites will minister in the things of God to the once rich and powerful.

Crummell's controlling thought in this sermon is a simple one: When God does not destroy a people but rather trains and disciplines them, God intends to make something great of them. The sermon functioned to empower his black listeners to press on to their destined greatness among the ranks of other civilized peoples despite their present hardships and struggles. He accomplishes this word of deliverance and empowerment by arguing for a redemptive purpose in suffering and shame. In Crummell's understanding of the passage, shame does not always suggest the hopeless confusion and utter destruction of the wicked; rather it can also stand for trial and punishment, which may correct and purify character. He argues here that two principles of discipline where shame may be manifest are at work in the universe. One is a principle of destruction.

> Some peoples God does not merely correct; He destroys them. He visits them with deep and abiding shame ... We read in our histories of the great empires of the old world; but when the traveler goes abroad, and looks for Nineveh and Babylon ... he finds nought but the outstretched graveyards which occupy the sites of departed nations.[29]

The other disciplining principle at work in the universe is a principle of restoration:

> Turn now to the more gracious aspects of God's economy. As there are peoples whom He destroys, so on the other hand there are those whom, while indeed he chastises, yet at the same time He preserves ... He disciplines; but when discipline has worked out its remedial benefits, he recompenses them for their former ignominy, and gives them honor and prosperity.[30]

In one instance, shame is the result of the utter destruction of a people; in the other, shame is redemptive, that is, it is used to correct and purify the nation to a higher purpose. Throughout history God has used this principle of discipline both to destroy and to correct nations. Crummell's interest in this disciplinary tool of God is directly related to the destiny of the race of people with which he is particularly concerned—the black race.

My purpose is to attempt, this morning, an investigation of God's disciplinary and retributive economy in races and nations; with the hope of arriving at some clear conclusions concerning the destiny of the Negro race.[31]

· Crummell has just cause to be concerned about issues of trials, punishments, and continued hardships. While we do not know the exact date when the sermon was originally preached, in the book in which it appears, *The Greatness of Christ*, it is styled as a Thanksgiving sermon preached in 1877,[32] which was a critical year in the life of black America, a fact surely not lost on the conscientious and studious Crummell. It was the year that marked the end of Reconstruction and the beginning of an extended period of retrenchment and backlash against blacks in white America.[33] So what did blacks have to be thankful for in 1877?

Crummell intends to demonstrate through his argument that they could be thankful in knowing that God could enter into a bad situation and bring good out of it. Not only would they be delivered from their present suffering, but they would actually prosper and attain new heights among their former captors. It is significant to note how Crummell uses an apocalyptic text to speak to a seemingly hopeless situation. On the basis of the text, he is promising his listeners not only deliverance from their captors but also empowerment and prosperity. He is arguing for more than mere survival; he is actually claiming superiority for his degraded and despised listeners. At such a time in their history, this claim could only be made possible through a mighty act of God.

The blacks of Crummell's day, like Israel in its Babylonian captivity, are in the relentless throes of a system that has systematically, capriciously, and arbitrarily discriminated against them. The forces that had historically sought to keep blacks economically disadvantaged and politically disabled seemed once again to be gaining the upper hand in the ideological struggle for the soul of the country. This Isaiah passage would undoubtedly have had special appeal to listeners who were entering an era of decline and reversal, an era in which it appeared they were once again at the mercy of insensitive whites and a callous and uncaring government.

To Crummell, this passage, which speaks of a restorative purpose to trial and punishment, seemed tailor-made to the issues of the day. It seems all the more appropriate for one whose thinking and religious upbringing had already been shaped by a longstanding belief in the power of almighty God to effect positive change in the face of overwhelming resistance and opposition. Crummell, in a carefully crafted argument, determines which type of discipline is being exacted upon a people at any given point in history. He points out that the current trials and hardships blacks are experiencing are clearly intended by God to be restorative, not destructive.

What is most important to remember about this argument, however, is his belief that none of this can come about except through the power of almighty God. Crummell consistently argues that God is in control of all earthly events and occurrences. God is actively engaged in the affairs of the nations of the world. Whatever befalls a nation—good or bad—is under the watchful eye of almighty God and serves some purpose in God's divine economy. When the discipline of shame is exacted upon a nation to its utter destruction, it comes from the hands of God:

> When I am called upon to account for all the loss of national and tribal life, I say that God destroyed them. And the declaration is made on the strength of a principle attested by numerous facts in sacred and profane history; that when the sins of a people reach a state of hateful maturity, then God sends upon them sudden destruction.[34]

When Crummell turns to the more palatable restorative principle, it too is implemented at the behest of a merciful and gracious God.

Throughout the sermon Crummell marshals both scriptural and nonscriptural examples to demonstrate to his listeners how God has liberated, lifted, and empowered despised races of people throughout history and ultimately brought them to their destined greatness. By citing the handiwork of God in such places as Nineveh, Babylon, Egypt, Assyria, Tyre, and Persia, Crummell intends to move blacks beyond the limited sphere of declining race relations in post-Reconstruction America in order to place them in the grand sweep of history. It is in that broad historical overview that one is better able to see the movement of almighty God.

In order to bring perspective to their current trials, Crummell lifts his people out of the hands of American political power as they are experiencing it and places them into the hands of a God who has dealt justly with nations and people throughout history. He wants his listeners to see that something more than American sociopolitical maneuvering is at work in their lives. He is determined to show how the paradoxical chastening in the divine economy of God will eventually lead to a better day for blacks.

Crummell's master lens of the mighty acts of God leads him to interpret history in a certain way. Things do not just happen on their own; rather they are under the direct control of a mighty God who acts, even through trial and punishment and the shame it causes, not only to destroy a people, but sometimes also to correct and purify them. Are there other possible ways to interpret the demise of once great civilizations? No doubt archaeologists, anthropologists, and theologians with a different theological perspective from Crummell's might interpret these events in a much different fashion. But Crummell's hermeneutic governs what he understands to be God's redemptive purpose in the Isaiah oracle.

In this instance the scripture selected by Crummell is clearly related to the power of God. It almost appears ready-made to the special needs of Crummell's listening congregation. The domain of experience in which this power is being manifested is corporate concerns, for God's power is made manifest on behalf of discouraged and demoralized blacks. A well-respected black pastor is speaking a word of exhortation and encouragement specifically to blacks. In his pairing of scripture and the black situation in life, Crummell predicts the superiority of blacks in every walk of life—political, educational, cultural, economic, and social. The extended metaphors through which the power is manifested may be described as deliverer and conquering sovereign who empowers the dispossessed. Both metaphors are interwoven throughout the sermon.

In summary, Alexander Crummell, a freeborn black Episcopal priest, appears to have been influenced by the understanding of God prevalent in the black religious experience of the nineteenth century. Given the nature of the times, blacks seemed intuitively to recognize that if they were to be lifted from the degradation of slavery and caste into first-class citizenship, their God had to be a God who was mighty to save. Crummell's preaching reflected an awareness and common usage of the biblical hermeneutic that I believe is central to black preaching. Although he preached a broad range of sermons, his pan-Africanist leanings made him more inclined to preach out of the social justice and corporate concerns domains of experience.

While Crummell's extensive writings allow us to see the hermeneutic more widely in his work, it can also be seen in the sermons of others who lived and preached in post–Civil War America. Francis J. Grimké is second to Crummell in the sheer quantity of published materials.

Francis J. Grimké (1850–1937)

For almost half a century Francis J. Grimké was regarded as one of the leading African American clergymen of his era. His perception of the conflict between Christian ideals and race prejudice led to his passionate denunciation of a wide variety of religious institutions and practices. As a lifelong member of the predominantly white Presbyterian church, his many protests within that denomination foreshadowed contemporary black caucus critiques of the white churches.[35] Born in Charleston, South Carolina, on November 4, 1850, Grimké was the middle son of a white planter and his slave mistress. Sold into slavery by his half-brother, Grimké was held in bondage until the war's end.[36]

While a student at Howard University, he decided to turn his thoughts toward ministry. In the fall of 1875, he entered Princeton Theological

Seminary to begin preparation for ministry. Upon graduation from the seminary in 1878, he accepted a call to the Fifteenth Street Presbyterian Church in Washington, D.C.[37] Throughout its history the church had included a high proportion of the city's African American aristocracy, who demanded, and received, an intelligent expression of Christianity as a religion that could nurture race pride and self-improvement. They also expected their pastor to be a strong "race man," speaking prophetically against the evils of race prejudice and on behalf of the rights of blacks as American citizens in the nation and as Christians in the church.[38]

As a craftsman of the homiletic art, Grimké was said to have few peers. His messages were consistently the product of careful and mature reflection, and they were delivered with power and conviction. Never one to compromise principle, Grimké habitually endeavored to proclaim truth as he saw it and as he understood it in his time. Much like his colleague and co-pastor in the city, Alexander Crummell, tactfulness was hardly one of Grimké's virtues. The central purpose of his life and preaching was the application of the gospel to the social order and its ills, particularly as that order related to the elevation of his people. He provided leadership in a time of great social ferment, having begun his public career shortly after America embarked upon the post-Reconstruction era. The dampened hopes of the black masses notwithstanding, Grimké never shied away from his belief that the lot of the Negro must and would be improved.[39]

Grimké, like the other ministers in our study, was not a systematic theologian; thus the best way to get at his understanding of God is through his sermonic material. Much of Grimké's published material comes at the end of the nineteenth and beginning of the twentieth centuries, from 1895 to 1915. This period has been described by many as the nadir of black life, that is, that time when it seemed that racial equality could never be achieved in America. Many blacks in this period believed the country was reneging on its promises of equality and attempting to roll back the gains made by blacks in the more progressive Reconstruction era just after the Civil War. Thus in Grimké's preaching one finds neither the trust in nor gratitude for government exhibited on numerous occasions by older ministers such as A.M.E. Bishop Daniel Alexander Payne. Grimké, true to the era in which he preached, saw it as his responsibility to call the government and the nation to account for their racism and retrenchment. At the same time he called white America to account, he also admonished blacks to continue to persevere in their pursuit of the American dream through thrift, labor, and moral rectitude.

From the sizable collection of historian Carter G. Woodson's edited volumes on Grimké's published sermons, one finds in his preaching the biblical hermeneutic of a God who acts mightily on behalf of the marginalized and powerless. On October 12, 1902, Grimké preached a sermon on racial issues surrounding an annual celebration in Washington, D.C.—the annual encampment of the Grand Army of the Republic. This day of celebration, from which blacks were apparently largely left out, prompted Grimké to search the scriptures for a word that would demonstrate to blacks why they have a right and a responsibility to participate in the governance and celebrations of a country where they were once held captive.

In his sermon titled "A Resemblance and a Contrast between the American Negro and the Children of Israel, in Egypt, or the Duty of the Negro to Contend Earnestly for His Rights Guaranteed under the Constitution,"[40] Grimké uses as his text a portion of the very familiar exodus story. The sociopolitical bondage of the Israelites seems to Grimké a most fitting comparison. Through the recounting of the exodus narrative, Grimké demonstrates to his people that God continues to act on behalf of those who are oppressed and marginalized by the powerful in society and how, in a providential turn of events, those who were once despised and rejected gain a place of prominence through loyalty and devotion in the country of their enslavement. Moreover, from that loyalty and devotion they also inherit a right and a responsibility to participate in the life of their country.

Grimké's text, taken from Exodus 1:9–10 (KJV), rehearses the story of the oppression of the Israelites at the hands of their Egyptian captors. However, it is much more than a tale of captivity and oppression; it is also the story of the eventual deliverance by God of God's chosen people. The exodus narrative that Grimké chose says volumes to his listeners about what he believes about the power of God, both to deliver and to provide for God's chosen people. No single symbol has historically captured more clearly the distinctiveness of African American Christianity, and subsequently its preaching, than the Exodus. The story of the exodus speaks especially to blacks, for it recounts the activity of God in the life of a degraded and marginalized people forcibly held against their will in the land of their captors.[41]

The domain of experience on which this sermon reflects and to which it is directed is social justice. Grimké is not seeking to overthrow the Constitution of the United States. Rather, he simply aspires to nullify the narrow interpretation of those who are attempting to exclude blacks from the guarantees of the Constitution. Grimké insists on equal treatment under the law and focuses on the earned right of captives to participate at every level in the life of the country of their enslavement.

The sermon functions to encourage American blacks to take their just and rightful places in the sociopolitical celebrations and pastimes of their country. The scriptural passage reads, "And he said unto his people, Behold, the people of the children of Israel are more and mightier than we: Come on, let us deal wisely with them; lest they multiply, and it come to pass, that, when there falleth out any war, they join also unto our enemies, and fight against us, and so get them up of out the land" (Exod. 1:9–10, KJV).

Grimké points out from the text parallels and dissimilarities between the Israelites and contemporary blacks in America:

1. Dissimilarity: Their Journeys into Captivity. Grimké points out an obvious dissimilarity in how the two peoples came into their respective captivities. Israelites, said Grimké, traveled to Egypt of their own free will, while blacks were seized by slave hunters.
2. Parallel: The Increase in Slave Population. Grimké notes the phenomenal increases in both populations in order to demonstrate that blacks, just like the children of Israel, multiplied in spite of their captors' effort to hinder the race.
3. Parallel: Captors Fearing Their Increasing Numbers. The Egyptians, alarmed at the rapid increase in Israelite numbers, sought several ways to diminish their population. So too whites, fearing the increasing number of blacks in America, engaged in a process of destruction to diminish their numbers.
4. Dissimilarity: Attitude of Captors toward Their Return. Grimké intends in this move to show a disparaging dissimilarity between the Israelites and blacks. First, he notes that the Egyptians feared their captives would find some way to escape. This fear did not grow out of love for the Israelites but rather out of practical concerns regarding a cheap labor supply. Second, Grimké points out that the Israelites never intended to remain in Egypt forever. Rather, they viewed their sojourn in Egypt as a temporary arrangement until the famine that had driven them there subsided. In their relationship to previously enslaved blacks, whites, unlike the Egyptians, preferred that blacks leave the country, but unlike the Israelites, blacks were in America to stay.
5. Parallel: Captors Feared the Enslaved Would Side with the Enemy. Both Egyptians and white Americans feared that, in the event of war, their slaves would side with the enemies of their captors, that is, not with the slaves' owners.

In pointing out the parallels and dissimilarities between the Israelites in Egypt and the blacks in America, Grimké is careful to leave no doubt that both captivities were under the control of almighty God. The exodus is important for Grimké because of what it says about the power and purpose of God. Just as there was divine purpose and intentionality in the captivity of the Israelites, there was also purpose and design in the captivity of

Africans in America. By juxtaposing the parallels and dissimilarities of the Israelites and the blacks, Grimké was not suggesting that the plight of the two enslaved peoples is identical. He was, however, attempting to show that the captivities of both peoples, although brutal and harsh, are nonetheless under the control and power of the sovereign God.

Grimké was not arguing for like situations but for the manifestation of the power of God in all situations of injustice and oppression. Even though it exacted much toil and sweat from both peoples, the providence of God eventually brought deliverance and freedom. In his fourth analogy where Grimké speaks of the Egyptians' fear of increasing Israelite numbers, he claims the providence of God as the cause of the Egyptians' failure to decrease the Israelite numbers:

> The Egyptians were alarmed at the rapid increase of the children of Israel, and sought in one way or another to diminish their number ... a decree was issued compelling parents to expose their own children to death. Under this decree, Moses ... would have perished had he not been providentially rescued by Pharaoh's daughter from an untimely death.[42]

In his fifth analogy where he addresses the length of the Israelites' stay in Egypt, Grimké observes that it was not in keeping with the divine plan that the children of Israel remain permanently in Egypt.

> When the children of Israel first went down into Egypt it was with no intention of remaining there permanently ... Nor was it in accordance with the divine plan that they should remain permanently, as is evident from the record, in forty-six of Genesis. "And God spake unto Israel in the vision of the night, and said, Jacob, Jacob ... fear not to go down into Egypt, for I will there make of thee a great nation: I will go down with thee into Egypt, and I will surely bring thee up again.[43]

Even when Grimké calls attention to the dissimilarity between the duration of the stay of the Israelites and of the blacks in the lands of their captors, it is still God who directs the affairs. Grimké believes it is God's will for blacks to stay in America even though their white captors, unlike the Egyptians, would prefer them to leave. He even rejects the black embrace of the highly touted and very popular theory of providential design, for he believes it to be contrary to the will of God for blacks.[44] No one, not even misguided blacks, is allowed to thwart or usurp the mighty acts of God. The point is clear: any action or initiative—even when it comes from blacks—that is contrary to an understanding of God's providential ordering of events must be rejected.

When Grimké speaks of the continued harsh treatment of the Israelites at the hands of their Egyptian captors, he observes that it was only allowed to continue "until it was reversed by the divine interposition, until God's righteous indignation was exacted, and the angel of death was sent forth." In like manner, says Grimké, oppressors the world over shall meet a similar fate:

> God is not dead—nor is he an indifferent onlooker at what is going on in this world. One day He will make requisition for blood; He will call the oppressors to account. Justice may sleep, but it never dies. The individual, race, or nation which does wrong, which sets at defiance God's great law ... will be sure, sooner or later, to pay the penalty. We reap as we sow. With what measure we mete, it shall be measured to us again.[45]

Never in the sermon is God depicted as anything other than the all-powerful and all-knowing God who acts mightily on behalf of the poor and oppressed.

Although Grimké draws pockets of truth from these analogies along the way, his chief purpose for selecting the Exodus passage comes into clearer focus as the structure of the sermon shifts to the main conceptual truth he wishes to draw from scripture that day. That truth, simply stated, is that blacks in America, just like the Israelites before them, had earned the right to participate in the civic and cultural affairs of the country of their captors.

Through loyalty and devotion as well as an unquenchable patriotism, blacks had obtained the right to be a part of the nation. In fact, blacks had been even more loyal to America than Israel had been to Egypt. This is especially true, according to Grimké, when one considers that God has apparently willed for blacks to remain in America, as opposed to returning to their homeland like the Israelites.

The target of Grimké's argument for black participation in the affairs of the nation is the yearly Encampment of the Grand Army of the Republic. Noting that the army was an organization made up of surviving veterans of the great Civil War, Grimké points out how blacks, even when held in slavery, participated and fought in that Grand Army of the Republic. He goes on to note that although blacks had been loyal to the country, the country had still not lived up to the promises of the Constitution.

Although the great amendments of the Constitution had been enacted, making blacks free people and citizens, blacks still had not been granted possession of their rights. Though blacks were denied their rights in a country for which they fought and died, they must continue to agitate for them nonetheless: "Be assured," said Grimké, "that these wrongs, from which we are suffering, will never be righted if we sit idly by and take no interest in the matter." Grimké would have his hearers know that it is God who is on their side in the struggle, and if they do not struggle for the rights God has enabled them to achieve, they will be doing themselves and God a disservice:

> If we are true to ourselves and to God the victory will be ours. It may be slow in coming, but come it will. Nothing is to be gained by withdrawing from the contest. Our duty is to remain firm; to plant ourselves squarely and uncompromisingly upon the rights guaranteed to us under the Constitution, and to hold our ground.[46]

Through the recounting of a portion of the Exodus narrative, Grimké draws one major conceptual truth about the purposive acts of God toward God's enslaved people. Both Israelites and blacks had been enslaved in the lands of their captors. In keeping with the will of God, however, both peoples eventually developed a loyalty and dedication that guaranteed them the right to participate in the life of the nation.

Grimké comes to this text with a prior understanding of the power of God. He sees in this narrative similar circumstances between the two peoples, but more importantly, he sees power and purpose in the plan of God. The domain in which God's power is demonstrated is social justice. Grimké, while speaking a word of encouragement intended especially for blacks, is calling for equality and justice for all, including blacks. The extended metaphors that inform the sermon are God as liberator and provider. The recounting of the narrative is so structured as to highlight this particular theme. Having established this truth on the basis of scripture, Grimké goes on to develop its implications in the lives of the blacks in post–Civil War America. They, according to Grimké, have earned their right to participate in the political and social affairs of the country.

Time and again throughout Grimké's preaching, one can see this foundational hermeneutic at work. Grimké goes to the text in search of answers that already contain some formulation of God, the mighty sovereign. His preconceptions of God help to frame the questions he will ask of the text concerning the situations faced by his people: What does God have to say this day to my people about the changes and challenges of their sociocultural situation? The pattern is repeated over and over again throughout his published sermonic material.

In a sermon titled "The Roosevelt-Washington Episode, or Race Prejudice,"[47] Grimké addressed head-on the uproar caused when President Theodore Roosevelt invited Booker T. Washington to the White House for dinner. Many whites, especially in the South, expressed outrage and alarm at this harmless gesture, the prominence of Washington notwithstanding.

Within two weeks of the dinner that took place on October 16, 1901, Grimké addressed the matter in his Fifteenth Street pulpit.[48] He selected Acts 11:2–3 for his text: "And when Peter was come up unto Jerusalem, they that were of the circumcision contended with him, saying, Thou wentest in to men uncircumcised and didst eat with them." (KJV)

Grimké's explication of the passage is clear and to the point: The Jews misunderstood their election by almighty God. The great blessings that came to them were intended to bring them nearer to God, to purify their hearts, and to fit them to do the work which he had mapped out for them, namely, to become his chosen instruments, in the fullness of time. This was the purpose which God had in mind in the training of the Jewish nation: to use them for the dissemination of the gospel among all peoples. Instead of viewing themselves as instruments, however, they viewed their election in narrow provincial terms that made them proud and arrogant. "They looked down upon all other races; held them in the greatest contempt. They felt that they were the special favorites of heaven."[49]

This same general feeling among the Jews—shrinking away from contact with others and regarding them as unclean—also affected Peter. When God wanted to use Peter by sending him on a mission to a certain Gentile named Cornelius, he actually had to work a miracle in order to prepare him. Grimké recounts the vision in the tenth chapter of Acts, where the heavens open and a certain vessel descends wherein are all manner of four-footed and creeping things of the earth. A voice says to Peter: "Rise, Peter, kill and eat." "But Peter said, Not so, Lord; for I have never eaten anything that is common and unclean. And a voice spake unto him again the second time, What God hath cleansed, that call not thou common" (Acts 10:14–15, KJV).

The vision makes clear that Peter is no longer to regard his narrow provincialism and Jewish exclusivity as being the will of God. As Peter mulled over the vision, men sent by Cornelius were inquiring where Peter lived. Peter went to proclaim the gospel to Cornelius and spent time in the home of the Gentile as his guest. For these actions Peter was bitterly denounced by his Jewish counterparts.

Grimké draws the parallel between the Jews and the whites in America:

> Poor Peter is not the only one who has been criticized for eating with a member of a supposed inferior race. Our good President is just now passing through a similar experience for inviting Booker T. Washington to dine with him. What a howl has gone up all over the South, and why? Because the President has seen fit to entertain at his table a colored gentleman ... who has been more lauded by the South than any Negro who has ever lived in this country.[50]

Grimké then outlines four reasons why he is glad that a black man has been invited to dine with the President in the White House. Underlying his reasoning is an implicit understanding about God, what God requires, and how God in God's own way eventually brings what God wills to pass. First, he says, it shows that the country has at last in the White House one who is every inch a man, one who has convictions and convictions in the right direction.

"It is a great thing," says Grimké, "to have the fear of God so implanted in the soul, and to have the love of right so strongly developed in us that we will not be turned away from the path of duty though confronted by all the powers of darkness." Roosevelt, by this controversial act, has shown himself to be a morally upright individual who views humankind in a manner consistent with the intentions of almighty God. Thank God, says Grimké, there has come at last into power a man who by this act has said:

> [W]hatever others may have done, so far as I am concerned, I shall know no man by the color of his skin. What I accord to white men I will accord to black men, I shall treat all citizens alike. That is the kind of President to have ...[51]

From his praise of Roosevelt it is clear that Grimké believes that the man worthy of the White House is one who does not view God's favoring of one race over another as a call to discriminate and oppress.

Second, the episode brought out the real feelings of the South toward the Negro:

> It doesn't make any difference what he becomes, what his achievements are, however pure his character, however culti-vated his mind, he is always to be treated as an inferior, to be kept in his place. Every Negro in the South may become a Booker T. Washington, and yet the brand of inferiority is to be stamped upon him.[52]

Grimké sees the uproar created by this invitation as an opportunity in one of the worst periods of race relations in America to call the country to account for the pernicious doctrine, which had steadily been growing in the North among supposed friends of blacks, that southern whites know best how to deal with blacks:

> There is but one ground upon which the North can or ought to accede to any such proposition, and that is that in its judgment the Southern white man ... has a larger sense of justice in deal-ing with the Negro ...[53]

The notion that the southern white man was more just was patently false to Grimké. "What hope is there for the Negro, left to be dealt with by men who object to Booker T. Washington dining with the President of the United States, and who denounce the President's conduct in inviting him as an 'outrage'?" The North has clearly grown weary of fighting the black man's battle and some thirty-five years after the Civil War, most whites have succumbed to a "let-alone policy," with regard to the South.

Grimké warns his northern friends that peace can never be obtained by yielding to evil:

> The men of this generation in the North may adopt the let-alone policy and permit things to go on as the South dictates, but they are simply laying up trouble for their children and their children's children. As the poet has expressed it:
>
> > "They enslave their children's children
> > Who make compromise with sin."[54]

For Grimké, it is no mere political squabble but a matter of dealing forthrightly with sin and evil. The ruckus caused by the South goes to the very heart of the issues of justice and fair treatment required by God.

Third, the issue would open the eyes of Professor Washington, who had taken a rather rose-colored view of things in the South and of the southern people. Although many whites viewed Washington as an instrument of God's will, because many of them believed he accepted their view of the race problem, Grimké is careful to point out that if Washington ever stepped beyond the boundaries of their limited aspirations for the Negro, he would not be tolerated by southern whites: "If he dares to entertain any other theory or ventures to step out in any other direction, the South must withdraw all sympathy from him and relegate him to the class of undesirable Negroes, Negroes who think themselves as good as white men."[55]

Even Washington—viewed by many whites as an instrument of God's will—must be called to account for his desperate attempts to appease the unfounded prejudices and fears of southern whites. Washington must know that second-class, subservient existence is not God's will for God's created order. And Washington, who has moved so often without incident in privileged circles, must see this episode as a reminder that he too is still regarded by many as little more than a useful tool of a decadent South determined to keep the African American in his place.

Fourth, the episode brought to view the fact that blacks still had some friends left in the North. The North had become so apathetic, so indifferent to blacks, that many had begun to feel their friends in the North were indeed few and far between. Men who were once identified with the cause of freedom were found fellowshipping with men who a few days earlier had remarked that "the action of President Roosevelt in entertaining that nigger will necessitate our killing a thousand niggers in the South before they will learn their place again."[56]

Grimké, however, thanks the northern press for speaking out against such men, who until the Washington incident had seemed to be gaining ground among those who were once counted as friends of blacks in their push for first-class citizenship. "What we need in the editor's chair," says Grimké, "as well as in the pulpit are men, God-fearing men—men who love righteousness and hate iniquity. And just in proportion as such men come to the front will public sentiment be moulded in the interest of justice and humanity. Let us not be discouraged. God reigns and the right will ultimately triumph."[57]

At the center of the organization of this sermon is God the mighty sovereign. Grimké viewed God as acting providentially in four specific instances. First, Grimké has shown the nation that in a very critical period in the country's race relations God has placed in the White House a man of honor and integrity. Second, God has used the dinner to expose whites who by the turn of the century have succeeded in convincing the North that the South knows best how to treat the black man. Third, the incident has opened the eyes of Booker T. Washington to the plight of his own people in the South, most of whom do not have the privilege of moving in the same circles of society as he does.

Finally, the incident reawakened some of the friends of blacks to continued vigilance on behalf of blacks. The domain out of which Grimké preaches is clearly social justice. He is insisting that blacks be treated as all other citizens of the country, which includes a dinner at the White House if the president so desires. Grimké seeks to reform the system he is critiquing so that it conforms once again to fundamental principles of fairness and equality, and he sees God's power being manifested toward that end.

These sermons by Grimké demonstrate that he also brought to scripture the master lens I claim is distinctive to black preaching. Whether dealing with social justice issues on a broad scale or personal piety concerns in the life of the believer, an examination of his published materials shows that he attributed all positive advancement to the will and power of God. Grimké saw God at work in every domain of black experience, and in God alone he placed his trust.

Daniel Alexander Payne (1811–1893)

The remaining nineteenth-century preachers I will discuss—Daniel Alexander Payne and Elias C. Morris—were roughly contemporaries of Crummell and Grimké but do not have their extensive publishing records.

Even in their limited publications, however, we see evidence of this central template.

Daniel Alexander Payne was born of free parents in Charleston, South Carolina, on February 24, 1811. In 1852, at the age of forty-one, Payne was elected a bishop of the African Methodist Episcopal Church (A.M.E.). He became the official historian of the African Methodists, their greatest educator, and perhaps the most influential bishop of the nineteenth-century black denominations.[58] In a ministry that extended across much of the nineteenth century, Payne constantly urged personal morality, domestic stability, thrift, industry, and education—virtues he believed would help shore up the black community.

He was a lifelong supporter of education and an educated ministry, as his own work in the founding of three schools and the purchase of Wilberforce University attests. He labored untiringly for the advancement of blacks in America, and while sympathetic to Africa, he never viewed colonization or repatriation to the motherland as a call or goal in his own ministry. His contribution to his race was to promote the intellectual, moral, religious, and social improvement of the people of color in the United States. This he did with unstinting zeal throughout the latter half of the nineteenth century as a bishop of the A.M.E. Church.

Payne's religious experience, like that of most of his contemporaries, was forged in the trying times of slavery. Though born free, he was not exempt from the ridicule, contempt, and flagrant racism heaped upon all blacks at that time in America. In his autobiography, whenever Payne recounts a sore trial or some heartrending situation for himself or his people, he responds by falling back on what he terms, "the strong arm of the Lord God Almighty."[59]

From early childhood he seems to have been imbued with a sense of the ultimate justice and vindicating power of God. When his first school was closed by a retroactive South Carolina law that forbade the teaching of colored students, Payne began to question the existence of God. "Is there no God?" he asked. But when he remembered that delay does not necessarily indicate denial, he contented himself with the promise of God's ultimate victory:

> But when there came into my mind those solemn words: "With God one day is as a thousand years and a thousand years as one day. Trust in him, and he will bring slavery and all its outrages to an end." These words from the spirit world acted on my troubled soul like water on a burning fire, and my aching heart was soothed and relieved from its burden of woes.[60]

The utter trust that Payne placed in God was no pie-in-the-sky, compensatory religious hope that caused him to be content with injustice and prejudice. Rather, it was this very belief in the justice and ultimate vindicating power of God that motivated Payne to look northward for a more productive teaching environment. His belief in God's ultimate power settled his mind, but it activated his will to make things better for blacks through education and moral refinement.

Examples abound of Payne relying on the ultimate power of God to set aright those things that were seriously wanting in America. On his election to the episcopate in 1852, feeling himself most unworthy for the task, he spoke of eventually yielding to the vote of the church because, "I felt that the omnipotent Arm that had thrust me into the position would hold me in it."[61] On another occasion, in an audience with President Abraham Lincoln, Payne informed the president that he never ceased to pray for his victory, and he prayed that God might impart such power to the Union government:

> We, the colored citizens of the republic, have been praying: "O Lord just as thou didst cause the throne of David to wax stronger and stronger ... we beseech thee cause the power at Washington to grow stronger and stronger, while that at Richmond shall grow weaker and weaker."[62]

In Payne's world, God caused things in God's own time, both good and bad. Payne believed in the ultimate power of God and trusted that that power was made available to, and used on behalf of, those who were just in their cause. During an 1865 missionary tour of the South, Payne attributed the devastation to God's indignation over slavery:

> All showed the devastating hand of war, and the hot indignation of that God who, when he stretches out his arm against the oppressor, never draws it back till every fetter is broken and slavery is free.[63]

Payne had a profound sense of the omnipotence of God and God's determination to set things aright. When put off a train because he would not sit in the section reserved for colored passengers, Payne refused to press charges against the railroad, preferring instead to put his case "in the hands of the Omnipotent." When later he was granted permission to ride first-class on the same train, he understood this as a clear signal that God was working on the hearts of the rulers of the earth.[64] In fact, Payne viewed his entire life's work as a plan of service mapped out for him by almighty God.

In reflecting on his long life, he considered himself an unworthy instrument in God's hand for the salvation of his people and the uplifting of his race.[65] This way of thinking about God, this constant sense of the presence and power of God, infused Payne's life. It is this same understanding of a God who acts mightily on behalf of the marginalized and powerless that Payne brought to his preaching. This understanding of God is the master lens through which he approached the scriptures and from which he drew relevant meaning for the listeners of his day. This hermeneutic is at the heart of Payne's most famous and widely heard sermon, "Welcome to the Ransomed; or Duties of the Colored Inhabitants of the District of Columbia."[66]

On April 11, 1862, Congress passed the District of Columbia Emancipation Act, intended to emancipate the slaves in Washington and compensate loyal masters for their loss of property. During this period President Lincoln received a visit from Payne, then presiding as bishop of the Second Episcopal District of the A.M.E. Church, with headquarters in the District of Columbia. Payne urged Lincoln to sign the bill but left without any assurances from the president that he would do so.[67] The black churches in Washington set aside Sunday, April 3, 1862, as a day of thanksgiving and prayer, hoping that the president would sign the act into law. At one of those services, Payne preached "Welcome to the Ransomed." Not long thereafter, President Lincoln signed the measure.[68]

Although Payne's sermon was intended to acclimate the newly freed slaves of the District of Columbia to the responsibilities that came along with freedom, it was also aimed at thousands of slaves from surrounding states who had fled into the camps of the Union soldiers near the city, seeking refuge and freedom. Shortly after the war began, Washington became a haven for slaves fleeing Virginia and Maryland. Though the sermon embodies the essence of the Protestant ethic—industry, sobriety, thrift, and piety—at the same time it clearly reflects the hermeneutic I claim is central to black preaching.

Payne chose to base his sermon on an epistle—1 Timothy 2:1–4 (KJV). Paul admonishes the Ephesian ministers and laity alike to make supplications, prayers, and giving of thanks for all people. For Payne, however, Paul's more specific admonition—that these acts be done for kings and for all that are in authority—appears to be the portion of scripture more appropriately suited to the recently freed slaves in Washington, D.C.

Initially, Payne attributes their freedom to the benevolent intention of the U.S. Congress, and because of this act of kindness, he tells his congregation of soon-to-be and newly freed people that Paul's admonition to pray for governing authorities is more binding upon blacks than it was for Christians in Paul's day. Paul lived under the bloody reign of Nero, who, having set Rome on fire, amused himself with drinking and music while the city was in flames. If Paul called upon Christians to pray for such "monsters of wickedness," how much more, asks Payne, "is it our duty to pray for a Christian government?"

> Congress needs our supplications, they shall have them. The
> President and his Cabinet need our prayers, they shall possess
> them ... Upon all these departments of law, authority, and
> power, we shall beseech the God of Nations to send the spirit
> of wisdom, justice, liberty ... To make supplications ... for these
> authorities, is the peculiar privilege of the Colored People in the
> United States.[69]

Recognizing that the welfare of each nation is bound up with its government, Payne urges the newly freed slaves to pray and give thanks for
the benevolent Christian authorities in Washington, D.C., for the same
three reasons outlined by Paul in his letter to Timothy: (1) that they may
lead quiet and peaceable lives in all godliness and honesty; (2) because it
is good and acceptable in the sight of God, our Savior; and (3) because
God will have all people to be saved and to come unto the knowledge of
the truth. The remaining structure of this deductive sermon follows the
contours of this outline of the text.

His insistence that they pray for and give thanks to the government
that freed them in order that they may lead peaceable lives is Payne's opportunity to spell out to the newly freed slaves the kind of life he thinks
they ought to live or, as we shall see later, the end to which the power of
God has been manifested on their behalf. In this regard, he ties the scripture directly to their sociocultural experiences. True to form, he welcomes
them to lives of personal morality, domestic stability, thrift, industry, education, and virtue:

> Enter the great family of Holy Freedom; not to lounge in sinful
> indolence, not to degrade yourselves by vice, nor to corrupt so-
> ciety by licentiousness, neither to offend the laws by crime, but
> to the enjoyment of a well-regulated liberty.[70]

Payne's sermon was more than an exercise in courtesy and decency; it
welcomed the freed people and at the same time outlined the "Duties of
the Colored Inhabitants of the District of Columbia."[71] They were welcome
to do those things that promoted and advanced the cause of freedom, but
they were not welcome to engage in those acts that would reflect negatively on free blacks or reinforce long-held white stereotypes. They were
admonished by Payne to attend church, cultivate their minds, and
sharpen their social skills through contact with other free blacks. Only after such meaningful engagements did Payne feel they would be morally
prepared to recognize and respond to all the relations of civilized and
Christianized life.

Although Payne thanked the government for its generosity and admonished the newly freed slaves to live lives worthy of such freedom,

there is more to this sermon than kudos for generous whites and timely advice for backward blacks. An overriding understanding of the power of God informs this entire sermon. One gets a sense of this understanding in the opening lines when Payne refers to emancipation as the boon of holy freedom. Why does he refer to freedom as holy? Why does he not characterize freedom in patriotic or human rights language? He refers to it as holy because this great deliverance has ultimately been made possible through the power of God:

> Now, if we ask, who has sent us this great deliverance? The answer shall be, the Lord; the Lord God Almighty ... Thou, O Lord, and thou alone couldst have moved the heart of the nation to have done so great a deed for this weak, despised and needy people![72]

This encapsulates the hermeneutic that undergirds the entire sermon. Even though he thanks Congress for the act of emancipation, urges the newly freed blacks to pray for the Christian government that freed them, and beseeches them to live lives worthy of such freedom, it is God who ultimately makes all of this possible. Why pray for governments? Because they are good? No! Because governments must ultimately conform to the power of God's redemptive purposes. Payne believes that government can be an instrument of that redemptive purpose but never an end in itself. With that in mind the apostle Paul and Payne urge us to pray for governments—good and bad—for ultimately God uses them to effect God's will.

Even in admonishing blacks to live good and upright lives, Payne does not encourage them to do this because the government is good but rather because God is good, and God has moved decisively in their lives to bring about their long-awaited freedom. The Union government is not good in itself; it is only good if it does what pleases God, for it is then that God's power is manifested on behalf of the nation and its people:

> If God has blessed this nation, neither internal foes, nor foreign enemies can crush it. But God will bless it if it will do right, administering justice to each and to all, protecting the weak as well as the strong, and throwing the broad wings of its power equally over men of every color. This is God-like, and God will bless his own image, be it in a nation or in a man.[73]

Even the higher moral life to which Payne is calling the newly freed slaves is not to be lived out of gratitude to the government but rather to God. He refers to their freedom as holy because he wants them to know that it comes from the hands of God and refers to more than mere physical freedom. They have also been freed spiritually, and this should be reflected in clean and decent living: "As you are now free in body so now seek to be free in soul and spirit, from sin and Satan. The noblest freeman is he whom Christ makes free."[74]

In 1862, when this act freeing slaves in the District of Columbia became law, blacks had not yet been granted the right to take up arms in defense of the government. While noting that Anglo-Saxons and "Anglo-Africans" alike had complained of this prohibition, Payne said he was rather glad of it. In fact, he could see the hand of God in such a decision, for Payne viewed the Civil War as a conflict among whites—"a sort of family quarrel." Blacks could be more useful by praying for God's power to be demonstrated on behalf of the Union government:

> But we can yield a power in behalf of the Government which neither rifled cannon, nor mortar ... nor bomb-proof walls resist. That power is the right arm of God—of God, who lifts up and casts down nations according as they obey, or disregard the principles of truth, justice, liberty.[75]

Blacks should not fret, he says, because they have not been granted the right to take up arms in defense of the country; they can still make a contribution to the cause by petitioning God to unleash God's power on behalf of those who are in the right. While men like Frederick Douglass and others who supported black involvement at all levels in the war would disagree with Payne's insistence that prayer, to the exclusion of taking up arms, was a sufficient weapon for blacks, Payne's argument is nonetheless consistent with the hermeneutic that informs his sermon—God acts mightily on behalf of the powerless.

The components of this formative hermeneutic are clearly present in this sermon. Underlying this textual sermon is an understanding of God that Payne brings to the scriptures prior to the selection of this particular passage. The formative hermeneutic that he brings both colors and impacts his sermon in a way that makes quite clear which lens he is using. It is the almighty God, working through the U.S. Congress and President Lincoln, who has acted with awesome power on behalf of the former slaves of Washington, D.C.

Payne's understanding of the sovereign God is a part of his worldview, his religious ethos. It is not just something he preaches because of the particular passage of scripture that is before him. Rather, it is the template he takes with him to the scriptures and which in turn shapes his construal and use of scripture. The particular genre selected for this sermon is an epistle, but the hermeneutic is operative irrespective of genre.

The domain of experience out of which he preaches is the present-day world of the corporate concerns of blacks in Washington, D.C., and later the entire South. His is a word of admonishment directed specifically toward recently freed blacks. The extended metaphors he uses to illuminate the power are those of the God who delivers and provides. Payne demonstrates that God's power was manifested both to free the slaves and ultimately to enable the Union to prevail and be victorious over the South. The power is connected to a moral, spiritual, educational, and economic context.

Because Payne was from the school of thought that believed moral virtue was foremost in the Christian life, the context he thought most appropriate to this display of power was that of a higher moral plane. His admonitions to thrift, hard work, education, and discipline were all born of a desire to see a higher moral standard exacted upon the recently freed Washington, D.C. slaves.

Though preachers like Crummell and Grimké would be less inclined than Payne to see goodness and Christianity in the American government, the same hermeneutic informs the preaching of all three men. They are all guided by a pattern they believe to be present in scripture—a God who acts mightily on behalf of the marginalized and powerless.

Elias Camp Morris (1855–1922)

Elias Camp Morris, a self-educated former slave, came to national prominence during the latter part of the nineteenth century. Morris was one of several leading black clergymen who were instrumental in effecting the union between the three African American Baptist bodies that came together in the last years of the nineteenth century to form the National Baptist Convention of the United States of America.[76] In 1895, at the age of forty, he was elected president of the consolidated conventions.

In religious and denominational matters, Morris was regarded as a "co-operationist" black minister, that is, he was counted among those who desired to maintain some ties of unity with the white Baptist establishment, although he saw the need for blacks to develop their own churches and leadership.[77] He rejected black nationalist calls for repatriation and back-to-Africa movements, and he supported the theory of providential design, primarily in its missionary emphasis. Morris believed that education, hard work, and a morally upright life were the keys to success in life.

Morris did not display the fiery rhetoric of Grimké, nor did he possess the pan-African sentiments of Crummell; but his understanding of God, like that of the other ministers in this study, was forged in the crucible of slavery and the hardships of race prejudice. Thus, he also brought to his preaching this perception of God that I claim is foundational to black preaching. From his one published volume of sermons and addresses, along with his presidential addresses scattered throughout other publications, one can ascertain three basic beliefs about God that permeated Morris's preaching throughout the latter part of the nineteenth century.

First, in terms of an overall worldview, he primarily understood God to be an immanent, real force in human affairs, controlling the universe and everything in it. Morris believed that even the black struggle for freedom and equality was under the direction of an unerring providence:

> I come to say that when the light from the eternal hills announced the birth of the nineteenth century, our race—our fathers and mothers—groaned in the grasp of slavery, and held the place of goods and chattels. But by the direction of an unerring providence, when a little past the meridian of the century, a decree was handed down that "the slaves are and henceforth shall be free."[78]

Second, Morris viewed God as using all human events and occurrences as agents of God's redemptive purposes. Whether in matters pertaining to white prejudice, racial solidarity, self-help, economic advancement, or other such issues, God uses humans to effect God's purpose:

> I firmly believe in the possibilities of the race and I believe also that he that hath begun a good work in us will perform it; that God began the emancipation of our race, and that no power on earth can prevent its complete disenthrallment. But in most of his dealings with men he has used human instrumentalities ...[79]

Third, Morris refused to cede to human hands alone the credit for the advancement of the race. Rather, whatever gains blacks had made are directly attributable to the leading hand of the Almighty; and to trust in anything less was both dangerous and deceptive:

> Some of the people of the race trusted in political parties to bring deliverance ... but the great masses of the people have trusted in God, and while political parties have come and gone ... this invincible race has moved steadily forward and is fairly well prepared to face courageously the second half century of its freedom ... Can we not truthfully say, "hitherto the Lord has led us," and we believe He will continue to lead us, until we shall have been fully established.[80]

Morris believed the omnipotent, all-wise God to be at work in a very practical and determined manner on behalf of black advancement despite overwhelming obstacles.[81] God was in charge of history, and the despised blacks were in God's hands. This perspective was central in Morris's preaching. In his published volume of sermons, Morris gives clear indication that this central template was part of his theological mindset.

Owing in part to his conservative beliefs and the influence of white Baptists on his theology, the domains of experience in which God's power is manifested, at least in Morris's published sermons, are primarily those of personal piety and care of the soul. He treated larger issues of social justice and corporate concerns, more often than not, in essays and presidential addresses but rarely in sermons.

Morris considered the conversion of the individual as one of the most pressing matters facing humanity, including the black race. Therefore, a pious and converted heart, exemplifying right conduct, is of prime importance in his sermons. Though the spheres in which he believes God's power to be operative are somewhat constricted with respect to his peers in the North, this same biblical hermeneutic nevertheless informs his sermon.

The personal piety that characterized much of the preaching in Morris's published sermons can be seen in his sermon titled "The Brotherhood of Man." His text is taken from Genesis 45, the story of Joseph being sold into Egyptian slavery by his brothers. The extended metaphor operative in this sermon is the parenthood of God: "The theme of our discourse carries us beyond blood relationships and introduces us to an unexplored field of humanity which recognizes one common Father—God, and one common brother—man."[82]

Morris then proceeds to argue for a doctrine of the brotherhood of man. He claims that the church has apparently gone to sleep on this great doctrine, allowing the political, economic, and social questions of the day to relegate it to the background. In so doing, according to Morris, the church has silenced one of the most effective weapons of the Christian religion.

That a biblical hermeneutic of a God who acts mightily on behalf of the marginalized and powerless forms the basis of this sermon is evident when Morris recounts Joseph's magnanimous spirit toward the brothers who sold him into slavery:

> Joseph hastily tells them that it was God's purpose that he should be thus sent ahead of them, that he might preserve life. We cannot always understand the purposes or plans of the All-wise God in his dealings with his people, nor are we at all times prepared to accept willingly the orders of his Providence or the wisdom of his counsel. But he surely knows what is best for us, for he can see the end from the beginning, and knows of every obstacle which lies in our path, from the cradle to the grave.[83]

Joseph's Egyptian bondage was not an event that occurred beyond the scope and power of almighty God, but God allowed it to occur through God's permissive will in order to save the lives of the Hebrew people. God acts at all times in the best interest of those who love and obey God, although we might not be able to see or accept the movement of God in all situations. Surely the blacks who heard Morris preach would know that even though he was recounting the trials of the Israelites, he was also speaking to their experiences as an enslaved people. And they would know that what he said about God's overarching care and providence for people in biblical days certainly applied to American blacks in the nineteenth and twentieth centuries. Morris points out that same divine purpose—the preservation of life—in the slave experiences of people throughout the world:

> Slavery has existed in some form or other in nearly all ages of the past. But in some instances it proved to be a blessing in disguise ... It has separated husband and wife, parents and children, brother and sister ... But these cruel separations do not, in all cases, last forever. Sometimes they are of short duration and work for the persecuted party "a far more exceeding and eternal weight of glory."[84]

The bonds of brotherhood remained tightly knit even through the harrowing ordeal experienced by Joseph and his brothers, for Joseph had the wisdom to understand that God was at work in his ordeal to preserve the life of God's people at a later, more trying time. The brotherhood of humankind is the expressed will of God, not the alienation and separation caused by dissension, division, and in-house squabbling.

Blacks as well as whites who believe this to be true should then be able to look beyond the American slave experience and see the broader, more perfect will of God for all God's created order. This task is made much easier, especially for those who were enslaved, if they believe that almighty God stands behind all such events to perfect God's will.

The brotherhood of humankind as the expressed will of God serves as the basis of Morris's shrewd play on white fears of religious equality. Morris, on the basis of the overarching will of God, distinguishes between a person's social life and religious life. He is willing to concede that whites are not bound to interact with blacks on a social level, for as Morris understands it, the doctrine of the brotherhood of man does not advocate the *social* equality of the races. However, he sees it as the inescapable duty of whites to interact with blacks on a religious level, for such is the will of God:

> But is there not a difference between our social and religious life? Is not every man our brother who has accepted Christ Jesus as his Saviour? The Syro-Phoenician woman had no legal, social or racial rights which would warrant her in approaching the Son of God, but she had a religious right, and she

contended for that right. Christ is not the Saviour of any particular race or class, but "whosoever will may take the water of life freely."[85]

Morris seems to suggest that while there may be whites living outside the will of God who do not wish to socialize with blacks at any level, there should be no whites who claim to be doing God's will yet refuse to interact with blacks on a religious level. Such is not in keeping with God's will. He then cites the biblical examples of the apostle Peter and Jesus Christ to prove that color cannot be a hindrance to the recognition of brotherhood among those who lay claim to the Christian hope:

> The commission which he [Christ] gives is without regard to race, color, or condition, but is that the Gospel be preached to every creature ... coming in direct contact with the people, all people ... "Christ Jesus came into the world to save sinners," not white sinners, nor black sinners, nor red sinners, but sinners.[86]

Although Morris is conscious that the church has not lived up to this high ideal, he nevertheless brings it forth as a principle of perfection to be reached by all of God's children:

> But let us not despair: the church will make to righteousness and put on her beautiful garments and her ministers will, ere long, declare that there be no North, no South, no East, and no West; no black and no white, but we shall be one in Christ Jesus.[87]

It is impossible to believe that Morris and his listeners considered this to be achievable outside of the will and purpose of almighty God. Morris begins this sermon by recounting to his listeners how almighty God was able to lead the children of Israel into slavery and out of it again. Although God's redemptive purpose may be slow in coming to pass, it comes nonetheless. Living in an era when social equality was much feared by whites, Morris sought to assure blacks that the brotherhood of man was the expressed will of God and that God had used circuitous routes in the past to effect God's will. Thus, they could rest assured that God was at work to effect God's will in their lives and times.

Because of the scarcity of Morris's published sermons, we cannot get a complete picture of the depth of his preaching, but we are able to determine that some of his sermons did in fact employ this central hermeneutic. Possibly owing to his conservative leanings and the temperament of the Baptist preaching of his day, Morris infrequently tackled social and political issues in his extant sermons. He seems to have been more inclined to deal with the personal and private domain of an individual's religious beliefs.

Conclusion

In summary, I have demonstrated the manner in which John Jasper, Alexander Crummell, Francis Grimké, Daniel Payne, and Elias Morris continually applied to scripture a hermeneutic of a God who acts mightily on behalf of the marginalized and powerless. Two of the preachers were highly educated and lived in the North—Crummell and Grimké—and were members of predominantly white denominations, Episcopal and Presbyterian respectively. Payne, a bishop of the African Methodist Episcopal Church, was born in the South but lived and worked most of his years in the North. Morris and Jasper were Baptists born in the South who spent their entire lives and ministry there. Morris was self-educated, while Jasper received little or no formal training.

Jasper and Morris, perhaps because of the influence of their white Baptist brethren, were more inclined to preach on matters of personal piety and care of the soul. They were less inclined to preach against whites and the government in general and were less strident in their public pronouncements pertaining to the educational, economic, and political concerns of blacks.

Bishop Payne, among the older of the five preachers studied, stands out as the centrist. A stern moralist, educator, and bishop par excellence, he could hardly be characterized as a folk preacher on the order of Jasper. He was from the school of thought that believed moral virtue was foremost in the Christian life. Thus, his sermons are filled with admonitions to thrift, hard work, education, and discipline. He sought to address blacks in every sphere of their existence. Yet in his preaching there is little or no agitation or stridency directed toward whites or those in powerful government positions. Payne was more inclined to see good in the American government and the power establishment than the other preachers in our study.

Grimké was the most strident and radical of the group. His sermons cover every conceivable aspect of black life, but always and everywhere, Grimké spoke out forcefully against injustice and mistreatment of blacks. Because he reached maturity during Reconstruction and lived well into the third decade of the twentieth century, his preaching reflects the changing moods in the American political climate.

One senses that Grimké was aware that he was preaching not just to the members of Fifteenth Street Presbyterian Church but to the country. At times he was conciliatory toward government and those in power; at other times he led the charge against policies and practices that he felt blacks simply could not abide. Grimké preached with the full confidence that his God of power and might would ultimately make things right for his lowly and despised people.

Political persuasions, denominational affiliations, and educational levels notwithstanding, there is a commonality in the sociocultural experiences of these preachers. They were all shaped by the sociocultural experience of being brought up black in America in an era of upheaval and great sociopolitical ferment. They sought to address the plight of their people in meaningful, practical, and immediate ways amid the critical times in which they preached. Thus, from the sermons of these five preachers, we may reasonably conclude four things:

1. Although they varied in levels of educational preparation, these preachers were knowledgeable about the times in which they lived, and they kept abreast of the crucial events and circumstances that impacted the lives of the people to whom they were preaching.
2. They made a conscious effort to apply the gospel in meaningful ways (i.e., ways that made sense in the lives of the listeners) to the various issues and adverse circumstances confronting blacks in post–Civil War America.
3. They sought a balance between the pastoral and the prophetic, that is, between matters of the heart relating to right behavior and private ethical/moral concerns and the broader interests of the black masses on issues of social justice and corporate concerns.
4. Above all, each had an unshakable faith in the power of God to bring about in their lives what no other power could do. This belief in the mighty sovereign conjoined with their everyday struggle for mere survival is the seed bed of black creativity and insightfulness in black preaching.

This way of conceiving of God has a distinct ring to it that can only fully be comprehended by those who live this experience daily and have been nurtured in its environs throughout their lives. Their sociocultural experiences shaped their perception of God and the Christian gospel to such an extent that the central component in their preaching centered on or found coherence in their perception of a God who acts mightily. Herein lies the distinctive source of African American preaching—the way in which blacks conceive of God and how they use that conception in the creation and organization of their sermons. We turn in chapter 3 to an examination of the sermons of several twentieth-century African American preachers to demonstrate how this longstanding hermeneutic continues to impact black preaching to this day.

A Hermeneutic of Power in Contemporary African American Sermons

The biblical hermeneutic that has informed African American preaching from its early beginnings in this country continues to serve as the template for the creation and organization of the black sermon. Having established the presence of this distinctly black hermeneutic in the preaching of post-slavery pastors, I shift in this chapter from garnering evidence for its existence to describing its presence and implementation in the sermons of twentieth-century preachers. I will analyze the sermons of six ministers who currently preach to large black gatherings on a consistent basis: Jeremiah A. Wright, Jr., Katie G. Cannon, A. Louis Patterson, Jr., Mozella Mitchell, Fred C. Lofton, and Carolyn Ann Knight.

Wright, cited by *Ebony* magazine as one of the fifteen greatest black preachers in America, is the senior pastor at Trinity United Church of Christ in Chicago, Illinois. Cannon is Associate Professor of Religion at Temple University in Philadelphia, Pennsylvania, and an ordained minister in the Presbyterian Church (U.S.A.). Patterson is the pastor of the Mount Corinth Missionary Baptist Church in Houston, Texas. Mitchell is pastor of Mount Sinai A.M.E. Zion Church in Tampa, Florida, and Associate Professor of Religious Studies at the University of South Florida.

Lofton is senior pastor of the Metropolitan Baptist Church in Memphis, Tennessee, and former president of the Progressive National Baptist Convention. Knight is assistant professor of homiletics at the Interdenominational Theological Center in Atlanta, Georgia. All are formally trained ministers with exceptional preaching skills. Though they differ in regional and denominational affiliation, they share this distinctive hermeneutic that shapes much of the preaching presently heard throughout black America.

My purpose in analyzing contemporary sermons is to help the reader see more clearly the internal dynamics that shape, inform, and give life to the creation and organization of the sermon in the black preacher's initial thought process. I am not attempting to provide a step-by-step procedure for the creation of a sermon.

Moreover, while the formative stage of interpretation is uppermost in my mind, I am not attempting to create an exegetical method that is separate and apart from accepted canons of biblical exegesis in their historical, traditional, or literary forms. I am, however, in search of that fundamental hermeneutic that informs the sermon in its beginning stages—the point where a passage of scripture is selected and one begins the first thoughts of how it is to be interpreted to a particular people on a particular day. I seek to uncover the characteristics of that longstanding interpretive principle that black preachers habitually rely upon, either consciously or subconsciously, in preparation for the sermon.

The preacher who would preach with a certain sense of authority and accomplishment in the traditional black church must always remember that at its heart the black sermon is about God—God's purposive acts in and for the world. The most effective preaching is preaching that conveys with clarity and insight how God acts in concrete situations in the lives of those who hear the gospel. People gather to be assured and reassured that God has acted and will act for them and for their salvation. Black preaching takes this mandate seriously.

With this understanding in mind—that we are in search of a particular habitus or mindset that leads us to view scripture a certain way—the reader is encouraged to pay close attention to the following three dynamics in the sermons of our contemporary preachers.

First, note the manner in which the preacher attempts to name God's presence in the text and in the sermon. Ask the following questions:

1. Based on a simple reading of the selected text, as far as you can determine, where is God, or where is the divine initiative in the text?

2. How does the preacher appear to interpret God's presence in the text? That is, on the basis of the content and shape of the sermon cite the particular ways in which the preacher perceives God to be acting in the text.

3. What are the circumstances surrounding the activity of God that the preacher chooses to focus on or highlight (e.g., the details of the narrative, parable, or epistle, certain historical facts, the discovery of some exegetical insight that sheds new light on the text, or painting a word picture of some biblical character's encounter with God)?

4. For whom or against whom does God act?

5. What, if anything, does God or the preacher do that makes God's presence and power the deciding factor in the text and ultimately the sermon?

Second, note the manner in which the preacher pairs the biblical text to the life experiences of the hearers. It is here that one gives consideration to the various domains of experience—personal piety, care of the soul, social justice, corporate concerns, and maintenance of the institutional church. Domains of experience are familiar ground to black listeners, for they characterize and typify the different kinds of events and occurrences that blacks encounter in life. For example, there are times in life when a person feels a deep longing for a closer, more intimate walk with God. In such a case, what is needed is some understanding of the teachings of scripture and one's theological tradition on matters pertaining to an individual's personal relationship with God. Most appropriate for such an experience would be a sermon that addresses the how-tos and benefits of that sphere of heartfelt desire.

At other times the person may have undergone some painful trial or crisis, such as divorce or a family member's catastrophic illness, and what he or she seeks in that experience is a word of consolation and care. On another occasion a parishioner might be grappling with some issue in the work place or community that cries out for a just resolution. A sermon that speaks to God's sovereignty over all affairs, including the social political order, would be fitting.

There could also come a time when people feel aggrieved as a group or must contend with issues that impact them as a distinct body. What they hunger for is some word from God that helps them cope with their lives as a part of this larger yet distinct social group. Finally, a sermon related to the growth and development of members within the church fellowship or the mission and meaning of the church beyond its four walls is also fitting from time to time and instructive for the life and witness of the gathered community of faith.

To understand which domain of experience the preacher has deemed most fitting for the people of God, the reader should ask the following questions of the sermon:

1. What area of human experience did the preacher address through scripture in the sermon?
2. Was the preacher seeking to instruct, exhort, or demonstrate some matter pertaining to upright living or personal moral conduct?
3. Did the preacher impart a word of healing, guiding, or sustaining to help the listeners cope with another day of struggle and survival?
4. Were the truths of the gospel directed toward sociopolitical concerns in the life of the local community or the larger world?
5. Did the preacher address an issue that particularly and peculiarly affects black people, for example, high black

unemployment rates, unrealized educational opportunities, or black-on-black crime?

6. Did the preacher speak to some concern that addressed the missionary or evangelical work of the institutional church or some matter related to the edification of the local body of Christ, such as stewardship, discipleship, and so forth?

These questions help the reader make some assessment as to the domain of black life being addressed through scripture that day.

Third, consider the end to which God's power is used. First, ask if God's power is used to liberate, deliver, provide, protect, empower, or transform. Second, attempt, when applicable, to identify the type of extended metaphor used to demonstrate the act in which God's power is made manifest.

Such questions provide us with some insight into the inner workings of the biblical hermeneutic so deeply woven into the fabric of black existence that it constitutes a part of the sacred story and affects and informs the black sermon from the outset. To ask these kinds of questions of the sermon helps the novice or uninitiated preacher bring to conscious reflection what most seasoned black preachers do by second nature, that is, find out where God is in any text, note God's involvement in and through that text, make a concrete, practical connection between God's presence and the lives of the listening congregation, and then demonstrate how God's power is used on behalf of God's chosen people.

With these thoughts in mind we begin our examination of the sermons of contemporary African American preachers. First, I consider the structure of each sermon through a detailed analysis of its organization and movement of thought. Sermons are a movement of language from one idea to another, each idea being shaped in a bundle of words.

Thus, when we preach we speak in formed modules of language arranged in some patterned sequence. This sequential unit of thought centered on a single meaning in consciousness is what David Buttrick defines as a "move."[1] Each move, which initially arises from the biblical text and then shifts to our own situation, is usually a lengthy paragraph or two in written form.[2] However, moves in the traditional black sermon can be longer than a couple of paragraphs for several reasons:

1. The black sermon as performed word usually runs longer than the traditional mainline sermon.
2. The black preacher often engages in a prolonged and precise detailing of some text, image, metaphor, or slice of life centered around one thought.
3. The listening congregation expects and has grown accustomed to following an elongated story plot without losing sight of the defining thought that occasioned the move.

Second, I evaluate the preacher's exposition of the scriptures and the manner in which that exposition is connected to the life experiences of the listeners. I point out how the various domains of experience are incorporated into the body of the sermon as the preacher seeks to make that vital connection between the living Word and concrete human experience. Finally, I will describe how the central foundational interpretive key permeates the black sermon, often so subtly that it goes almost unnoticed.

Jeremiah A. Wright, Jr.

WHAT MAKES YOU SO STRONG?

The moves of the sermon:

1. Recounting of centuries of black achievement despite oppression	→	2. Exposition of biblical narrative: Deliah's question and Samson's weakness— foreign women and revealed secrets	→	3. The necessity of guarding one's special relationship with God	→	4. Dangers inherent in revealing one's whole heart— bondage and blindness	→	5. The symbol and the source of Samson's strength: God's Spirit.

In a sermon titled "What Makes You So Strong?"[3] Jeremiah A. Wright, Jr. demonstrates the power of the mighty sovereign at work in the lives of black people in twentieth-century America. This sermon focuses on the root of black strength and survivability. Wright makes clear throughout the sermon that the source of all strength, and especially of black strength, is none other than the Spirit of God. He recounts the story of Samson and Delilah to warn blacks that trouble awaits them when they do not take care to guard their very special relationship with God. Wright reminds his parishioners that the preeminence of God in black life has long been the source of blacks' strength. Perils that threaten their very existence are sure to come when blacks give their hearts to lesser ideals and depart from the course of life set forth for them through the grand design of God. The sermon is also a word of encouragement to blacks that their continued strength and advancement is made possible through the might and power of the Spirit of God.

Recalling the pain and suffering inflicted on blacks throughout human history, Wright opens the sermon with numerous examples of black men and women from antiquity to the present who have survived injurious, inhumane treatment and gone on to prosper in their particular fields of endeavor. "How is it," he asks, "that after all this country has done to you, you can still produce a Paul Robeson, a Thurgood Marshall, a Malcolm X (el-Hajj Malik el-Shabazz), a Martin King, and a Ron McNair? ... I don't care what field we pick, you produce a giant in that field. What makes you so strong, black man?"[4] From his opening sentences, Wright moves to instill pride in his black listeners by parading before them a black hall of fame, people whose lives exemplify the struggle, survival, and conquest of a maligned race of people. Wright skillfully interweaves tragedy and triumph into the heart of his message:

> They told you that you were not allowed in the field of medicine and here you come with a black M.D. graduating from medical school in the 1800s ... They told you no women were allowed in the male-dominated field of TV journalism, and here you come with a Melanie Lawson and an Oprah Winfrey ... No other race was brought to this country in chains ... and yet no other race has done so much starting out with so little ...[5]

In preparation for the move that will turn his congregation to the word of God for the day, Wright expands his query about black strength by offering several possible answers: "How were you able to do that? What makes you so strong, black people? Is it something in your African blood? Is it something in your African psyche? Is it something in your African soul? Is it something in your African spirit?"[6]

Making a decided connection between black achievement and God's power, in his second move Wright shows that the question—What makes you so strong?—really has its origin in scripture and is a question of such importance that a precipitous answer could be disastrous. The question that provides the refrain for Wright's sermon is actually the question put to Samson by Delilah in the Judges 16 passage that serves as the text for Wright's sermon. Samson was a judge from the tribe of Dan, famous for his superhuman strength, associated with his uncut hair, and for his exploits against the Philistines. The story of Samson and Delilah resonates with blacks for it is an Old Testament narrative with which they are quite familiar. Blacks see their life experiences in many of the angles, pitfalls, and implications of the Samson story. Wright, aware of his listeners' identification with this story, shrewdly interweaves Samson's plight with present-day black experiences:

> If you read this whole biography of Samson, you discover that Samson had several problems. He never did get that love thing straight ... he never could pull off that right combination in terms of a committed relationship ... His people were constantly under attack. They were assaulted by the twin demons of assimilation and segregation. Though Samson ruled suc-

cessfully for twenty years politically, he never was quite able to put it all together in his personal life ... He was absolutely no judge of character and a complete failure when it came to judging the opposite sex or choosing relationships with them.[7]

Wright's congregation identifies with Samson through Wright's skillful retelling of the particulars of Samson's life. A part of the genius of black preaching is that it still seeks to make contemporary life conform to the story world of the biblical witness. Blacks continue to believe the Bible depicts life as it is meant to be lived in the presence of God. Consequently, the details of biblical narratives in particular as well as the Bible in general are of utmost importance to the black preacher. True to traditional black preaching, Wright labors for a while on the details of the Samson story, while never losing sight of the overall function of the sermon, which is to assure his listeners that in order to survive and prosper they must maintain their special relationship with God and completely rely upon God's strength. Samson achieved a measure of success in spite of the oppressive environment in which he had to live as have many of the blacks in Wright's congregation. His success notwithstanding, Samson still found some areas of his personal life sorely lacking—"He never did get that love thing straight." Even for those who achieve great success, there remain seemingly unsolvable personal problems that defy easy answers. Even successful people, strong on numerous fronts, can be blindsided and undone by unwise decisions and premature actions. Vigilance is required at all times.

"Everyone," says Wright, "has got a certain weakness in life." Samson's weakness was foreign women and a loose tongue. His weakness for those women led to even greater difficulties in his life. His biggest problem, according to Wright, was that he told somebody who didn't care anything about him something that was of ultimate importance in his life. Successful Samson, strong on many fronts, is about to allow a miscalculation in his personal life to pull him down.

In the third move of the sermon, Wright expounds on the personal problems in Samson's life in order to help the listeners better understand how easily they too can be brought down and why it is so important that they guard their special relationship with God and look continually to God for their sustenance and strength. On the surface it could appear that Wright's sermon is collapsing into superficial moralizing. But on closer inspection one recognizes that such is not the case. The emphasis here is not on moral laxity but on the many pitfalls that threaten a person's close, intimate walk with God.

The King James Version of that passage says, "he told her all his heart" (Judges 16:17). The Hebrew word is *leb*, connoting

feeling, will, intellect, the center of everything ... She vexed
him ... until he told her his whole heart, that which was of ultimate importance in life. He told her what my mama used to
call the God's honest truth.[8]

Wright is not here moralizing, rather he is speaking about a personal
difficulty in the life of an otherwise decent man that enticed him to reveal
his special relationship with God. Samson revealed his secret to his enemy
(to this one who cared nothing about him). "He allowed his desire for her
to take precedence over his devotion to God. Watch out! Don't let what
somebody can do to you or do for you become more important than what
God wants to do *in* you and *through* you." God, according to Wright, had
set the terms for Samson's life and labors long before Samson was born,
because God had work to do in and through Samson. His desire for Delilah
momentarily distracted him from the grand design of God, but clearly in
this sermon the emphasis is on God and God's steadfast love for those
who conduct their lives according to God's purpose.

Wright wants the congregation to understand that what made Samson
so strong was the work of a sovereign God who created Samson for a special work in life even before his birth. What weakened Samson and eventually brought him down was an attraction to Delilah that he allowed to
take priority over his special relationship with God. At this point in the sermon, Wright makes an explicit connection between Samson, African
Americans, and the purposive acts of almighty God on behalf of those
whom God destines for a special work:

You see, God has a work that he wants to do through African
Americans—a people who have known hatred, yet who still
have the strength to love ... God has a work of redemption and
healing to do through African Americans. God will do through
you individually, not only corporately ... Watch out for what
somebody can do to you and for you. Don't let that become
more important than what God wants to do *in* you and *through*
you. Samson allowed a relationship that he wanted to have but
could not have get in the way of the relationship that he already had with God.[9]

What makes you so strong? The answer to this question is found in the
foreordained purposes of almighty God: It is God's favor and God's
strength that has sustained blacks throughout their history in this world.

In the fourth move of the sermon, Wright cites the dangers inherent in
revealing one's whole heart to others. Even when you know the source of
your strength, you should be careful in how you answer and to whom you
answer. Samson revealed his secret to his enemy; he told Delilah about his

relationship with God. Then, he shared with her what symbolized his special relationship with God. According to Wright, Samson suffered dire consequences as a result of that revelation. "See what happens when you reveal your whole heart to others? First, they put you in chains ... They'll put your eyes out so you can't even see what's happening to you." Imprisonment and blindness take on metaphorical significance when Wright applies Samson's plight to present day blacks:

> You give them your heart; they chain your body and then your mind ... They'll put your eyes out so you can't even see what's happening to you. You can't see the psychological chains ... the economic chains ... or even the drug addiction chains they've put you through.[10]

Samson's desire for a foreign woman leads him to answer a question concerning his intimate relationship with God. The answer given to the enemy in a weak moment signals the downfall of this once proud and strong servant of God.

But all is not lost. In the fifth and final move of the sermon, Wright points his listeners to the true source of both Samson's strength and present-day black strength. While Samson gave his enemies the edge by revealing what symbolized his strength—his uncut hair—he also revealed the source of his strength, about which his enemies could do little. The source of Samson's strength (as is the source of the listening congregation's strength) was none other than the Spirit of God:

> They didn't listen to his whole answer. His hair was the symbol, not the source. Look at his whole answer. He said, "My hair has never been cut." That's a symbol. Why? "Because I have been dedicated to God as a Nazirite from the time I was born." Now that's the source of his strength ... "The LORD's power began to strengthen him."[11]

It is apparent to Wright that the source of Samson's strength was God. He cites several passages of scripture in which God's power is manifested in an unusual manner on Samson's behalf. So too with respect to the source of his strength, God's power is the driving and saving force in Samson's life.

In the final stage of the sermon Wright moves into the arena of rejoicing and celebration that black congregations anticipate when there has been a demonstration, reaffirmation, or even the promise of some mighty work on the part of God. Celebration at its best in black worship is an affirmative, joyful event that signals that the worshiping community has grasped some sense of what the sermon intended to say and to do. When the listener has not grasped the essence of the sermon, celebration becomes little more than sounding brass or tinkling cymbals. Wright's listeners are encouraged to celebrate if they truly believe the same divine power made available to Samson in his hour of peril is open to them in the changes and challenges of their lives. The sermon ends, as it began, with Wright engaging in a roll call of biblical characters and contemporary people of faith who have been delivered time and again by the mighty hand of God. David, Isaiah, and Martin Luther King, Jr. were all made strong by none other than God. "Our strength comes from the Spirit of God. This same Spirit of God will empower you as he empowered our Lord, Jesus Christ. Jesus promised that he would give the spirit to you. He has never failed any of his promises. This is what makes us so strong."

Summary

Since Wright's sermon is our first example of the formative dynamics at work in twentieth-century African American preaching, I will summarize the moves of his sermon and recount once again the interpretive strategies at work in the initial stages of the sermon. Wright's sermon is based on a familiar Old Testament narrative. It may rightly be characterized as a sermon with two domains interacting with equal weight upon one another. While it clearly has characteristics of corporate concerns in its appeal to race pride and racial solidarity, it also displays features of care of the soul in its word of hope and encouragement to blacks, intended to sustain and guide them through the ups and downs of life. Wright is reminding his congregation that it is their special relationship to God that has made them strong and successful. It is that relationship that they are to guard with all their hearts. Their destinies lie within the grand design of God and not the manipulative machinations of humankind. God's power and overall protection are made available to them in the present day to help them to overcome and to prosper, irrespective of the obstacles thrown in their paths by those who seek to hinder and hurt them. The guiding force at the center of this sermon is God the mighty sovereign.

With the two broad domains of the sermon clearly before us—corporate concerns and care of the soul—and the overall focus of the sermon in view, let's review once again the three dynamics that inform the hermeneutic at work in the sermon: the acts of God, the life experiences of the believer, and the type of power manifested by God. First, we take up the matter of Wright's understanding of the purposive acts of God in this passage. Again, the following questions help us to gain a better insight into God's presence and action in the text and the sermon:

1. In terms of a simple reading of the text, what is God doing, explicitly or implicitly?

2. How does the preacher interpret God's presence in and through the text?
3. What are the circumstances surrounding the activity of God (e.g., the details of the narrative)?
4. For whom or against whom does God act?
5. What does God do that makes God's presence and power the deciding factor in the text?

In terms of a plain-sense reading of the passage itself, God is first mentioned in this chapter by Samson when he tells Delilah that no razor has ever been used on his head because he has been set apart to God since birth. Wright takes this passage to mean that God had a work to do in and through Samson before he was born. Before Samson was conceived, his destiny was in God's hand and under the control of God's purposive acts. Thus all the grand achievements accomplished by Samson were not only known to God but in keeping with God's plan for Samson's life. Despite the many obstacles and impediments in Samson's life he met with great success because God was in charge of his life.

As to the circumstances surrounding the activity of God, Samson has been fooled by a woman who is being used by his enemies to defeat him. Delilah does her best to find out the secret to Samson's great strength—a secret known only to God and Samson. Cunning enemies, a deceitful lover, and a foolhardy Samson are not sufficient to undermine the purposive will of God. Samson's strength does not ultimately lie in his hair but in his God.

God clearly acts in this story on behalf of those who honor and recognize God's sovereignty and against those who attempt to thwart or usurp the promises of God. God empowers Samson for one final act of bravery and gallantry—humiliated, blinded Samson brings down the walls of the temple. It is clear from Samson's prayer before this final act that he believes it can only be possible through the divine aid and assistance of the sovereign God. Thus Samson prays to God to remember and strengthen him for one last battle against the Philistines (Judg. 16:28). Notice, Wright does not focus on Samson's folly in following after foreign women nor does he chide Samson for his downfall. The focus is on God and what God can and will do for God's covenant people.

The second dynamic involves the ways in which the preacher pairs the biblical text to the life situation of the hearers. Wright, aware that he is speaking to people for whom life has not been easy, uses the details of the Samson narrative to draw meaningful insights into the lives of his listeners. He allows his listeners to walk around in the text and feel its relatedness and relevance to their own lives.

Samson's life was filled with extreme ups and downs. He achieved great success in spite of the oppressive environment in which he had to live. His success notwithstanding, he still had some weaknesses to overcome. Samson, a person of so much promise, could not get "the love thing" straight, was inclined to talk too much, and was led astray by a personal flaw he could not easily overcome. In spite of Samson's weaknesses, God saw to it that God's plans for Samson would not ultimately be defeated. The listeners discern some similarities and some hope between their lives and Samson's very human struggle.

Wright's ability to use the details of the biblical narrative to draw his congregation into the story world of the text is not done through mere happenstance. He does not luck upon a relevant message. From the story world of the text, Wright, consciously or subconsciously, decides upon a specific domain of experience in which to pair the particulars of the text to the life situation of the hearers. It is equally conceivable that Wright's pastoral sense led him to the Samson passage as the most fitting text to address the care of the soul and corporate concerns of his congregation for that day. Be it the domain interacting with the text or the text interacting with the domain, the result is the same—a vivid encounter between concrete contemporary experience and the story world of the text.

On this particular day to this particular people, Wright utilizes a biblical text to reflect on and preach out of two spheres of black life—corporate concerns and care of the soul. He could just as well have decided to move in the direction of social justice or singularly in the direction of care of the soul. He purposely chose, however, to address the spiritual, physical, and mental well-being of blacks by focusing on obstructions and impediments that peculiarly affect them as a distinct group of people in the United States. Thus, his is a bifocal word of consolation and corporate concern to black people who are engaged in a daily struggle to survive and prosper in what for many appears at times to be a mean and unfriendly world.

The third dynamic calls for consideration of the end to which God's power is used. What does God do in the sermon to make a difference in Samson's life and how does God use God's power to make that difference? God takes a proactive stance of protection and empowerment for those who own God as their sovereign Lord and live their lives according to God's grand design. In this passage God was Samson's deliverer and battleax.

The end result of Wright's skillful employment of this biblical hermeneutic and its identifiable components is a sermon that is faithful to scripture and meaningful to the congregation's life experiences.

Jeremiah A. Wright, Jr.
UNEXPECTED BLESSINGS

The moves of the sermon:

1. Examples of unexpected blessings	→	2. Excursus on importance of going to church— Jesus and Satan attend	→	3. Exposition of primary passage— Jesus' visit and Peter's unexpected blessing	→	4. Praise: the key to unexpected blessings!	→	5. Slice of life: an elderly gentleman blessed by God

A second sermon preached by Wright, titled "Unexpected Blessings," follows the contours of the hermeneutic described in the previous sermon. This oration is based on Mark 1:21–31, the passage that involves the cleansing of a man with an unclean spirit in the synagogue and the healing of Peter's mother-in-law. The unexpected blessing comes to Peter when he leaves the synagogue and takes Jesus home to his ailing mother-in-law, who is then healed of her sickness and begins to minister to Jesus and those who are with him. What is interesting about this sermon is that while Jesus is at the center of the action in this narrative, God's mighty acts implicitly permeate the entire sermon.

In the opening move of the sermon, Wright asks his parishioners if they have ever been engaged in their normal routines when all of a sudden the Lord stepped in and blessed that situation beyond their wildest dreams. Although Wright says "the Lord" stepped in and blessed the situation, examples of the unexpected blessings he cites to support his claim explicitly come from the hand of God: Sarah giving birth to Isaac long past her child bearing years; Moses encountering the voice of God in a burning bush, calling him to lead God's people; Hannah, the mother of Samuel, praying for a child and subsequently giving birth to one who far exceeded her expectations; and Isaiah's life-altering encounter with God in the Temple in the year that King Uzziah died. "The biblical record," according to Wright, "is replete with instances of unexpected blessings—folks following their normal routine, doing what it is they usually do, when all of a sudden the Lord steps in and blesses in ways that could not have been imagined." While it is common practice in black religious life to use the term "Lord" interchangeably for "God" and the "Lord, Jesus Christ," the examples cited by Wright are clearly from Old Testament passages that involve God's action on behalf of those who received the unexpected blessings.

In the second move of the sermon, Wright begins with the explication of his selected passage but then quickly digresses into an excursus on the importance of attending church. Jesus went into the synagogue, or as Wright, in the vernacular of the people, puts it: "Jesus went to church to worship God ... In fact, verse 39 says that wherever he went, whatever town he was in, the Lord's day found him in the Lord's house." Implicit in this excursus is some understanding that attending church can also be a source of unexpected blessings. But the healing scene in the synagogue is merely a precursor to the healing at Peter's home.

After his brief digression on the importance of going to church, Wright opens the third move of his sermon which is, in fact, the central focus of his entire message—how Peter takes Jesus home after church and eventually finds his unexpected blessing:

> Immediately after church, Jesus, his disciples ... left the church and went straight to Peter's and Andrew's house ... and what they experienced was an unexpected blessing ... When the churchgoers got home, Peter's mother-in-law was in bed with a fever. Somebody told Jesus about the situation ... he went straight to Peter's mother-in-law, touched her, took her by the hand, and helped her up. One touch and the fever was gone.[12]

Peter's unexpected blessing has come through a wonderwork of Jesus Christ. Jesus went to the bedside of Peter's mother-in-law, took her by the hand, helped her up, and the fever was gone. Wright draws two truths from this scene: First, the Lord works in your own house just like he works in the church house. Second, Jesus is good for what ails you. In spellbinding oratory Wright enfleshes the gospel on those two points.

In the fourth move of the sermon, as Wright prepares to tell the congregation how they too can put themselves in line for unexpected blessings, the hermeneutic that informs the entire sermon overtly surfaces once again. The unexpected blessing in the text clearly comes through a work of grace on the part of Jesus of Nazareth. The key, however, to unexpected blessings for Wright's parishioners comes expressly from God, and it is praise to almighty God that puts one in blessing range:

> But the key to God's using and giving unexpected blessings is lost when we let problems get in the way of praise. Think about how problems in your life cause you to say, "I don't want to pray. Lord, just leave me alone." But when you praise God in spite of problems, it is precious, and it is priceless, and God will bless you unexpectedly.[13]

Jesus, the Christ, in the act of grace demonstrated toward the mother-in-law of Peter, does the will of God. Unexpected blessings come from the hand of God to those who continue to praise God and acknowledge God's guidance and direction in their lives. At the heart of this sermon, based on a New Testament passage, is the power of God at work in unexpected ways on behalf of God's people.

The final move of the sermon is a slice of life that provides a tangible image of how unexpected blessings come to us in contemporary times. Wright tells of a story he heard about an elderly gentleman in the Northeast who learned to place his trust in God at an early age. The man received unexpected blessings from God when he acted on his faith and walked eight miles to church, gave every dime he had in the offering, and returned home broke but happy. On the way home, the elderly gentleman received showers of blessings. He found money he did not expect, met a woman who told him where he could find work, and was given extra money by the bus driver. Wright, confident that his parishioners have gotten the point of the story, joins them in a celebratory close by assuring them over and over, "God will fix it for you. Won't he fix it? He's a good God!"[14]

It is interesting to see how Wright has interpreted the presence and power of God in this passage. First, he uses "Lord" and "God" interchangeably. In the first move of his sermon, where he is citing examples of unexpected blessings, all the blessings come from the hands of God. Having assured his readers that the biblical record is replete with instances of unexpected blessings, Wright then moves to the exposition of his text for the day. The unexpected blessing that Wright will expound on comes from the "Lord." Wright sees the work of Christ as an extension of the work of God, the mighty sovereign. Throughout his exposition it is the Lord at the center of this work of grace—the healing of Peter's mother-in-law. However, when Wright tells his listeners how they too can receive unexpected blessings, he reverts to the term "God," and uses "Lord" and "God" interchangeably throughout this section where he makes the primary point of his sermon:

> But the key to God's using and giving unexpected blessings is lost when we let problems get in the way of praise. Think about how problems in your life cause you to say, "I don't want to pray. Lord, just leave me alone." But when you praise God in spite of problems, it is precious, and it is priceless, and God will bless you unexpectedly. Peter and Andrew went to church anyhow and praised the Lord, and the Lord blessed them. They had a problem at home but they went to church to praise.[15]

The biblical hermeneutic that informs Wright's sermon is so overpowering that Wright sees God at work through the wonder-workings of Jesus Christ and uses the names of the Deity interchangeably to make his point about unexpected blessings. As Wright sees it, even a mighty act of Jesus Christ ultimately comes from the hands of God. He is faithful to the text in his exposition of the passage, for he repeatedly uses the word "Lord" throughout the narrative, but he is also faithful to the hermeneutic that informs his sermon when he pairs and applies the ancient text to the contemporary situation of his hearers: Unexpected blessings come from God.

This sermon is born of reflection on the care of the soul domain. It is God who provides for God's people in surprising and unexpected ways. They are sustained and strengthened in their lives through a remarkable, unanticipated manifestation of God's power on their behalf. Wright is a colorful, gifted, and extremely articulate preacher. He opens up to his listeners in very unique ways many insights into scripture. He employs keen powers of observation in the pairing of scripture to the human situation. He seems to have a knack for knowing when and how to tie scripture to the life experiences of his listeners. Like the other ministers in this study, Wright brings with his considerable preaching gifts this distinctive biblical hermeneutic so crucial to powerful black preaching. At the center of his preaching is a mighty God who acts in meaningful ways in the lives of God's people. Wright skillfully points out to his congregants how and where this God they have come to trust is at work in their lives.

Katie G. Cannon
TO TELL THE TRUTH

The moves of the sermon:

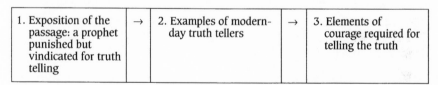

1. Exposition of the passage: a prophet punished but vindicated for truth telling	→	2. Examples of modern-day truth tellers	→	3. Elements of courage required for telling the truth

The focus of this sermon is speaking the truth at all costs. Katie Cannon opens the sermon, which is based on a narrative from 1 Kings 22, with a simple explanation of the passage that begins with a treaty between King Ahab and King Jehoshaphat. Ahab, king of the ten tribes of the North, asked Jehoshaphat, king of the two southern tribes, to join with him in forming a united front against King Aram, who had taken Ahab's land in an earlier confrontation. Before Jehoshaphat would join Ahab, he first wanted to inquire of God if God would be on their side in the battle. Ahab agreed and called some four hundred prophets into his court. All the prophets lied and told Ahab there was no doubt he would win the war. King Jehoshaphat, still not satisfied, asked Ahab if there was not another prophet of God. King Ahab threw up his hands and said: "Yes, there is yet one man who is a prophet. His name is Micaiah, son of Imlah, but he never prophesies anything good for me; only disaster."[16]

When Micaiah appeared before the kings, Ahab said to him, "Micaiah, shall we go to battle in Ramoth-gilead ..." Micaiah replied, "O King, if you go to war, you will be defeated ... An enticing, lying spirit is in the mouths of the other prophets. If you go to war, God has decreed disaster for you"[17]

Ahab, full of anger, ordered his guard to throw Micaiah into prison and feed him only reduced rations of bread and water until the battle was won and the king emerged victorious. Micaiah's prophecy notwithstanding, Ahab and Jehoshaphat prepared their armies to go to war, where Ahab was mortally wounded. The words of the prophet Micaiah came to pass.

In the second move of her sermon, Cannon moves from Micaiah's prophecy and Ahab's subsequent death to the importance of always telling the truth in present-day situations, irrespective of the outcome. She draws upon several slices of life as she describes the harm we do to ourselves and others when we refuse to be truthful in any and all circumstances:

> There used to be a popular program called *To Tell the Truth* ... Whenever this game show came on, people would gather around the television and listen to the affidavit so that we could judge for ourselves who was the real person and who were the two impostors ... So many of us live out our days as impostors ... wherein we refuse to speak out the truth that God lays on our hearts in times of crisis simply because we lack the courage to be true prophets of God.[18]

Even at this point, where Cannon is outlining the conceptual principle upon which her sermon will be based, it is important to note that she urges her listeners not just to speak the truth but "to speak out the truth that God lays on our heart of hearts ..."[19] The truth that we must speak is the truth that has been revealed to us by God:

> Sometimes God will lay something on our hearts to say to another person or to a committee or to those who control our paychecks ... Our concern today is that for us to be silent when God has given us a message to deliver to God's people is to be guilty of lying. To sit still with our lips sealed ... not to mumble a word when God has revealed a specific truth to us that our community is in dire need of hearing, results in our living a lie.[20]

God's proactive presence is at work urging us to tell the truth, and our refusal to do so not only harms us and the community, but it also entails intentional disobedience to the will of God, who, according to Cannon, has laid the truth upon our hearts.

After describing the serious implications of not telling the truth that God has set before them, in the third move Cannon takes a very practical stance in outlining ways in which they can "discover, define, and develop elements of courage that relate to telling the truth," in order that they might live as true prophets in the name of the Lord their God.[21] Following the contours of a typical deductive sermon, Cannon expands on the abovementioned propositional truths that listeners must embrace if they are to tell the truth in keeping with the will of God. Behind all three propositions is the proactive presence and promise of the mighty God, who has revealed the truth to the one who is now being urged by Cannon to speak it openly and truthfully:

1. "The first element of courage we must embrace related to telling the truth is that we must discover what the divine gift is that God has given us." An awareness of our God-given gifts centers us on our responsibilities and prevents us from trying to be all things to all people. It helps us to zero in on our particular contribution. Micaiah, the prophet who served in Ahab's court, was fully aware of the message that God sent him to proclaim to the king. He was able to stand against the other four hundred prophets because he had a clear understanding of God's will for his life and he had the courage of his convictions. According to Cannon, if we are going to be modern-day Micaiahs, then we too must know in our heart of hearts the task that God is calling us to do, the message that God is commanding us to communicate, and the truth that we must tell so that our living will not be in vain. It is an awareness or discovery of the gifts that God has given that enables us to know with some degree of assurance what God has called us forth to declare.

2. The second element of courage we must embrace related to telling the truth is that we must define the revelation God gives us. To define the revelation gives us the courage of our convictions and allows us not to shrink back from the enormity of the truth we are called upon to tell along with its broad implications:

> Too often we want to select and handpick the people with whom we share the Good News. We want to voice our opinions among two or three behind closed doors. But the Bible is telling us that we must prepare ourselves to speak the truth before powers and principalities, against spiritual wickedness in high places.[22]

Defining the revelation that God gives to us emboldens us to say whatever God wants us to say. Returning to Micaiah in the text, Cannon persuasively argues that even when the messenger located the prophet and wanted him to go along with the majority opinion and not to speak against the desires of the king, Micaiah refused. This, according to Cannon, is the essence of defined truth—to know beyond the shadow of a doubt what message we need to share in those places where crucial decisions are being made so that our living will not be in vain.

3. The third and final element of courage is that we must develop a God-consciousness. God-consciousness is made possible through a direct relationship with the almighty God. Because truth is active and dynamic, it requires a personal relationship with the one who is Truth. "If we want the strength and power to be truth tellers, we must stay in touch with the Creator and Sustainer morning by morning, day by day."[23] Cannon now makes explicit reference to the God who has been active and present throughout the sermon:

> Each of us needs a direct relationship with Almighty God. Truth cannot be absolutized once and for all and squeezed into a permanent mold because truth is active and dynamic. If we want the strength and power to be truth tellers, we must stay in touch with the Creator and Sustainer morning by morning, day by day ... To develop courage as tellers of truth, we must keep the lines of communication open between us and the Deity so that we can speak truth to particular situations at specific times.[24]

Staying in touch with the source of all truth gives us strength and courage to put an end to the lie of silent consent and, in turn, stand forth courageously as true prophets so that our living will not be in vain.

The passage before us is an Old Testament narrative that speaks of a true prophet of God acting justly even in the face of reprisals and recriminations. The interpretive key of God, the mighty sovereign, acting mightily on behalf of the marginalized and powerless shapes this sermon from beginning to end. In terms of a plain-sense reading of the text, the story begins with one king asking another king for help in settling a score with a common enemy. King Jehoshaphat, before agreeing to join King Ahab in battle, demanded that they discover what God wanted them to do. Ahab agreed that it was fitting and proper to find out if God would indeed be on their side.

Four hundred prophets in Ahab's court assured the king that God would be on his side in his attempt to win back his land. King Jehoshaphat, still not satisfied, asked Ahab if there was not another prophet of God. Ahab then told Jehoshaphat of Micaiah but assured him that this prophet never had anything good for him. A messenger who found Micaiah warned him that if he valued his life, he had better agree with the four hundred prophets from Ahab's court, who had already assured the king that he would be successful in battle. But Micaiah, according to Cannon, said without fear or trembling, "Whatever God wants me to say, that I will say. Whatever God lays on my heart of hearts to tell the king, that is what I will tell him."

Micaiah went before King Ahab and assured him that if he went to war he would most certainly be defeated because God had decreed disaster for him. Ahab, full of anger, ordered Micaiah thrown into prison and placed on reduced rations until the battle was won and the king had returned victorious. Ahab went to battle and lost his life just as Micaiah had prophesied. One sign of an authentic prophet was whether or not the prophecy came true. Micaiah emerged from shame and humiliation victorious when Ahab was felled by a mortal blow on the battlefield. The consequences notwithstanding, Micaiah told the truth and was vindicated by God.

Powerful kings, with the power of life or death over their subjects, inquire through the prophets of the land as to whether they will be successful in battle. Four hundred prophets, fearing the outcome of a negative prophecy, lie to the kings, while one lonely prophet, relying solely upon the vindicating power of God, tells the kings the truth. In a clear demonstration of the negative consequences of earthly power, Micaiah is punished immediately for telling the truth. But in an equally clear demonstration of ultimate vindication by divine power, Micaiah is eventually liberated through the actions of God. The point is obvious: God inexorably delivers those who speak the truth from God. It is God and God alone who is the source and sustenance of all who live their lives in the light of God's truth, temporal consequences notwithstanding. At the center of the story is a faithful and devout prophet who will only speak the truth as he perceives God has given it to him.

Note how Cannon makes no extended comments on the fact that King Jehoshaphat initially inquires of God as to whether the battle could be won. Even after being assured by four hundred excited prophets from Ahab's court, Jehoshaphat yet inquired about one other prophet in the land. That this king initially sought guidance from God could be a possible angle for the sermon. The thrust of Cannon's sermon, however, is guided by the template that she brings to the interpretive process—God, the mighty sovereign, at work on behalf of those who have been mistreated and rejected and who have no other hope but God. A king who seeks the favor of God is commendable, but a maligned, powerless prophet who speaks the truth for God is more in keeping with the hermeneutic that drives this sermon. Micaiah, the faithful prophet, though oppressed and imprisoned, is determined to obey God at all costs and in the end is delivered through an act of God. The contemporary listeners who are being urged by Cannon to tell the truth are not likely to miss the parallels she has drawn. They will surely understand that they too can rely on that same power that delivered Micaiah in his time of peril.

Based on the examples Cannon cites of the times in which we are afraid to speak the truth, the domain of experience to which the sermon is addressed centers on social justice. We are required to act justly in personal matters as well as in those areas pertaining to broader concerns:

> Sometimes God will lay something on our hearts to say to another person or to a committee or to those who control our paychecks, but instead of standing our ground and speaking the truth that is revealed to us, far too often we follow the crowd, get on the bandwagon, shrug our shoulders, and muzzle ourselves, acquiescing to the tyranny of the majority.[25]

In every walk of life a person is called upon to speak and to do the just thing, the right thing in any given situation. God empowers the individual to act with justice in any situation and in every sphere of life. To keep silent and refuse to speak the truth is to deny ourselves a meaningful contribution to the human situation. What we say is not taken seriously and is reduced to noise without content:

> The serious danger with this is that if we keep on being silent in time of speech, if we keep on living as impostors instead of authentic Christians, if we keep on living as liars instead of tellers of truth, then our lives will amount to no more than noisy gongs and clanging cymbals ... which are "full of sound and fury, signifying nothing" (Shakespeare).[26]

Cannon views God as an empowerer of truth-tellers and a way-maker for those who have the courage and fortitude to tell the truth, notwithstanding the end result.

A. Louis Patterson, Jr.
HOW TO KNOW YOU ARE IN THE KINGDOM

The moves of the sermon:

1. Characteristics of a person who is not far from the kingdom	→	2. Two reasons why we are close but not in	→	3. Explanation of what it means to love God fully

A. Louis Patterson, Jr., true to the conservative Baptist heritage out of which he comes, preaches a propositional/textual sermon in which the text provides the subject and the major points of the sermon. The particular domain of experience to which the sermon speaks is that of personal piety, that area of reflection primarily concerned with individual matters of the heart such as prayer, moral discipline, and the maintenance of a person's right relationship with God. The structure of the sermon follows the contours of the textual sermon while the content concerns itself with an emphasis on the individual's personal, intimate relationship with God. The text is taken from Mark 12:34: "And when Jesus saw that he answered discreetly, he said unto him, Thou art not far from the kingdom of God, And no man after that durst ask him any question" (KJV).[27]

After some brief introductory remarks to the audience gathered for the conference of preachers for whom this sermon will be given, Patterson informs his listeners that what he will engage in is a simple exposition of the divinely inspired written Word of God. Having assured them that he will speak nothing but the true word of God, he urges upon them three things that will enable them to receive the word with greater clarity and insight:

> First, step back and watch the miraculous ministry of the Holy Spirit operate in your concentric circle of contacts ... I want us to recognize that what I am going to say is the Word of God ... Secondly, I want us to respond to the Word of God in your own heart ... the third thing I want us to do is to rush out and put it into practice.[28]

Patterson urges his listeners to trust that what he is about to say is the actual Word of God, intended for their individual hearts and meant to be lived out in their personal lives immediately. Without a doubt this sermon addresses the personal piety domain—one of the more popular domains addressed by black preachers in the proclaiming of the gospel.

After several illustrative anecdotes that describe how a person can be close to something while not actually being in it, Patterson cautions his assembly that, in like manner, it is not enough to be close to the kingdom, but in order to benefit one must be in the kingdom. Following the text closely for the propositions he intends to develop in his sermon, in his opening move Patterson poses a rhetorical question to his listeners: "What are the characteristics of a person who is not far from the kingdom?" The first mark of a person who is not far from the kingdom yet not in the kingdom is that he comes to Jesus. Verse 28 says:

> One of the scribes came to Jesus ... The reason he is not far from the kingdom is because he came with a crowd. He came; he was wise enough to come. But just because I come to the Astrodome in Houston and see the Rockets play is no suggestion that I am a member of the team. Close and yet not in.[29]

Patterson, aware that he is speaking primarily to a gathering of professional clergy, reminds them that it is not enough to come to church with the crowd but that they must actually be committed to the work of the kingdom.

The next three reasons why the scribe in the text is characterized as being close but not in the kingdom are quickly enumerated by Patterson:

> One of the scribes came with the crowd and having heard ...
> This word carries the connotation of having comprehended the
> content ... But he does something else here. He reasoned and
> perceived. That means he concluded correctly, because when
> Jesus spoke back to him, Jesus said to him that you have an
> swered discreetly; or, in other words you have thought this
> thing out ... The next thing the scribe did in this verse is, he
> asked Jesus a question. This means that he communicated his
> concerns.[30]

In describing the four characteristics of this scribe who is close but not in the kingdom—he came, heard, reasoned, and questioned—Patterson says he has just given a description of a person who can sit in a congregation for forty years and still not be in the kingdom.

In the second move of the sermon Patterson poses another rhetorical question: "But why is it that he [the scribe] is still away from the kingdom although he is not far from the kingdom? Because, says Patterson, the scribe omitted two very important things:

> The first thing he omitted was that he did not confess his own
> condition. The second thing he omitted was that he did not
> commit himself to Christ. All he did was come with the crowd,
> comprehend the content, conclude correctly and communicate
> his own concerns. But he made no commitment to Christ which
> is predicated upon what theologians suggest is "homologeo":
> the confession, the acknowledgment, the announcement, the
> agreement from God's point of view of his present condition.
> That's why he was not far from the kingdom.[31]

Patterson further elucidates the two reasons he has declared to be essential for entry into the kingdom: confession to God and commitment to Christ. He stresses the importance of confession in the individual's life:

> When was the last time you heard somebody actually confess?
> I find that people have a sense of self-sufficiency. I find that a
> person can be filled with troubles and trials and tribulations,
> can know nothing except fear and frustration, and fracture and
> fruitless failure, can be miserable underneath the skin, cynical
> and disillusioned, and hard to get along with, and will blame

somebody else for his present pilgrimage. There is a distinct absence of confession of our own waywardness.[32]

Again, the emphasis here is on the condition of the individual believer before God. Patterson outlines the dire straits of humankind and why it is so necessary for us individually to confess our sinful state to God and commit our lives to Christ:

> We are sinners by choice of our own desire to dictate the agenda, dominate the audience and demonstrate our authority; and we have a conversation that is wicked because our throats are open sepulchres. Our conduct is miserable because our feet are swift to mischief ... and Jesus says to us "you are not far from the realm, the rule, the reign and the righteousness of the sovereignty of God." ... God has a beautiful blueprint drawn up by the Divine Architect of your life. And the reason you are here is because He wants to build a super structure on the foundation of your commitment to Christ.[33]

A commitment to Christ, which in actuality is a commitment to God's rule and God's reign, is the only way to leave behind the woeful plight of the sinner and step into the divine will of the sovereign reign of God. This commitment enables the hearer to embrace the principles of "spiritual aerodynamics" and rise above the smothering grip of sinful gravity.

In the third move of his sermon, Patterson further expounds on what the commitment to Christ entails. The commitment that assures that one is in and not just close is this: "And thou shall love the Lord thy God with all thy heart ..." Love of Christ with all of one's being assures entry into the kingdom. Patterson, again by way of a detailed exposition of this text, delves into an elaborate explanation of what it means to love the Lord your God with all your heart, soul, and mind and how to distinguish this love from lust or sentimental feelings. First, he declares that this love must be in the believer's heart. Heart, according to Patterson, is the biggest word in the Bible. "Everything that makes me underneath the skin is categorized as the heart. And that, of course, will include the mind, emotions and will." Entrance into the kingdom is assured when one loves Christ with one's whole heart. It is within the private sphere of the heart that one's soul is laid bare before God:

> Let me tell you how to know if you are in the kingdom. I am in the kingdom when I am in private on my knees before God in my heart. What I am in private is what I am period ... Any preacher not praying is playing. And any church not praying is straying ... That's why God navigates the circumstances of life sometimes and lets the floods of life come because He is trying

to get my attention ... He says that the way you get that done,
Al Patterson, is to love me in your heart.[34]

Patterson then explains what it means to love God with all of one's soul and mind.

This type of sermon is much beloved in the traditional black church. It is a direct appeal to one's personal relationship with almighty God. Patterson, following the contours of the text, outlines in a very clear and precise manner the hindrances and requirements for gaining entry into the kingdom of God. He stresses the individual's right relationship with his or her God and reminds his group time and again that what they are in private before God is what they really are. There is no mention of race, larger societal problems, or systemic evil. There are no calls for social justice, no appeals for self-help, or racial solidarity. No interest is expressed in matters that peculiarly affect black people as a race. Those who appreciate this kind of sermon would not expect Patterson to delve into the broader issues of social and systemic concerns. To do so, in the eyes of many, would do irreparable harm to a sermon that grows out of reflection on an individual's personal relationship with God. A right relationship with God must come first; then the individual is ready to branch out into the heady waters of broader social and systemic concerns.

A sermon that urges involvement at the corporate level before there has been an acceptance of God's saving grace in an individual's heart is viewed by many in the black church as premature and unwise—flowers cut from their roots. First things first! The emphasis in this sermon is on private matters of the heart. What is most important to Patterson is the individual's personal standing and right relationship before God. The scribe in the text comes to Christ, but he does not confess and commit his life to him. It is only when he commits himself and expresses that commitment by loving the Lord his God with all his heart, soul, mind, and strength that he can gain entry into God's rule and reign upon the earth.

Here we have a propositional/textual sermon, containing quotable propositional truths with a healthy smattering of illustrative anecdotes, outlined by Patterson in a clear and lucid manner. Patterson urges his listeners to confess their sins, shun self-sufficiency, and rely on the promised strength and guidance of the Divine Architect, God Almighty. The implicit understanding of this sermon is that God's power is made available to help all who desire to be in the kingdom by confessing their sins and asking Christ to come into their lives. God, the mighty sovereign, stands ready to help God's sinful, finite, struggling creatures come into the fullness of God's intentions for them.

It is the compelling need to be in a right relationship with the sovereign God that drives this sermon. Its title, "How to Know You Are in the Kingdom," suggests that what should be uppermost in the listener's mind is how to know whether or not he or she is within the realm and rule of God. Patterson assures his listeners that if they will follow the biblical principles he has outlined, their entry into the kingdom of God will be at hand. He reminds them that it is God who has navigated the circumstances of life and brought them together under the authority of God's word in order to do something in them, for them, and through them. We can never attain complete fulfillment in life until we have gained entry into the kingdom. This is Jesus' answer to the scribe who was not far from the kingdom, and it is Patterson's answer to those who hear the gospel today.

Mozella Mitchell
Pro-vi-dence

The moves of the sermon:

1. Definition of providence and personal testimony	→	2. Exposition of scripture: God's care for Elijah in the famine	→	3. The widow's faith response to Elijah's plea	→	4. Contrapuntal: Defense of miracles in modern times	→	5. Assurance of God's care in dire situations

Mozella Mitchell preaches a simple yet profound sermon in the black preaching tradition. Titled *Pro-vi-dence*, it consists of five moves, with a running commentary about the providential goodness of almighty God. Mitchell takes an Old Testament narrative and shows God's providential care in the lives of the obedient and faithful. Her sermon reconfirms the wisdom of the pulpit sages of old, who constantly reminded their young proteges that the first rule of good preaching is that one be able to tell the story. As the plot of this miracle story unfolds, Mitchell pauses at each new turn in the narrative to give her listeners helpful insights into the ways of God. She opens the sermon with a definition of the word "providence" (*Pro-vi-dence*) and a testimony to God's providential care in her own life. In the opening sentence she moves to identify with her congregation and to assure them with her simple and direct language that they are about to hear a sermon with which they can easily and readily identify:

> Very often we hear people say, "I believe in the farsighted goodness of God." That means God cares for us and looks out for us and provides for our needs.[35]

In the second move of the sermon, she begins her explication of the passage. Mitchell explains each development in the narrative and straightaway provides her listeners with a running commentary on the import of that particular development in their own lives. Expository preaching in the hands of an inexperienced preacher can quickly lose its central focus and end up being three or four sermons bundled into one. Such, however, is not the case with Mitchell. This is not an undisciplined preacher, carelessly jumping from pillar to post. Mitchell has done her exegetical homework and is therefore able to keep the sermon focused on the providential care of God throughout the retelling of the narrative. She identifies the principal characters in the story: the Phoenician widow and the prophet Elijah:

> In the story in the seventeenth chapter of First Kings, God's goodness came to the poor widow of Phoenicia in the hour of her greatest need. We see at least two good things happening in this story. First of all, the prophet of God is following the leadership of God and ministering to the woman who is in need. And at the same time, God is providing for the needs of both the prophet and the poor widow. God has worked these two things together so well that it just amazes you.[36]

She then introduces conflict into the narrative. An unexpected famine in the land is the precipitating factor that necessitates the imposition of the providential hand of God. Allowing for the possibility that some members of her congregation would question the goodness of a God who allowed such suffering to come upon the land, Mitchell quickly inserts the justifying scenario into this unfolding plot: The Israelites, following a weak king married to a strong pagan woman named Jezebel, are led to the worship of the idol god Baal. Because of this great sin, the Lord sends a great famine upon the land. "God is good," says Mitchell, "but God will permit things to happen to us in order to bring to our awareness the source of our blessing." Even when God's people sin and go astray, God uses those things in the grand design and triumph of God's ultimate purpose.

The sermon then moves to the individual care God provided for those who remained faithful and obedient. Because of Elijah's dreadful prophecies against the sinful king and his people, he was forced to go into hiding. He survived on water from a brook near the Jordan and food provided by ravens in the mornings and evenings. In an effort to demonstrate the lengths to which God will go to provide for God's own, Mitchell inserts a few sentences about the raven to show that a raven bringing food can only happen through an act of God:

> Now you know how ravens are. They prey on others and ordinarily wouldn't bring you anything. But God found a good use for them here.[37]

At each step along the way, it is faithful Elijah's response to the initiatives of almighty God that assures his needs will be met. God instructs the raven to send food. When the brook dries up, God sends Elijah to the poor widow of Phoenicia.

Upon Elijah's arrival at the widow's home, Mitchell turns the focus of the story to the widow. In the third move Elijah instructs the poor woman to fix him food before she and her son eat. According to Mitchell, Elijah assures her that if she acts in keeping with his instructions, the Lord will provide. "God has sent me to tell you that the jar of meal shall not be spent, and the cruse of oil shall not fail until the day that the Lord sends rain upon the earth." The poor woman in the story opens herself to the special providence of God when she responds obediently to the request of Elijah:

> Now, this woman didn't know what was going to happen, but she did as she was asked to do. And not only did the jar of meal and cruse of oil not give out, but her son was also restored to health after a grave illness. She knew then that Elijah was a man of God.[38]

Having outlined the providential care of God for those who trust and obey, Mitchell then begins to elucidate on the great faith this woman must have had in order to respond obediently to the request of Elijah. This elucidation she does through the intricate detailing and embellishment of circumstances that, while not recorded in scripture, help to draw the listener into the story world of the text. Reveling in the picture-painting creativity that characterizes the best of black preaching, Mitchell recreates the impoverished straits in which the widow found herself:

> Now, you can imagine how serious the situation was. It has been a long time—years—since it had rained. All the crops had failed, and all the rivers were drying up. The people all around the countryside were dropping dead of hunger, of thirst, and disease. Maybe this poor widow's husband had passed away for the same reason ... I imagine the widow and her son had gone on for several days now without eating ... Now the time had come when they could hold out no longer ... Just at this critical moment entered the man who'd been sleeping out by the brook ...[39]

Mitchell, through her imaginary reconstruction of the details of this story, is inviting the congregation to think over their lives and the many hindrances that could preclude them from responding positively to the initiatives of almighty God. As she assembles the imagined details to this narrative, she constantly reminds her listeners that God would do a mighty work in this woman's life if she had enough faith to trust God:

> The woman must have been puzzled by the audacity of this stranger. She must have stared at him long and hard. Yet, there must have been something persuasive about this man, or the spirit of God must have moved in the heart of the woman in a special way. For she went ahead and prepared the mite of meal for the man as he had asked.[40]

This is a wonder of wonders, for as the woman responds in faith, miraculous things begin to happen. Mitchell believes it is all attributable to God. "And the next day and the next day and on and on, the meal kept coming, and the oil kept flowing because God had his hand on the woman, on the meal and oil, and on the man whom she had fed. God is so good. That's why they call God Providence." The focal point of the resolution of this conflict caused by a famine in the land is the mighty acts of the sovereign God.

In the fourth move Mitchell anticipates a counter point concerning the miracle in this narrative. Conscious of modern day doubts about the miraculous, she assures her congregation that she—a respected pastor and scholar—needs no explanation about the actions of God because she is convinced that God can do anything. She reminds her predominantly black listeners of their struggle in this country, where every possible means has been employed to keep them down and to destroy them. They continue to rise and survive because God has performed miracles in their lives.

In the final move Mitchell reminds her congregation that they too are in a famine of sorts. Much uncertainty surrounds them in present day America. She reminds them of the depressed economy, the high crime rate, joblessness, and the general insecurity of the times. While taking care to make them no promises she cannot support, she assures them that they are in the hands of a higher power:

> What I can say to you is that you're in the hands of a good God, and God will take care of you! Now, how God will do it, I don't know. But I do know that your jar of meal shall not be spent and your cruse of oil shall not fail if you respect God and obey.[41]

In a sermon with five simple moves, Mitchell has invited the listeners into the story world of the text. The biblical hermeneutic she brings to the text is clearly that of God, the mighty sovereign, acting powerfully on behalf of the marginalized and oppressed. The domain of experience upon which she is reflecting and to which her preaching is directed is plainly care of the soul. The extended metaphor she draws upon is that of God as provider.

Where is God, and what is God doing in this passage as Mitchell perceives it? Without a doubt, Mitchell sees God as being proactive and in complete control of this desperate situation from beginning to end. God brings the prophet and widow together in their hour of greatest need and ministers to both through their obedience to God. The harsh famine in the land is permitted by a God who works in mysterious ways to bring the people to their senses and to the source of their blessings. But even in the land of famine God takes care of God's own children and provides for them. On the heels of Elijah's dreadful prophecies to a sinful king, God tells Elijah to go and hide by the brook near the Jordan and commands the ravens to bring bread and meat to him.

When the brook dries up, God sends Elijah to the poor widow of Phoenicia. It is the power and presence of God that gives Elijah the courage to approach this poor widow whose plight is just as bad as Elijah's. But, says Mitchell, the widow was talking to a man who knew that God could provide. It was God who moved in the heart of the woman in a special way and caused her to respond favorably to Elijah's plea. The contents of the meal and oil containers remained the same because God's hand (power) was upon the woman. Without question, God's power and presence are indispensable to this narrative.

God is shown by Mitchell to be on the side of those who trust and obey God even in the midst of desperate circumstances. The connection Mitchell makes between the ancient text and the contemporary situation is the providential goodness of God, irrespective of time and place. Mitchell acknowledges that while the narrative from which she was preaching took place many centuries ago, God has always been good, and thus she has a right to expect the same goodness from God as Elijah and the widow. If Mitchell has a right to expect this same goodness, then by extension those who are listening to her interpret this passage also have a right to embrace this promise. Mitchell assures her listeners that God is at work in all desperate situations to bring about good to those who trust and obey.

In this narrative God initially acts against a sinful king who wants to kill Elijah, but in the case of the widow who is suffering as a result of the famine, Mitchell demonstrates that God also acts against nameless forces and uncontrollable circumstances when they join hands to defeat those who respond positively to the initiative of God. Through a skillful weaving of ancient text and contemporary situation, Mitchell reassures her congregation that God is at work on its behalf. While God takes care of all God's children, God's special care is reserved for those who obey and live according to the sovereign's promises.

Fred C. Lofton
BAD BLACK DUDE ON THE ROAD

The moves of the sermon:

1. Focus on race and definition of "bad dude"	→	2. Disadvantages of the eunuch—physical and psychological castration—from African American world view	→	3. Benefits of authority and responsibility; words of admonition to blacks	→	4. The eunuch as God-fearer: blessings for those who seek God's guidance

Fred C. Lofton's sermon titled "Bad Black Dude on the Road"[42] is a prime example of a sermon that reflects on and speaks out of experiences in the corporate concerns domain—the domain that speaks specifically to black interests and concerns. His text is taken from Acts 8:26–39—the story of Philip's encounter with the Ethiopian eunuch on the road to Gaza. The focus of the sermon is that handicaps are not barriers to productive living when one has been empowered by God through Jesus Christ. While noting that much preaching on this passage has centered on Philip and his missionary activity, in the opening move of the sermon, Lofton redirects the focus from Philip to the black presence from Ethiopia—the bad dude. He defines "dude" as someone who is fastidious in manners, dress, bearing, and skill. He recognizes that in the eyes of many in his listening congregation, it is a great compliment among the commoners in the black community to refer to a person as a "bad dude." Among blacks it is a flattering term that evokes cunning, skill, and an ability to stay above the fray "without breaking a sweat."

Having redirected the focus of the text to the Ethiopian, in the second move Lofton picks up on particulars in this narrative that he believes will have a direct appeal to a large number of blacks, even though such details have been discounted by some biblical scholars. He declares the eunuch to be black, castrated, and deprived:

> But I choose to place attention on the Ethiopian, the black man receiving the good news of the gospel of Christ from Philip. Here was a man stripped of his manhood, as we African—American men are today … The Ethiopian experienced living in hell as a result of physical castration. But the hell was both physical and psychological. In the days of Queen Candace of Ethiopia, in whose service the Ethiopian labored, it was mandatory that a man who worked in the service of the queen submit to castration. It was, in other words, both a condition of

employment and a requirement of existence. This Ethiopian, like our own black men today, had to forgo his manhood as the price for his continued existence.[43]

The Ethiopian's psychological castration came from the fact that he would have to live with physical castration for the rest of his life. Drawing on this theme of a black person castrated and deprived simply in order to exist and survive, Lofton turns his attention to the analogous castration of black men in America:

> African American males find it hard to function adequately as males because of the hell they live in ... America castrated black people when they brought us from Mother Africa, and we remain victimized by that crippling legacy. Many African-Americans worked jobs and never received a promotion. Others with less experience, education, and know-how stepped up the ladder of success while we stood by discouraged, disappointed, disgusted and dismayed.[44]

From the outset of the exposition of this text, Lofton is determined to interpret it in a manner quite unlike a minister from a traditional mainline church. The focus is not on the missionary activity of the early church and the spread of the gospel, but on an aggrieved "black dude" who is trying to survive despite his physical and psychological castration. Blacks listening to Lofton can identify with the perils encountered by this eunuch, although there is little in the text to suggest that the eunuch perceived his condition in such a damning light. In a creative move, typical of the freedom granted to black preachers to say and do what they wish in the preaching of the gospel, Lofton seizes upon a general understanding of the plight of eunuchs to speak a word of hope and encouragement to his black listeners.

After more examples of blacks who have been stripped of their manhood by disingenuous whites, Lofton returns to his exposition of the biblical narrative with a more positive twist. Having assured his listeners that he intends to preach this text with their interests and concerns in mind, in the third move he shifts the tone of the sermon from the eunuch as a despised black man to a smart, creative, and powerful black person. At this point in the sermon, the eunuch and blacks are one and the same. While acknowledging that blacks have had a hard time making their way in this country, Lofton also speaks a word of encouragement to them about their God-given gifts of survival and prosperity:

> His boss, Candace, the queen, had bestowed great power and authority upon him. He maintained responsibility for her

financial affairs, "in charge of all her treasure" (v. 27). The eunuch had been commissioned to journey to Jerusalem to seek further knowledge of the religion of Israel. This was truly a bad black dude … The man in this narrative must have been a financial wizard, someone who knew how to hold and handle the queen's money wisely.[45]

He uses his laudatory comments about the Ethiopian eunuch as an opportunity to issue his first words of rebuke and exhortation to his listeners. It is in the corporate concerns domain that the preacher is allowed to say things to blacks that only another black should say. Lofton, speaking of the wizardly and financial acumen of the eunuch, cites two areas in which blacks must be encouraged to do better. The first area concerns itself with brothers, who unlike the eunuch in the story, have a problem working under strong women:

Some of the brothers encounter problems working with sisters in authority over them, and can't deal with it. I experience no difficulty in this kind of situation. If the sister's got more—education, ability, grace, gifts, and whatever—she's just got it. And brothers, we must learn to admit it, accept the reality, and learn to work for and with her.[46]

The second word of admonishment comes when Lofton speaks about the eunuch being entrusted with the financial arrangements of the queen. Blacks, he says, should take pride in other blacks who know how to handle and invest large sums of money. But Lofton chides his congregation for being skeptical about black ability in this area:

What is wrong with black people that we can't handle our own money? Explain for me this twisted love affair we have with white folks in the economic arena. Why take the fruits of our labor and give them to the affluent for the uplifting of their community and elevating of their people, while our own black communities plead for life and liberation? I pray that Almighty God will let me live to see a reversal of this pitiable situation someday.[47]

Here we see words of strong rebuke to black people being spoken by another black person. Black men are chided for their male chauvinism in refusing to work under qualified black women, and blacks in general are chastised for their refusal to bank and spend their money among their own people. Such strong words to blacks can only come from another black whom they admire and/or respect. This type of stinging critique from a white preacher to a predominantly black congregation would not be well received. In fact, most blacks would be insulted and highly offended if a white preacher were to say such things to them in any setting. However, in the hands of a seasoned black pastor such criticisms are heard and received, even if not acted upon.

Lofton well understands that he is speaking out of the corporate concerns domain, saying what only a seasoned black preacher can say to his or her black parishioners. Young black preachers, however, should be slow to engage in this kind of rhetoric. Admonitions and chastisements that can grow out of corporate concerns preaching should be left to experienced pastors who have the wisdom to gauge the appropriate level of critique.

In the fourth move Lofton identifies the eunuch as a man who feared God, noting that on the way back to Ethiopia from Jerusalem, the eunuch sat in his chariot reading Isaiah the prophet. Lofton attributes his reading of scripture to a desire for spiritual direction from almighty God:

> Not only was this man entrusted with the treasury of the powerful queen, but on the spiritual side, he feared God. God's Word says he came to Jerusalem to worship, and on his way back to Ethiopia he sat in his chariot reading Isaiah the prophet. This black man sought spiritual guidance, and at this point in his life the Lord intended to reward him abundantly.[48]

It is in this move that Lofton heads toward a very explicit understanding of the hermeneutic that informs this sermon. This mistreated but smart eunuch seeks guidance and direction from almighty God, who, according to Lofton, is prepared to bless him abundantly. Lofton assures the congregation that a way will be made for all who truly seek God's guidance. He provides a personal testimony of how God opened doors for him during his school days at Morehouse College. "I had no father to count on, nor any Merit Scholarship, Pell Grant, financial aid, or work-study program to help me. But I had a praying mother and an almighty God on my side." Again, as on the previous occasion, when Lofton speaks of the opportunities made possible through the providence of God, he criticizes young blacks for complaining about their lack of opportunity:

> It is disturbing to hear young African-American males and females complaining today because of the lack of this or that— no family, no father, no "wheels," sometimes no nothing. I hasten to remind them if they possess a creative positive attitude combined with whatever other blessings that have come their way—good health, sharp minds, strong bodies—they already hold all that they need. If a young person is endowed with one or a combination of these attributes, along with a willingness to work and succeed, and a willingness to seek and serve God, "God will surely make a way!"[49]

Throughout this sermon Lofton simultaneously lifts and chides. The same word that upholds also humbles. In one instance he describes how the scriptures model the best of black life, and in another instance he describes how black life is so out of character with the scriptures. He is dividing the word of truth as only a skillful black pastor can, saying what should only be said when both sender and receiver are black.

After another word of admonishment to black parents concerning the love and attention they owe their children, Lofton returns to his interweaving of text and contemporary situation. Philip, upon seeing the eunuch in the chariot, approaches him and asks if he understands what he is reading. The eunuch replies, "How can I, except some man should guide me?" Lofton sees the eunuch's plea for assistance as another sign of an intelligent black dude—a person who is unafraid to seek divine guidance from those in the know:

> No matter how successful, prosperous, or upwardly mobile you are on the job and in society, you need somebody to interpret God's Word for you. You may be conversant with power brokers, skilled in the courtroom, adept in the halls of Congress, at home within the walls of academia, a genius in the operating room, the science lab, or the cockpit of the mighty 747—but you still need the guidance of a spirit-filled man or woman of God to help you wrestle with the life-giving, soul-sustaining, eternal, and powerful Word of God.[50]

The eunuch is wise indeed to seek a clearer understanding of the scriptures, for the Word Philip preaches to him leads to salvation. As the eunuch responded positively to the good news Philip proclaimed to him, he became even more intellectually and spiritually enlightened. His unspeakable joy leads him to urge Philip to baptize him with water from a nearby stream. The eunuch's further enlightenment and subsequent rejoicing are made possible through none other than God's saving power:

> This eunuch in Candace's cabinet, this bad black dude, when he came up out of the water, "went on his way rejoicing," because he'd experienced and accepted the love and mercy of God. He now held within his heart and mind a story to tell to all he met regarding God's saving power.[51]

Not content to leave the grand exploits of the eunuch to the witness of scripture, Lofton adds extrabiblical materials to the narrative to demonstrate the grand and noble purposes to which a life can be put when it is placed at the service of almighty God. Lofton informs his listeners that some people believe this eunuch established the Coptic Church in Ethiopia, the oldest consecutive Christian community on the continent of Africa. Again, another feature of corporate concerns preaching is an appeal to race pride and accomplishments. The eunuch was able to accomplish so much in life in spite of hardships and handicaps because, although physically castrated by human beings, he was spiritually empowered by God in and through Jesus Christ.

In a sermon intended specifically for a black congregation, Lofton recounts the trials and tribulations of an Ethiopian eunuch who was able to overcome and persevere in the face of overwhelming odds. The eunuch was given great responsibilities by Queen Candace and went on to even greater accomplishments for God, because God was at work in his life in a providential and empowering way. Undergirding the unfolding events of the eunuch's life is a powerful God who enabled the eunuch to turn setbacks into blessings throughout his life.

The domain on which Lofton reflects and to which the sermon is addressed is most certainly that of corporate concerns. His somewhat untraditional handling of the text no doubt had great appeal for its intended gathering. But Lofton is not simply a cheerleader for black pride, solidarity, and uplift, he also sees this sermon as an occasion to chide and criticize blacks when they fall short of God's will for God's created order. Lofton, the seasoned black pastor, knows that what he is saying by way of exhortation and admonishment should only be said to blacks by another black. The extended metaphors implicit throughout the sermon are God as provider and empowerer.

Carolyn Ann Knight
IF THOU BE A GREAT PEOPLE

The moves of the sermon:

1. Leadership and continuity	→	2. People of color dispute and challenge allotment of territory	→	3. Hindrances to the promised inheritance	→	4. Jesus Christ: the ultimate example of triumph of greatness

This sermon by Carolyn Ann Knight, titled "If Thou Be a Great People," may also be categorized under the rubric of corporate concerns but has an equal bearing upon the maintenance of the institutional church domain.[52] She preaches from an Old Testament passage made famous in black circles by Sandy F. Ray, a gifted black preacher from an earlier generation.[53] Knight acknowledges Ray's widely acclaimed sermon and continues with the theme of struggle and triumph, but develops the text in a new and creative manner, basing it on insights from contemporary experiences.

The sermon is styled as a liberation sermon in the edited volume in which it originally appears. However, some of the oppressive ideas Knight seeks to counteract come from within neighborhoods and institutions under black control. Outside oppressive forces are mentioned, but African Americans are also charged with hindering their own progress in their own locales and settings. Thus, the liberation terminology currently in vogue is not the only way, or maybe not even the best way, to understand the organizing theme and structure of this sermon.

The sermon's audience was a conference of pastors and lay people, that is, people whose primary responsibility is the maintenance of the institutional church.[54] Thus in its essence, this sermon is really about empowerment—the empowerment of a great people who have a long history of involvement with the sovereign God. Knight calls to mind the proven track record of this God for a new generation of blacks, who stand poised and ready to tackle the difficult challenges of life awaiting them in the next millennium.

To the end that a liberation sermon helps the oppressed recognize and repent of their own forms of sin, this sermon may be narrowly construed as such. But in its broader implications, it is really a word of empowerment to black people, in black churches, about what will be required to sustain and enhance their people, their community, and the primary institution that has loved and nurtured so many of them in the past—the black church. Looking at the sermon through the lenses of corporate concerns and maintenance of the institutional church allows us to see more clearly its creativity and ultimate aim.

The sermon opens with a propositional statement on the importance of continuity in leadership in any movement. Knight notes how blacks in contemporary America are searching for a leader who can galvanize the black masses in the same way that Malcolm X, Martin Luther King, Jr., Adam Clayton Powell, Jr., and others did in the past. She then contrasts black America's leadership vacuum with Israel's smooth and swift transition from Moses to Joshua:

> Such was not the case with the people of Israel. After the death of Moses, the transfer of leadership was swift, smooth. Joshua was a fitting successor to Moses because Joshua had great courage and vision ... Because Joshua was able to see the invisible and believe the impossible, he inherited the role of leader. After the conquest, the children of Israel were ready to cease their wanderings in the wilderness. Joshua had the assignment of dividing the territory among the twelve tribes.[65]

The second move of the sermon introduces conflict and race into the narrative. The people of Israel lose their leader. Joshua swiftly takes up the leadership mantle. The children of Israel conquer the land of Canaan, and all is well until it comes time to divide up the land, among the tribes. The allotment proceeds without difficulty until Joshua gets to Ephraim and Manasseh.

The first indication the reader has that a predominantly black audience is the intended focus of this sermon comes with Knight's opening examples of great leaders in the African American community. Her explicit focus on race, however, takes a more open turn in her second move where she describes Ephraim and Manasseh as people of color. Knight explains to her listeners that Ephraim and Manasseh were the children born to Joseph's Egyptian wife, Asenath, and later adopted by their grandfather Jacob and given a share in his inheritance along with Jacob's other children. After explaining the racial origin of the two tribes, Knight then engages in what could be perceived as double entendre when she says:

> Now if I understand my geography, Egypt is in northern Africa, which means that Ephraim and Manasseh were an Afro-Asiatic people: people of color. Upon receiving their inheritance, Ephraim and Manasseh began to grumble and complain that their share of the allotment was too small ... Because of their history and family lineage coupled with a personal and abiding relationship with God Almighty, they insisted that their share of the land should be more.[66]

This line of argument before a predominantly black group could be interpreted in different ways. It could mean that the two tribes of color, with their great and noble African ancestry, felt they were being undervalued, or worse yet, discriminated against in their allotment of territory. Or it could mean, in a humorous way, that no real dissension arose in the apportionment process until it came time to give the people of color their land. The humor lies in the acknowledgment that even among great people of color there are those who will never be satisfied with their lot in life and will always find something about which to grumble. Either way, the listener by now clearly understands that the sermon will have as its focus the particular challenges facing people of color.

After setting the sermon in a racial milieu, Knight then makes an explicit connection between the people in the text and the people at the church conference. Joshua's admonition to the biblical people of color becomes Knight's admonition to contemporary people of color:

I believe this passage is a word to this New Millennium Pastor's Conference as we prepare to face life in the twenty-first century. "If thou be a great people go up into the hill country and clear a place for yourself there!" At this uncertain point of our perilous pilgrimage upon this planet, we must recognize who we are as a people and appropriate our rightful inheritance in God and in this world. If thou be a great people ... a great preacher/pastor, a great community, a great family, a great sister, a great brother ... the challenge of the hill country awaits you.[57]

Having stated to her listeners that their rightful inheritance will involve them in tough and at times seemingly impossible challenges, Knight is careful at this point not to turn the sermon into a xenophobic disquisition on the unparalleled greatness of blackness, a pitfall all too common among sermons in the corporate concerns domain. Instead, she issues a disclaimer:

Mind you, we are not here talking about great as a perception that is based on race or gender or class alone. I am talking about greatness as a way of harnessing and husbanding the best of our spiritual, intellectual, financial, educational, and political resources and empowering our communities and enriching this society.

Knight wants it understood that the greatness of which she speaks is not solely determined by one's race, gender, or class but by one's relationship with the sovereign God:

I am not talking about greatness as a way of exalting everything that is African and trashing everything that is European. I am talking about the greatness that the Bible says is in all of us who claim to be the people of God.[58]

While her sermon is directed to the particular interests of African Americans—thus its corporate concerns focus—its call for a great people to stand up to the challenges before them is based on those inherent possibilities that the Bible declares to be within *all* those who enter into covenant with the mighty God. True to the biblical witness, Knight recognizes that the genuine source of greatness in all human beings is not gender, race, or class but God. If the tribes of color are to overcome challenges and receive their rightful inheritance, it can only come about by calling forth that which the mighty God has granted unto them.

Still, in her second move—people of color disputing their allotment of territory—Knight continues her interweaving of ancient text with contemporary situation. When the tribes of Ephraim and Manasseh grumble about their allotment, Joshua challenges them to go and possess the rugged, unclaimed land of the hill country. Knight enumerates two ideals that made these Afro-Asiatic people believe they could take on such a challenge—a healthy self-identity and their long-standing covenant with God. She in turn ascribes these two traits to contemporary people of color. With respect to a healthy self-identity, Knight says present-day blacks, like the Afro-Asiatic tribes, practice the art of self-definition:

> They refused to be defined by circumstances, or environment, or culture, or class, or race. We know who we are. We have a unique sense of somebodyness. We have a good memory. We know our oral tradition. We are well aware of our ancestors. Our father, Joseph, was Jacob's favorite son. Jacob, our grand-father, was a schemer, but one night by the ford of Jabbok, he wrestled with God and prevailed. Isaac, our great-grandfather, was the only son of our great-great-grandfather Abraham, a friend of God who received the promise by faith. Oh yeah, we come from good stock.[59]

Although the appeal is implicitly made to a healthy black self-identity, their memory of the history of that identity is based on the biblical narratives of God's involvement with Israel.

The second thing Ephraim and Manasseh, and by implication contemporary blacks, had going for them that assured them of their greatness and ultimate triumph was their covenant with God. "God promised," says Knight, "through Abraham and Sarah never to forsake us. That our family would be as numerous as the stars in the heavens and the sand on the seashore. Throughout history the blessing of God has been upon us."

Mindful of their great heritage and their covenant with God, the tribes of color are not discouraged when Joshua urges them to accept the challenges of the hill country:

> Great people are not condemned by the conditions of their birth, or locked into Euro-centric thought patterns. You have enough imagination, ingenuity, intelligence, and integrity to make a place for yourselves. Do not linger on the low plains of life crying and complaining, fretting and fuming, moaning and groaning about what you cannot do or what you do not have. Be creative. Accept the challenge of the hill country.[60]

Using the example of ancient people of color, Knight assures her listeners that black people possess an inherent will to triumph. What present day blacks are currently experiencing is not their promised lot in life but rather a wilderness that requires the empowerment of a rugged and forthright people:

> I submit that what we are experiencing right now—ethnic cleansing in Bosnia and Mississippi and Arkansas, bombings in New York and Oklahoma, Birmingham and Atlanta; high unemployment, no health care, poor child care, insecure social security, babies dangling from bridges, babies with bullets, children with guns, runaway teenage pregnancy, children with no hope, mothers who can't cope, fathers on dope; more black men in jail than in college; women forgotten too soon; men gone too soon; children dying too soon, sisters waiting to exhale ... many of us kept out, kicked out, knocked out, locked out, pushed out, put out, pulled out, phased out; the hopelessness and despair that pervades our communities—what we are experiencing right now is an aberration. We are wandering in a wilderness called the United States. This is not who we really are.[61]

Having established the greatness inherent in all people of God, Knight reminds the gathering that the dysfunctional social milieu in which blacks currently find themselves is not indicative of the great people they have been and are presently called to be. Moreover, it is not the inheritance promised to people who have entered into covenant with God and trusted God from generation to generation.

In spite of the many hindrances and setbacks blacks are currently experiencing, Knight appeals to black pride and determination by reminding her listeners that God has always done great things through Africans. She urges blacks to remember their healthy self-identity as well as their covenant with God. She calls to mind the many contributions of Africans to science and medicine, literature, the arts, religion, and business. Acknowledging that many blacks struggle with low self-esteem because they are more familiar with the American side of who they are than the African side, she admonishes blacks to get in touch with the African side in order to know that they are a great people, and what God has done through them to make them a great people:

> We are a great people with a great history. We must stop reciting the failure studies that have been done on our communities. We must never forget that God has always done great things through Africans. We are formed out of adversity. From it we have fashioned our unique perspective on humanity and divinity. They gave us straw. We gave them bricks. They gave us seed. We gave them cotton. They gave us sorrow. We wrote

> songs ... They called us failures. We gave them Fisk ... They gave us hell. We gave them Howard.[62]

Knight previously declared that greatness was not determined by race, color, or gender but by God. Having established that all-inclusive criterion for greatness, she now feels free to speak particularly of God's mighty acts on behalf of the black race. She pointedly declares God to be at work in black greatness through the African side of African Americans. According to Knight, Africanness "is an instrumentality that God uses to enrich the world ... And God wants to use us to make a contribution to this world. You see, we are a great people."

Knight continues to interweave Joshua's admonition with the plight of present-day blacks as she seeks to encourage her listeners, through her explication of the scriptures, to make a place for themselves in spite of the setbacks and adversities they encounter:

> Joshua said to the tribes of Ephraim and Manasseh and to us ... Stop fighting over these petty plots of land. Stop fighting over insignificant positions and titles ... You have a great work to do: churches to build, families to save, children to nurture, men to redeem, women to empower, marriages to mend, colleges to revitalize ... a drug epidemic to rout out, an AIDS pandemic to cure, sin to conquer, salvation to gain, songs to sing, poems to write, hell to avoid, heaven to gain. If thou be a great people, the hill country awaits you.[63]

In the third move the tone of Knight's sermon changes from upbeat encouragement to dire warning as she cautions the assembly about the hindrances and obstructions that threaten to imperil the inheritance promised by God to a great people. What is needed in order to overcome the many obstacles that await them is a renewed sense of empowerment by God, not liberation from oppression. The opposition and danger that threaten contemporary blacks in their metaphorical hill country are only in part from powerful outside forces. Knight cites only two references to systemic oppression—white-collar businessmen who tamper with financial institutions, health care, and Social Security and a Democratic president who cuts the heart out of welfare. She goes into much greater detail about the harm that comes to blacks at the hands of other blacks in their own community:

> All of our opposition is not from people who look different than we do. There are people in our communities who do us harm. We have leaders among us who violate our trust and destroy our integrity. We must cut them down, vote them out, and

replace them! There is even opposition among churches and in the churches. There are Christians who think that their church or denomination is the only ticket in town. They build themselves up by putting you down.[64]

The problems of the hill country come, in part, at the hands of outside forces but even more so from people within the camp. What is needed is not so much a liberation from outside powers but rather a strong resolve from those within the tribes to live up to the greatness God has instilled in all God's children. What is needed for the challenge of the hill country is empowerment. They've already been liberated. They are in the land of promise. They need to be empowered for the challenge of triumphing over that which God has already promised and delivered. The strength they need in order to succeed can come only through the mighty sovereign who has brought them this far by faith. Building on black pride, Knight assures her listeners, by recounting their grand history, that God has had God's hands on blacks throughout the ages, and that God intends to continue to do great things through the black peoples of the world, including Africans in America.

In her fourth and final move, Knight places Jesus in the hill country, indicating that he went there and made a name for himself by making it a highway to heaven. True to traditional understandings of how to close the black sermon, she ends her message with a celebrative reference to Jesus Christ. In so doing, however, she unintentionally dilutes the general thrust of this well-crafted sermon with her late insertion of a new idea and her somewhat awkward referencing of Jesus Christ. While it is always proper to point to Jesus Christ as God's ultimate revelatory act, it can confuse the listeners when the Old and New Testaments lack continuity and Jesus appears to be an afterthought tacked on to the end of an Old Testament passage.[65]

A variety of other possible closings would have allowed Knight to include Jesus Christ while at the same time maintaining the integrity of her Old Testament focus. Knight could have (1) presented Jesus as the highest and best of all that we ultimately aspire to achieve in our greatness; (2) portrayed Jesus as the ultimate overseer of all those who overcome the challenges of life's hill country; and/or (3) shown how God's empowerment made the difference in the challenges faced by the historical Jesus in his own season of struggle and triumph. Those concerns notwithstanding, Knight has crafted an excellent sermon that reflects in the best way on God's active involvement in experiences that grow out of corporate concerns and the maintenance of the institutional church domains.

This sermon speaks to corporate concerns because Knight is clearly of the opinion that greatness has come to black people through their Africanness and not their Americanness. Throughout the sermon she urges the listeners to get in touch with their African side and call to mind once again their greatness as a people of color. The sermon also speaks to the maintenance of the institutional church, for if one takes note of Knight's examples as she outlines the challenges and obstructions of the hill country, they nearly all concern themselves with matters pertaining to the maintenance—prosperity and well-being—of the institutional church.

At one point in the sermon, she urges her listeners to stop fighting over insignificant positions and titles. At another place, when she reminds them that they have a great work to do, the first example of that great work is the building of churches.[66] When she speaks of opposition in the community, she mentions church rivalries and infighting. Thus, her call to the challenges of the hill country is clearly directed to the participants in the organized church.

While God has no active role in the text per se, God's power and presence are the motivating forces behind the actions of the people in the text and the preacher of the sermon. The tribes of Ephraim and Manasseh, according to Knight, considered themselves to be a great people "because of their history and family lineage coupled with a personal and abiding relationship with God almighty."[67] Because of their ancestral achievements and their personal relationship with God, the Afro-Asiatic tribes thought they should have a greater share of the land. Building on this understanding of family lineage and personal encounter with God, Knight urges contemporary blacks to lay claim to their "rightful inheritance in God and in this world," as they face the challenges of their own hill country.

Convinced that if blacks are going to succeed in the new millennium, they must go forward with a heightened sense of the greatness of their ancestry and the awesome strength of their God, she wills her listeners forward with a pro-black interpretation of God's actions in biblical history. It is, after all, God who calls a people to greatness and God who sustains them in their forward movement and onward march:

> You are a great people. You have an internal mechanism to help restore our families, save our babies, empower our women, and reclaim our men ... You are not going into the hill country alone. God never sends us where God has not already been. God never sends us without first preparing the way.[68]

A proactive God is central to this sermon and central to an understanding of the one who empowers blacks for the changes and challenges that lie ahead of them.

Conclusion

It is clear that the common thread running throughout the sermons of our contemporary preachers is the biblical hermeneutic they bring to the sermon preparation process. The hermeneutic of God, the mighty sovereign who acts mightily on behalf of the powerless and oppressed, is the long-standing template blacks place on the scriptures as they begin the interpretive process. This template informs and affects much of what they see in scripture, and it helps blacks to discern God at work in and through the scriptures they proclaim in very creative and interesting ways. Blacks historically and to this present day believe God is proactively at work on their behalf. This is what they bring to scripture, see in scripture, and preach from scripture.

There are those who believe black preaching is predominantly Christocentric in its focus.[69] They base this assertion, in part, on the fact that many black preachers close their sermons by recounting the events surrounding the crucifixion, death, and resurrection of Jesus Christ. Proponents of this view claim that the entire African American sermon is built around this much-anticipated celebrative moment. While it is true that many blacks close their sermons in this manner, what is often overlooked in the Christocentric argument is the climactic conclusion of the narrative where the fate of Jesus is completely in God's hands. What equally claims the attention of the black preacher in the crucifixion story is the power of God made manifest when God raises Jesus from the dead. The black church and the black preacher well understand that even when you clothe it in poetic language and picturesque speech, if you simply detail the events surrounding the death of Jesus you have not given a full account of God's ultimate redeeming act.

After describing in great detail the crucifixion and death, the black preacher proclaims—with equal and in some instances even greater fervor—the church's faith that *early* Sunday morning God raised Jesus from the dead. Again, the emphasis, in what many regard as a purely Christocentric event, is ultimately placed on God's faithfulness and power in resurrecting Jesus. Jesus did not rise on his own; he was raised by the power of God. Resurrection emanated from the throne room. It is true that many black sermons end with the sweet moan of the black preacher crying out, "*He died on Calvary, yes he did.*" But the good news is not complete until the preacher also proclaims, "*But early, early on the third day morning God raised him from the dead ...*" No one who hears the complete story can deny the black preacher is also celebrating the redemptive power of God manifested on behalf of Jesus, the crucified One.

Blacks have long believed that it is the Creator God who works mightily in human history to accomplish God's purposes. Their enduring emphasis on the might and majesty of God has been a persistent theme in black religious thought. The demonstration of God's power is the fundamental key to understanding what drives, motivates, and gives shape and life to the creation and organization of the black sermon. Time and again in countless sermons from blacks who span the centuries and hail from different denominational, educational, and geographical backgrounds, one finds this foundational hermeneutic at work. It is the distinctive factor in black preaching.

4

The Basic Dynamics of the African American Sermon

Though not intended as a how-to manual on sermon preparation, this book does seek to reflect on the formative influences and preconceptions that impact and shape the black sermon in its embryonic state. It seeks to uncover the foundational dynamics at the heart of the black sermon. Through my investigation of the manner in which blacks interpret and apply scripture, I have determined that there are three crucial interpretive dynamics at work in the early stages of the African American sermon preparation process:

1. An understanding of what blacks believe about power and the sovereign God and how that belief has traditionally informed their sacred story.
2. An awareness of and sensitivity to the history and culture of black life in America.
3. An insightful competence in describing and addressing the many and varied life situations (domains of experience) that blacks experience daily in America and an ability to wed the scriptures to those experiences in a practical and relevant manner.

Power and the Sovereign God

As a result of their historical marginalization, what became most important to blacks in their encounter with Christianity was an intimate relationship with a powerful God, who exhibited throughout scripture a willingness to side with the downtrodden in very concrete and practical ways. The belief that the scriptures consistently showed God acting in this manner in time became a way of construing and using all of scripture. The powerful river of black preaching has its origin in this conceptual framework. Deeply embedded in the black sacred story is the belief that God is unquestionably for blacks in every aspect of their existence. This is not to suggest that God is at work only for blacks or that God is not the God of all creation. It is to say, however, with power and conviction that the powerless and oppressed have not been left out of the redemptive purposes of almighty God. A once despised and maligned people have historically believed that they have found unconditional favor in the mighty sovereign's sight. This is the preconception that blacks bring to the study table in preparation for preaching, and it is the template that governs their exposition of scripture.

Powerful black preaching speaks forth the things of God. I am not arguing that every sermon ought to have the word "God" in it, but each sermon should concern itself with God's essence and actions—God's divine initiative and revelatory activity, especially as that activity is manifested through the work and person of Jesus Christ, biblically witnessed and historically confessed. According to David Buttrick, "Christian preaching involves a '*bringing out*' or a '*bringing into view*' of convictional understandings—understandings of God, of God's mysterious purposes, and of unseen wonders of grace in human lives."[1] This bringing out and bringing into view is accomplished in the sermon through many different rhetorical means—depiction, analogy, metaphor, explanation, analysis, and creedal explorations—but such rhetorical instruments must have as their aim some understanding, inference, or attestation to God.

The key to the powerful black sermon that consistently strikes a chord in the hearts of the listening congregation is simple yet profound: The sermon must be about God! It must bring the listener to some understanding of who God is and what God is about. At its core the black sermon is not about what blacks have had to endure in America or their peculiar place as a people of color in this country. All peoples have had to endure something. While the life experiences of blacks certainly impact and color their interactions with God and scripture, it is the sovereign God at work in and through those experiences that characterizes the essence of powerful black preaching. Black Christian faith and concomitantly black Christian preaching involve the positive response of the total person to the initiatives of almighty God.

Crucial to the comprehension of what makes for powerful black preaching is the way in which African Americans conceive of God. An understanding of God in the African American religious experience must rest upon realistic ideas that relate God's revelatory activities to the life experiences of the people being addressed. Only blacks can fully speak of God as God is related to their black condition. Consequently, the manner in which blacks conceive of God may best be viewed through a cursory examination of black theologians' thoughts about God. Historically, along with the classical conceptions of God, four themes have been central to the ways in which African Americans understand God to be at work: freedom and partiality; love and partisanship; personhood and creativity; and survival and liberation.

Freedom and Impartiality

African Americans have traditionally experienced God as an impartial judge of human character and motives. That God is "no respecter of persons" is one of the major affirmations of the African American Christian community. Black Christians affirmed that God was impartial because they lived in a society in which European Americans claimed the divine right of race, denied the humanity of African Americans, and decided who would receive the benefits of that society based solely on the color of one's skin.[2]

God's impartiality also disassociates God from the unjust and discriminatory structures of a racist culture, thereby accentuating one of the central biblical emphases of the nature of God, that is, God's freedom. Freedom is essential to God's character. In African American theological thought the emphasis is not so much on God's freedom as an abstract quality of God's being as it is on what that freedom means in relation to the struggle of black people for liberation and wholeness.[3]

Love and Partisanship

African American Christians have claimed the impartiality of God, but they have also affirmed the seemingly contradictory claim that God is on the side of the oppressed. They recognized in the Exodus story and in the writings of the prophets of Israel a God who takes sides in human conflict, not only rendering judgment on those who oppress but exercising what Latin American liberation theologians have referred to as "a preferential option for the poor."

This affirmation, like the previous one, must be understood in relation to its social and political contexts. Black Christians asserted that God was on their side because they lived in a society where European Americans made *absolute* claims on the divine legitimation of their dominance. Put another way, the oppression of African Americans was often justified by implying that they were abandoned by God. However, the reality of the experience of God among African American Christians convinced them that not only were they not abandoned by God but also that God had taken their plight as God's own.[4] By affirming the partisanship of God, African American Christians expressed their faith that God had not abandoned them in their struggle for survival and liberation. In essence, God's partisanship was a tangible sign of God's care for the lowly.

Personhood and Creativity

In addition to the impartiality and partisanship of God, African Americans have declared that God is personal. The personhood of God is foundational to the doctrine of God in black theological thought. A criterion for belief in a God that matters in the black theological tradition is the affirmation that God is a personal being. Not only is God the supreme and ultimate source of all reality emanating from God's self alone but also is God that being of goodness and love who fundamentally upholds the world, because God wants to, for God's own good pleasure, and for the world's good. Of God alone can one speak of a self-existent, absolute reality who is also a good and loving person.[5]

Survival and Liberation

For James Cone, the major developer of black theology in America, the essence of God's nature is to be found in the concept of liberation. Consequently, thoughts about God that are not directly related to the black struggle for liberation are at best an intellectual hobby and at worst blasphemy. Cone understands every doctrine of God to be based on a particular theological methodology. The point of departure for black theology is the biblical God's relation to the black struggle for liberation. The key question posed by that point of departure is: How do we dare speak of God in a suffering world, a world in which blacks are humiliated because they are black?[6]

Concomitantly, there are two hermeneutical principles—revelation and liberation—that are operative in Cone's analysis of the doctrine of God. (1) The Christian understanding of God arises from the biblical view of revelation, a revelation of God that takes place in the liberation of oppressed Israel and is completed in the incarnation, in Jesus Christ. (2) The doctrine of God in black theology must be of the God who is participating in the liberation of the oppressed of the land. This hermeneutical principle arises out of the first. Because God has been revealed in the history of oppressed Israel and decisively in the Oppressed One, Jesus Christ, it is impossible for the proponents of black theology to say anything about God without seeing God as involved in the contemporary liberation of all oppressed peoples. The God of black theology, then, is the God of and for the oppressed. For Cone, any other approach is a denial of biblical revelation.[7]

Black Theology and Classical Conceptions of God

While it is important to have some sense of how black theologians view God, attempts to name God's presence and actions in a balanced manner also require an awareness and familiarity with historical understandings of the faith, that is, classical theology and traditional methods of interpretation. Though black Christians bring a different perspective to the hermeneutical table because of their sociocultural experiences, they can never forget that they too are part of a larger whole. They must remember that the gospel proclaimed by African Americans as well as other Christian preachers is always larger than any particular theological formulation of it. Theological God-talk that focuses exclusively on the narrow purview of black experience alone will never be sufficient to speak to the broad range of human existence that is more than but not other than the multifaceted situations in black life.

Historically, the traditional black church has not viewed its broad belief system to be along the narrow confines of black theology alone. Samuel D. Proctor, in *The Certain Sound of the Trumpet*, forcefully argues against a one-dimensional style of preaching and calls for a broader understanding of the multidimensional aspects and needs of the black church.

> The social prophet [is] the one who every Sunday looks at the failures of the institutions of society and the unraveling of the social fabric. Indeed, courageous criticism of public discord is in keeping with Isaiah, Micah, Amos, and Jeremiah—and was very much a part of Jesus' ministry. ... However, along with this social and prophetic word, the people need education in religious matters and comfort in life's crisis moments; they need to be given an impetus to serve, to participate, and to create alliances to address the issues that are so glaring in the pastor's sermons. So the social prophet must remember the total menu and the need for a complete diet in the weekly sermons.[8]

It is this broader, multidimensional interpretation that one historically finds in much of black preaching.

Moreover, while the emphasis in black theology over the last thirty years has been placed on sociopolitical liberation, James Evans and other African American theologians have been right to move us into the broader, multidimensional understandings of liberation. Evans has taken up the task of a more detailed outlining of the dimensions of liberation that are operative in black life. To James Cone's sociopolitical liberation, he has added physical, spiritual, and cultural understandings of liberation.[9] According to Evans, these added dimensions must be seen as one piece:

> *Physical liberation* refers to the innate desire of all human beings to enjoy freedom of movement and association and the rights of self-determination. *Spiritual empowerment* is that dimension of the liberation struggle in which African Americans come to understand and reclaim their intrinsic worth as human

beings. *Cultural liberation* refers to freedom from negative self-images, symbols, and stereotypes.[10]

An overemphasis on any one of the three dimensions leads to an imbalance in the others. Consequently, Evans cautions against viewing the liberation motif as unidimensional.[11] In its unidimensional extremes, it tends to be identified with sociopolitical justice at one end or a mere inward spiritual piety at the other. For example, Dwight Hopkins, a liberation theologian, contends that the essence of the gospel is justice for the poor:

> Christians must judge everything—culture, politics and theology—from the perspective of the "least of these" in society. If one does not side with the poor, then one is not a true Christian.[12]

At the other end of the spectrum, Joseph Jackson, former president of the National Baptist Convention, Inc., maintains that while liberation from oppression, which also includes justice for the poor, is indeed valid in its own right, it is much too narrow to accommodate the universality of the Christian gospel of liberation. According to Jackson, liberation theologians tend to overlook that aspect of liberation that has to do with the individual's victory over the temptation and the demonic forces within humankind that must be conquered before one can be considered totally liberated.[13]

Hopkins and Jackson are thus representative of the two diverse interpretations of the liberation motif that are quite common in black religious life and consequently black preaching. Their contrasting interpretations of the essence of the gospel suggest that a narrow understanding of black theology in either extreme does not cover the broad spectrum of thoughts on God that seeks to address life in all its dimensions. Thus the need for the crucial balance in black preaching is made possible, I believe, through constant reflection on the particular concerns of black theology with respect to God and the wider implications of the classical understandings of God.

In recent decades the tendency has been to view the respective theologies—classical and black theologies—as either/or rather than both/and. The "both/and" approach, however, is closer to the manner in which the black church has historically approached its understanding of God-talk. Granted, a theology that seeks to address the specific needs and concerns of the black situation in life is a must for those whose primary task will be to proclaim the gospel in a setting of marginalization and struggle. Thus there is a pressing need for the continued study and development of black theology. But for at least three reasons, black theology alone cannot be the sole arbiter of reflection, interpretation, and proclamation in the black church.

First, few ministers and lay persons who labor in black churches are even aware that black theology is a discipline of study and reflection. According to C. Eric Lincoln's study on the black church, interest in and understanding of black theology barely exists among the majority of persons in the seven major traditionally black denominations.[14]

Second, black theology's lack of acceptance is not born of lack of knowledge alone. Even among knowledgeable black pastors, there is the perception that black academicians who construct theology outside of the practices of the church are largely out of touch with the very people about whom they claim to write. James H. Harris argues that because of this perception, few black ministers read and teach the works of prominent black theologians such as James Cone, Gayraud Wilmore, J. Deotis Roberts, C. Eric Lincoln, or Major Jones. And, says Harris, even fewer laypersons are familiar with the tenets of black liberation theology.[15]

Third, because the major formulators of and subscribers to black theology hail from the intellectual elite of the black church (theologians, scholars, and divinity school students), they have been unable to move beyond their middle-class origins, even though a major tenet of black theology is to do theology from the "bottom up," that is, from the perspective of the oppressed in society.

Lincoln suggests two ways to work toward the broader acceptance of black theology: (1) A much more intense educational effort on the part of the intellectual elite is required before black theology is fully acceptable, or (2) the theological formulation itself must undergo major revision.[16]

The point I am arguing is this: While black theology should be taught to young, aspiring black preachers and seasoned black pastors alike, in the interest of balance and the whole counsel of God, it cannot be taught to the exclusion of the broader, classical understandings of the faith. Affirmations about God from theologians whose point of departure is the black religious experience, as well as understandings of God derived from historical and traditional understandings of the faith, must be taught concomitantly. Together, they are ideal places to begin our quest for black understandings of the sovereign God.

THE BLACK SOCIOCULTURAL CONTEXT

The second dynamic at work in the creation of the African American sermon is the black sociocultural context. As is true of other faith communities, the pattern that blacks ascribe to scripture is determined by the ways in which they have experienced God and scripture in their faith community. The African American understanding of God grows out of the unique social situation in which blacks find themselves in America. The distinctly black experience of marginalization and struggle is crucial to understanding what gives depth and dimension to black preaching.

The ongoing significance of this experience and how it informs the black sermon is one of the foundational components of a truly African American biblical hermeneutic. One's preaching is greatly enhanced when there is an awareness of the formative influences out of which one preaches. James Cone rightly asserts that there is no truth for and about black people that does not emerge out of the context of their experience.[17] Their sociocultural milieu and its ever-present reality is intricately tied to the manner in which blacks hear and process the gospel.

Included in this sociocultural experience of blacks is the awareness that they are both black and American. Their reality and the issues with which they must contend grow out of and are bound by this fact. Evans Crawford coined the word "biformation" to express the dual nature of the spiritual formation that must be cultivated in the preacher in order to give life and substance to black preaching:

> It may be proper to talk of an African-American biformation, a shaping of identity, perspective, and expression that flows from being both African and American ... That term keeps before us the particular legacy of being black in America ... [It] reminds us that the developing musicality of black preaching through history involves more than simply the reformation of one dominant cultural stream.[18]

The preparation process for black preaching must take into account this dual reality. When the preacher is searching for possible avenues into the hearts of the listeners, he or she must be able to analyze and explicate situations and slices of life that stem from this biformation reality.

The creative genius of the best of black preaching is found, in part, among blacks who take seriously the complexity of the dual nature of African American identity. The psychic energy released by this overwhelming, obsessive burden of duality is an enormous factor in the black preacher's imaginative projections and in his or her ability to "paint a picture" in preaching that resonates with black congregations in a meaningful way.

This duality of existence should not be overlooked or denied but rather analyzed, cultivated, and developed as fertile ground for black sermonic thought and construction. The black preacher's social location on the boundary of the dominant culture continues to provide creative perspectives that are usually unavailable to those standing within the center of power.[19]

For example, historian Donald G. Mathews noted how black preachers have historically had the ability to deal with such themes as suffering, pain, and redemption in ways quite unlike those of their white counterparts. Blacks, according to Mathews, did not merely preach on suffering in the Bible, they seemed actually to embody the suffering in their proclamation.[20] Their ability to preach with such sensitivity and insight is derived, I believe, in part from their experiences as marginalized people in this country. Such insights into scripture have been characterized by some as the "hermeneutical privilege of the poor and oppressed," the notion that the poor and downtrodden can hear the gospel better because of their low estate in life.[21]

Insights that lead to creative and imaginative preaching can only be brought to consciousness, developed, and subsequently taught in preaching when one takes seriously the milieu out of which they arise. In order to tap into this reality, the crafter of the black sermon must weigh what it means to heed the claims of the gospel as both a black and an American. A black homiletic, then, must seek to bring greater clarity to one's understanding of how God and scripture have historically been perceived in the community of the marginalized and powerless, for it is this community that gives formation and shape to the black preacher's identity and proclamation.

God's presence in this faith community must be wrestled with, grasped, and proclaimed in a way that is mindful of the faith community's past and faithful to the Christian gospel. The fallacy of the traditional all-purpose homiletic is that it assumes a similar background for Christian identity. Such is not now the case nor has it ever been. Though black churches since the late nineteenth century have tried in earnest to imitate the theology and lifestyle of the mainline white denominations, there has always been a strain of protest in the black religious experience that recognized a distinct difference between black and white existence in this country. While there is much that binds us together as Christians, there is much that separates us as people with distinct worldviews.

Unfortunately, for a variety of reasons many black preachers are not as well informed as they should be about black history and culture and their impact on their religious beliefs. Consequently, all too many come to the interpretation of scripture not with a broadly based understanding of their rich black religious heritage and the implications of their marginalized status, but with a truncated view of an imitative theology that seeks, in the main, to be evangelical and conservative in its outlook. It is a view that too often rejects a broader social witness in favor of a more constrictive, privatized religious hope.

In order for black exegetes to appreciate and reflect on the marginalization and struggle so integral to the particular community in which they will expound on the scriptures, this understanding of and constant exposure to the history, theology, and biblical motifs of the black sociocultural context should be considered an indispensable component in black preaching

VARIETIES OF BLACK EXPERIENCE

Understanding the multifaceted life situations of blacks is important to the crafting of the sermon because of the manner in which black listeners process the gospel. Blacks are more inclined to hear the gospel through life experiences rather than through codified theological formulations. It is not that blacks have no theology, but rather that their theology tends to be more implicit than explicit in both their thought processes and in the preached word. For example, if a black preacher preached a series of sermons on the importance of stewardship to the life and witness of the church, he or she would not initiate the pros and cons of such a sermon with a disquisition on the Reformed understanding of stewardship, detailing how John Calvin, Martin Luther, and others theologized on the subject.

In all likelihood the preacher would approach the sermon with some examples of the historical importance of the church and its outreach to the black community. He or she would then draw scenarios of how one could faithfully maintain that witness in the present day through the commitment of one's time, talents, and finances. The insights of Luther and Calvin could and should inform the sermon, but a biblical passage on the order of Romans 12—"many members ... one body in Christ"—paired with the idea of the well-established importance of the church in the life of the community would serve the interests of the stewardship sermon much better than the chapter and verse citing of Reformed theology.

When examining the structure of a traditional black sermon, one can see that its initial formation comes to life through scripture reflecting on the common life experiences of the people of faith. Consequently, a sermon is best heard when an insightful perspective on lived experiences takes the lead in creating and organizing the sermon and not the specific enunciation of a theological formulation. For this reason an understanding of situations, or domains of experience, and how to name them and build upon them is crucial in the development of the black sermon.

Domains of experience call for a role reversal in the very conception of the sermon. In black religion thoughts about the best way to develop a sermon have tended to focus on the person of the preacher. This is to say, the content and shape of the black sermon were initially determined by the way in which the preacher conceived of his or her calling. Thus we have thought more about the self-understanding of the person doing the preaching and not enough about the congregation to whom the sermon was preached. In fact, exploration into the makeup and nature of congregations is a glaring deficiency in contemporary preaching theory. Leonora Tisdale, in *Preaching as Local Theology and Folk Art*, argues persuasively for a sermon preparation process that takes congregational "contextuality" as seriously as it does biblical "textuality."[22]

African American models for preaching have centered on preacher-oriented ideal types such as pastor, priest, prophet, politician, and nationalist, with little or no consideration for the persons in the congregation. In black religious life there has been a tacit assumption about a certain kind of homogeneity among black congregations; a homogeneity that allowed many to believe the call and personality of the preacher determined, in large part, the thought and worldview of the congregation gathered around the preacher. This is especially true in black religion where so much power and authority are centered in the person of the preacher.

While it is true that people are drawn to a congregation, in part, on the basis of the personality and character of the preacher, it is also the case that the needs, interests, and concerns of a congregation are more complex than a preacher's personal sense of call and self-understanding.

Domains of experience allow the sermon to have its conception in the life of the people as opposed to a single-minded focus on the person of the preacher. They help the preacher to think more broadly and to preach with greater depth because they allow or even force the preacher to consider other areas of experience and reflection that do not necessarily stem from his or her own personal convictions regarding call and vocation.

For example, a preacher brought up to believe that clean living and a right relationship with God are central to the gospel can come in time, through reflection on domains of experience, to understand that while personal piety concerns are indeed important, a just social order where all God's people are treated with dignity and respect is also central to the proclamation of the gospel.

While personal piety may continue to be a preacher's primary emphasis because of the formative influences of his or her faith community, in time that preacher can develop sermons that speak to other areas of experience and reflection that are equally important to the work and witness of one's faith community.

Those who emphasize one domain to the neglect of others are doing black preaching a disservice. Historically, the black church has continually maintained a dual focus on personal and social empowerment and transformation. In its more personal dimensions the church has emphasized that *personal* conversion, moral renewal, and sanctification are ideals that should also manifest themselves in the more *corporate* acts of justice, charity, and service in the wider world.[23]

The best of black preaching, with an eye toward the broad sweep of all five domains of experience, has consistently proclaimed that we were saved for some purpose beyond our private, individual selves. A personal faith without a commitment to the wider world, or a commitment to the wider world without a personal faith, is at best a skewed, truncated view of the Christian witness. Cornel West sees the necessity of juxtaposing the social/political and the personal/spiritual:

> The social and political aspects of the Christian faith are insep-
> arable from, though not identical with, the spiritual and per-
> sonal aspects of the Christian faith. Politics always has and al-
> ways will be a poor vessel for healthy and longstanding
> transcendence for persons who undergo illness, dread, despair,
> and death in any social system.[24]

West contends that seminaries and divinity schools should be preparing ministers for the multidimensional practice of the Christian ministry to the people of God.[25] The preacher who would craft meaningful sermons on a consistent basis must learn to observe God's presence and actions in a wide range of human experiences. Preaching in a disciplined manner out of identifiable domains of experience helps the preacher to sharpen these powers of observation, which are more likely to produce sermons that resonate in a powerful way with the listeners.

Domains of experience also help the preacher to craft a practical sermon, that is, a sermon that deals with pressing life situations currently being experienced by the parishioners. A God who acts mightily in concrete and practical ways is foundational to black preaching. Thus black preachers rarely spend precious time in the pulpit engaged in abstract thought. The black quest for God has been based on the immediate hopes and aspirations of an oppressed community often discouraged and beaten back by life. Thus the black congregation desires to know if there is a word from the mighty Sovereign, whose power is made known through and reflected in their everyday life experiences.

This insistence on the practical has led some to accuse African American preaching and the African American church of anti-intellectualism. William B. McClain has rightly noted that it may be more accurate to say that there is little tolerance in the pews for rarefied abstraction:

> The African American preacher can discuss anything of philo-
> sophical and theological import as long as it is presented in
> such a way as to make sense of life and relate to the lives of
> the hearers. How an issue is presented is more often more
> important than what the issue is. People such as Gardner C.
> Taylor, Howard Thurman, George Outen, Vernon Johns, and

Martin Luther King, Jr. have proved that African American preaching can contain intricate historical, political analyses while at the same time feeding the flock.[26]

Black congregants struggling to practice the Christian faith are much more interested in what God has done and can do to help them with their particular concerns and problems. These concerns are often related to the harsh realities of life such as sickness, hunger, death, family problems, inadequate housing, crime, and lack of opportunities for education. They expect the preacher to have the knowledge and faith to assure them of God's power, not to question or doubt it.[27] Black preachers are often reminded by their congregations to preach their declarations and not their doubts.

Every preacher, because of his or her life experiences, will have certain preferences in terms of the domains of experience upon which they reflect and out of which they preach. Considering the many sermons I have read and heard, I believe domains of experience are preached on in the following order: personal piety, care of the soul, and maintenance of the institutional church. The social justice domain would be the next most frequently utilized sphere, with corporate concerns following closely on its heels. Effective preaching that will build and sustain a congregation requires frequent preaching on all five domains. A steady diet of any one of the five to the exclusion of the other four does irreparable harm to a congregation and greatly circumscribes the preacher's ability to name God's presence and action in every realm of black existence. Wise, well-rounded preachers will train themselves to preach effectively in all five areas.

Conclusion

Black preaching has been, and continues to be a very complex and convoluted system of preaching. It involves many facets, perspectives, and outlooks from a cross-section of denominational beliefs, educational levels, regional affiliations, and numerous other considerations. There are, however, some formative influences central to its interpretive process that cause this kind of preaching to sound forth with a note of conviction and authority that many admire and seek to emulate. I believe the three crucial dynamics central to this style of proclamation are:

1. a longstanding belief in an all-powerful sovereign God;
2. a black sociocultural context of marginalization and struggle; and
3. five identifiable categories of life experiences that grow out of black history and struggle and through which the black listener learns to process the gospel.

These foundational dynamics have been woven into a template that becomes the lens through which the black preacher interprets scripture and subsequently pairs it to black lived experiences. While those who are not in this tradition may never be able to fully engage the milieu that surrounds it, all can benefit from an awareness of the three broad dynamics at the heart of the black preaching tradition—belief, context, and life experiences. It is an amalgamation of these three components that undergirds and sustains the powerful black sermon.

APPENDIX

Sermons

The Sun Do Move[1]

John Jasper   (Josh. 10:13, KJV)

Allow me to say that when I was a young man and a slave, I knew nothing worth talking about concerning books. They were sealed mysteries to me, but I tell you I longed to break the seal. I thirsted for the bread of learning. When I saw books I ached to get into them, for I knew that they had the stuff for me, and I wanted to taste the contents, but most of the time they were barred against me.

By the mercy of the Lord a thing happened. I got a room fellow—he was a slave, too, and he had learned to read. In the dead of night he gave me lessons out of the New York Spelling book. It was hard pulling, I tell you; harder on him, for he knew just a little, and it made him sweat to try to beat something into my hard head. It was worse with me. Up the hill every step, but when I got the light of the lesson into my noodle I fairly shouted, but I knew I was not a scholar. The consequences were I crept along mighty tedious, getting a crumb here and there until I could read the Bible by skipping the long words, tolerably well. That was the start of my education—that is, what little I got. I make mention of that young man. The years have fled away since then, but I ain't forgot my teacher, and never shall. I thank my Lord for him, and I carry his memory in my heart.

About seven months after my getting to reading, God converted my soul, and I reckon about the first and main thing that I begged the Lord to give me was the power to understand His Word. I ain't bragging, and I hate self-praise, but I'm bound to speak the thankful word. I believe in my heart that my prayer to understand the Scripture was heard. Since that time I ain't cared nothing about nothing except to study and preach the word of God.

Not, my brethren, that I am the fool to think I know it all. Oh, my Father, no! Far from it. I don't hardly understand myself, nor half of the things around me, and there are millions of things in the Bible too deep for Jasper, and some of them too deep for everybody. I don't carry the keys to the Lord's closet, and He ain't told me to peep in, and if I did I'm so stupid I wouldn't know it when I see it. No, friends, I know my place at the feet of my master, and there I stay.

But I can read the Bible and get the things that lay on top of the soil. Outside of the Bible I know nothing extra about the sun. I see its course as he rides up there so grand and mighty in the sky, but there is heaps about that flaming orbit that is too much for me. I know that the sun shines powerfully and pours down its light in floods, and yet that is nothing compared with the light that flashes in my mind from the pages of God's book. But you know all of that. I know that the sun burns—oh, how it did burn in those July days. I tell you he cooked the skin on my back many a day when I was hoeing in the corn field. But you know all of that, and yet that is nothing to the divine fire that burns in the souls of God's children. Can't you feel it, brethren?

But about the courses of the sun, I have got that. I have ranged through the whole blessed book and scored down the last thing the Bible has to say about the movement of the sun. I got all that pat and safe. And let me say that if I don't give it to you straight, if I get one word crooked or wrong, you just holler out, "Hold on there, Jasper, you ain't got that straight," and I'll beg pardon. If I don't tell the truth, march up on these steps here and tell me I am a liar, and I'll take it. I fear I do lie sometimes—I'm so sinful, I find it hard to do right; but my God don't lie and he ain't put no lie in the Book of eternal truth, and if I give you what the Bible says, then I'm bound to tell the truth.

I got to take you all this afternoon on an excursion to a great battlefield. Most folks like to see fights—some are mighty fond of getting into fights, and some are mighty quick to run down the back alley when there is a battle going on, for the right. This time I'll escort you to a scene where you shall witness a curious battle. It took place soon after Israel got in the Promised Land. You remember the people of Gibeon made friends with God's people when they first entered Canaan and they were mighty smart to do it. But, just the same, it got them into an awful mess. The cities round about there flared up at that, and they all joined their forces and said they were going to mop the Gibeon people off of the ground, and they bunched all their armies together and went up to do it. When they came up so bold and brave the Gibeonites were scared out of their senses, and they sent word to Joshua that they were in trouble and he must run up there and get them out. Joshua had the heart of a lion and he was up there directly. They had an awful fight, sharp and bitter, but you might know that General Joshua was not up there to get whipped. He prayed and he fought, and the hours got away too [fast] for him, and so he asked the Lord to issue a special order that the sun hold up awhile and that the moon furnish plenty of moonshine down on the lowest part of the fighting grounds. As a fact, Joshua was so drunk with the battle, so thirsty for the blood of the enemies of the Lord, and so wild with the victory that he told the sun to stand still until he could finish his job. What did the sun do? Did he glare down in fiery wrath and say, "What are you talking about my stopping for, Joshua; I ain't never started yet. I've been here all the time, and it would smash up everything if I were to start"? No, he didn't say that. But what does the Bible say? That's what I ask to know. It says that it was at the voice of Joshua that it stopped. I didn't say it stopped; ain't for Jasper to say that, but the Bible, the Book of God, said so. But I say this; nothing can stop until it has first started. So I know what I'm talking about. The sun was traveling along there through the sky when the order came. He hitched his red ponies and made quite a call on the land of Gibeon. He perched up there in the sky just as friendly as a neighbor that comes to borrow something, and he stood up there and he looked like he enjoyed the way Joshua waxed those wicked armies. And the moon, she waited down in the low grounds there, and poured out her light and looked just as calm and happy as if she was waiting for her escort. They never budged, neither of them, long as the Lord's army needed a light to carry on the battle.

I don't read when it was that Joshua hitched up and drove on, but I suppose it was when the Lord told him to go. Everybody knows that the sun didn't stay there all the time. It stopped for business, and went on when it got through. This is about all that I have to do with this particular case. I have shown you that this part of the Lord's word teaches you that the sun stopped, which shows that he was moving before that, and that he went on afterwards. I told you that I would prove that and I have done it, and I defy anybody to say that my point is not made.

I told you in the first part of this discourse that the Lord God is a man of war. I suppose by now you begin to see it is so. Don't you admit it? When the Lord came to see Joshua in the day of his fears and warfare, and actually made the sun stop stone still in the heavens, so the fight could rage on until all the foes were slain, you are obliged to understand that the God of peace is also the man of war. He can use both peace and war to help the righteous, and to scatter the host of the aliens. A man talked to me last week about the laws of nature, and he said they couldn't possibly be upset, and I had to laugh right in his face. As if the laws of anything were greater than God who is the lawgiver of everything. My Lord is great; He rules in the heavens, in the earth, and down under the ground. He is great, and greatly to be praised. Let all the people bow down and worship before Him!

But let us get along, for there is quite a big lot more coming. Let us take next the case of Hezekiah. He was one of those kings of Judah—a mighty sorry lot, I must say, those kings were for the most part. I'm inclined to think Hezekiah he got sick. I dare say that a king when he gets his crown and finery off, and when he is prostrated with mortal sickness, he gets about as common looking and grunts and rolls, and is about as scary as the rest of us poor mortals. We know that Hezekiah was in a low state of mind; full of fears, and in a terrible trouble. The fact is, the Lord stripped him of all his glory and landed him in the dust. He told him that his hour had come, and that he had better square up his affairs, for death was at the door. Then it was that the king fell low before God; he turned his face to the wall; he cried, he moaned, he begged the Lord not to take him out of the world yet. Oh, how good is our God! The cry of the king moved his heart, and he told him he was going to give him another show. It is not only the kings that the Lord hears. The cry of the prisoner, the wail of the bondsman, the tears of the dying robber, the prayers of the backslider, the sobs of the woman that was a sinner, mighty apt to teach the heart of the Lord. It looks like it's hard for the sinner to get so far off or so far down in the pit that his cry can't reach the ears of the merciful Savior.

But the Lord does even better than this for Hezekiah—he told him he was going to give him a sign by which he would know that what he said was coming to pass. I ain't acquainted with those sun dials that the Lord told Hezekiah about, but anybody that has got a grain of sense knows that they were the clocks of those old times and they marked the travels of the sun by those dials. When, therefore, God told the king that He would make the shadow go backward, it must have been just like putting the hands of the clock back, but, mark you, Isaiah expressly said that the sun returned ten degrees. There you are! Ain't that the movement of the sun? Bless my soul. Hezekiah's case beat Joshua's. Joshua stopped the sun, but here the Lord made the sun walk back ten degrees; and yet they say that the sun stands alone still and never moves a peg. It looks to me he moves around mighty briskly and is ready to go anyway that the Lord orders him to go. I wonder if any of those philosophers are around here this afternoon. I'd like to take a square look at one of them and ask him to explain this matter. He can't do it, my brethren. He know a heap about books, maps, figures and long distances, but I defy him to take up Hezekiah's case and explain it off. He can't do it. The Word of the Lord is my defense and bulwark, and I fear not what men can say nor do; my God gives me the victory.

Allow me, my friends, to put myself square about this movement of the sun. It ain't no business of mine whether the sun moves or stands still, or whether it stops or goes back or rises or sets. All that is out of my hands entirely, and I got nothing to say. I got no theory on the subject. All I ask is that we will take what the Lord says about it and let His will be done about everything. What that will is I can't know except He whispers into my soul or writes it in a book. Here's the Book. This is enough for me, and with it to pilot me, I can't get far astray.

But I ain't done with you yet. As the song says, there's more to follow. I invite you to hear the first verse in the seventh chapter of the book of Revelation. What does John, under the power of the spirit, say? He says he saw four angels standing on the four corners of the earth, holding the four winds of the earth, and so forth. Allow me to ask if the earth is round, where does it keep its corners? A flat, square thing has corners, but tell me where is the corner of an apple, or a marble, or a cannon ball, or a silver dollar? If there is any one of those philosophers that's been taking so many cracks at my old head about here, he is cordially invited to step forward and square up this vexing business. I here tell you that you can't square a circle, but it looks like these great scholars have learned how to circle the square. If they can do it, let them step to the front and do the trick. But, my brethren, in my poor judgment, they can't do it; it ain't in them to do it. They are on the wrong side of the Bible; that's on the outside of the Bible, and there's where the trouble comes in with them. They done got out of the [bres'wuks] of the truth, and as long as they stay there the light of the Lord will not shine on their path. I ain't caring so much about the sun, though it's mighty convenient to have it, but my trust is in the Word of the Lord. As long as my feet are flat on the solid rock, no man can move me. I'm getting my orders from the God of my salvation.

The other day a man with a high collar and side whiskers come to my house. He was one nice Northern gentleman what think a heap of us colored people in the South. They are lovely folks and I honor them very much. He seemed from the start kind of strict and cross with me, and after a while, he broke out furious and fretted, and he said: Allow me, Mister Jasper, to give you some plain advice. This nonsense about the sun moving that you are getting is disgracing your race all over the country, and as a friend of your people, I come to say it's got to stop. Ha! Ha! Ha! Master Sam Hargrove never hardly smashed me that way. It was equal to one of those overseers way back yonder. I told him that if he'll show me that I'm wrong, I'd give it all up.

My! Ha! Ha! Ha! He sail in on me and such a storm about science, new discoveries and the Lord only knows what all, I never heard before, and then he told me my race is against me and poor old Jasper must shut up his foul mouth.

When he got through—it looked like he never would, I told him John Jasper ain't set up to be no scholar, and don't know the philosophers, and ain't trying to hurt his people, but is working day and night to lift them up, but his foot is on the rock of eternal truth. There he stands and there he is going to stand til Gabriel sounds the judgment note. So I said to the gentleman that scolded me up so that I heard him make his remarks, but I ain't heard where he gets his scripture from, and that between him and the word of the Lord I take my stand by the Word of God every time. Jasper ain't mad: he ain't fighting nobody; he ain't been appointed janitor to run the sun: he's nothing but the servant of God and a lover of the Everlasting Word. What I care about the sun? The day comes on when the sun will be called from his race-track, and his light squinted out forever; the moon shall turn to blood, and this earth be consumed with fire. Let them go; that won't scare me nor trouble God's elected people, for the word of the Lord shall endure forever, and on that Solid Rock we stand and shall not be moved.

Do I have you satisfied yet? Have I proven my point? Oh, ye whose hearts are full of unbelief! Are you still holding out? I reckon the reason you say the sun don't move is because you are so hard to move yourself. You are a real trial to me, but, never mind; I ain't getting you up yet, and never will. Truth is mighty; it can break the heart of stone, and I must fire another arrow of truth out of the quiver of the Lord. If you have a copy of God's word about your possession, please turn to that minor prophet Malachi, that wrote the last book in the old Bible, and look at the first chapter, verse eleven; what does it say? I better read it, for I have a notion you critics don't carry any Bible in those pockets every day in the week. Here is what it says: For from the rising of the sun even until the going down of the same My name shall be great among the Gentiles. My name shall be great among the heathen, says the Lord of hosts. How does that suit you? It looks like that ought to fix it. This time it is the Lord of hosts himself that is doing the talking, and He is talking on a wonderful and glorious subject. He is telling of the spreading of his Gospel, of the coming of his last victory over the Gentiles, and the worldwide glories that at the last He is to get. Oh, my brethren, what a time that will be. My soul takes wings as I anticipate with joy that millennium day! The glories as they shine before my eyes blind me, and I forget the sun and moon and stars. I just remember that along about those last days that the sun and moon will go out of business, for they won't be needed anymore. Then will King Jesus come back to see His people, and He will be the sufficient light of the world. Joshua's battle will be over. Hezekiah won't need a sun dial, and the sun and moon will fade out before the glorious splendors of the New Jerusalem.

But what's the matter with Jasper? I almost forgot my business, and almost go to shouting over far away glories of the second coming of my Lord. I beg pardon, and will try to get back to my subject. I have to do as the sun in Hezekiah's case—fall back a few degrees. In that part of the Word that I gave you from Malachi—that the Lord himself spoke—He declares that His glory is going to spread. Spread! Where? From the rising of the sun to the going down of the same. What? It doesn't say that, does it? That's exactly what it says. Ain't that clear enough for you? The Lord pity these doubting Thomases. Here is enough to settle it all and cure the worst cases. Walk up here, wise folks, and get your medicine. Where are those high-collared philosophers now? What are they sulking around in the bush for? Why don't you get out in the broad afternoon light and fight for your colors? Ah, I understand it; you got no answer. The Bible is against you, and in your conscience you are convicted.

But I hear you back there. What are you whispering about? I know; you say you sent me some papers and I never answered them. Ha, ha, ha! I got them. The difficulty about those papers you sent me is that they did not answer me. They never mentioned the Bible one time. You think so much of yourself and so little of the Lord God and think what you say is so smart that you can't even speak of the Word of the Lord. When you ask me to stop believing in the Lord's Word and to pin my faith to your words, I ain't going to do it. I take my stand by the Bible and rest my case on what it says. I take what the Lord says about my sins, about my Savior, about life, about death, about the world to come, and I take what the Lord says about the sun and moon, and I care little what the haters of my God choose to say. Think that I will forsake the Bible? It is my only Book, my hope, the arsenal of my soul's supplies, and I want nothing else.

But I got another word for you yet. I have worked over those papers that you sent me without date and without your name. You deal in figures and think you are bigger than the archangels. Let me see what you say. You set yourself up to tell me how far it is from here to the sun. That's what you say. Another one said that the distance is 12,000,000; another got it to 27,000,000. I hear that the great Isaac Newton worked it up to 28,000,000, and later one of the philosophers gave another ripping raise to 50,000,000. The last one gets it bigger than all the others, up to 90,000,000. Don't any of them agree exactly and so they run a guess game, and that last guess is always the biggest. Now, when these guessers can have a convention in Richmond and all agree upon the same thing, I'd be glad to hear from you again, and I do hope that by that time you won't be ashamed of your name.

Heaps of railroads have been built since I saw the first one when I was fifteen years old, but I ain't heard tell of a railroad built yet to the sun. I don't see why if they can measure the distance of the sun, they might not get up a railroad or a telegraph and enable us to find something else about it than merely how far off the sun is. They tell me that a cannon ball could make the trip to the sun in twelve years. Why don't they send it? It might be rigged up with quarters for a few philosophers on the inside and fixed up for a comfortable ride. They would need twelve years rations and a heap of changes of raiment—mighty thick clothes when they start and mighty thin ones when they get there.

Oh, my brethren, these things make you laugh, and I don't blame you for laughing, except it's always sad to laugh at the follies of fools. If we could laugh them out in counting, we might well laugh day and night. What cuts into my soul is, that all these men seem to me that they are hitting at the Bible. That's what stirs my soul and fills me with righteous wrath. Little care I what they say about the sun, provided they let the Word of the Lord alone. But never mind. Let the heathen rage and the people imagine every vain thing. Our King shall break them in pieces and dash them down. But blessed be the name of our God, the Word of the Lord endureth forever. Stars may fall, moons may turn to blood, and the sun set to rise no more, but Thy kingdom, O Lord, is from everlasting to everlasting.

But I have a word this afternoon for my own brethren. They are the people for whose soul I got to watch—for them I got to stand and report at the last—they are my sheep and I am their shepherd, and my soul is knit to them forever. It ain't for me to be troubling you with these questions about those heavenly bodies. Our eyes go far beyond the smaller stars; our home is clean out of sight of those twinkling orbits; the chariot that will come to take us to our Father's mansion will sweep out by those flickering lights and never halt until it brings us in clear view of the throne of the Lamb. Don't hitch your hopes to no sun or stars; your home is got Jesus for its light, and your hopes must travel up that way. I preach this sermon just for to settle the minds of my brethren, and repeat it because kind friends wish to hear it, and I hope it will do honor to the Lord's Word. But nothing short of the pearly gates can satisfy me, and I charge, my people, fix your feet on the solid Rock, your hearts on Calvary, and your eyes on the throne of the Lamb. These strifes and griefs we'll soon get over; we shall see the King in His glory and be at ease. Go on, go on, ye ransom of the Lord; shout His praises as you go, and I shall meet you in the city of the New Jerusalem, where we shan't need the light of the sun, for the Lamb of the Lord is the light of the saints.

The Destined Superiority of the Negro

Alexander Crummell   (Isa. 41:7, KJV)

The promise contained in the text is a variation from the ordinary rule of the divine government. In that government, as declared in the Holy Scriptures, shame signifies the hopeless confusion and the utter destruction of the wicked. But in this passage we see an extraordinary display of God's forbearance and mercy. Shame, here, is less intense than in other places. In this case it stands, indeed, for trial and punishment, but for punishment and trial which may correct and purify character. The allusion is supposed to refer to the Jews after their restoration, and the passage is regarded as teaching that, for all their long-continued servitude and suffering, God, in the end, would make them abundant recompense. Great shame and reproach He had given them, through long centuries; but now, when discipline and trial had corrected and purified them, He promises them double honor and reward.

The allusion is supposed to refer to the Jews after their restoration, and the passage is regarded as teaching that, for all their long-continued servitude and suffering, God, in the end, would make them abundant recompense ... As thus explained, the text opens before us some interesting features of God's dealing with nations; by the light of which we may, perchance, somewhat determine the destiny of the race with which we are connected. My purpose is to attempt, this morning, an investigation of God's disciplinary and retributive economy in races and nations; with the hope of arriving at some clear conclusions concerning the destiny of the Negro race.

1. Some peoples God does not merely correct; He destroys them. He visits them with deep and abiding shame. He brings upon them utter confusion. This is a painful but certain fact of Providence. The history of the world is, in one view, a history of national destructions. The wrecks of nations lie everywhere upon the shores of time. Real aboriginal life is rarely found. People after people, in rapid succession, have come into constructive being, and as rapidly gone down; lost forever from sight beneath the waves of a relentless destiny. We read in our histories of the great empires of the old world; but when the traveler goes abroad, and looks for Nineveh and Babylon, for Pompeii and Herculaneum, he finds nought but the outstretched graveyards which occupy the sites of departed nations. On the American continent, tribe after tribe have passed from existence; yea, there are Bibles in Indian tongues which no living man is now able to read. Their peoples have all perished!

When I am called upon to account for all this loss of national and tribal life, I say that God destroyed them. And the declaration is made on the strength of a principle attested by numerous facts in sacred and profane history; that when the sins of a people reach a state of hateful maturity, then God sends upon them sudden destruction.

Depravity prepares some races of men for destruction. Every element of good had gone out of them. Even the most primitive virtues seem to have departed. A putrescent virus has entered into and vitiated their whole nature. They stand up columnar ruins! Such a people is doomed. It cannot live. Like the tree "whose root is rottenness," it stands awaiting the inevitable fall. That fall is its property. No fierce thunder-bolt is needed, no complicated apparatus of ethereal artillery. Let the angry breath of an Archangel but feebly strike it, and, tottering, it sinks into death and oblivion!

Such was the condition of the American Indian at the time of the discovery of America by Columbus. The historical facts abide, that when the white man first reached the shores of this continent he met the tradition of a decaying population.

The New Zealand population of our own day presents a parallel case. By a universal disregard of the social and sanitary conditions which pertain to health and longevity, their physical constitution has fallen into absolute decay; and ere long it must become extinct.

Indeed, the gross paganism of these two peoples was both moral and physical stagnation; was domestic and family ruin; and has resulted in national suicide! It came to them as the effect, the direct consequence of great penal laws established by the Almighty, in which are wrapped the punishment of sin. Hence, if you reject the idea of direct interference in the affairs of people, and take up the idea of law and penalty, or that of cause and effect, it amounts to the same thing. Whether through God's fixed law, or directly, by His personal, direful visitation, the admission is the same. The punishment and ruin come from the throne of God.

The most striking instances of the working of this principle of ruin are set before us in the word of God. The case of Egypt is a signal one. For centuries this nation was addicted to the vilest sins and the grossest corruption. There was no lack of genius among them, no imbecility of intellect. It was a case of wanton, high-headed moral rebellion. As generations followed each other, they heaped up abominations upon impurities of their ancestors, until they well-nigh reached the heavens. Then the heavens became darkened with direful wrath! The earth quaked and trembled with God's fearful anger; and judgment upon judgment swept, like lava, over that doomed people, assuring them of the awful destruction which always waits upon sin. And the death of the first-born at the Passover, and the catastrophe of the Red Sea, showed that the crisis of their fate had come.

In precisely the same manner God dealt with the wicked people of Assyria, Babylon, Tyre, and Persia. Read the prophecies concerning these nations, and it seems as though you could see an August judge sitting upon the judgment-seat, and, of a sudden, putting on his black cap, and, with solemn gesture and choked utterance, pronouncing the sentence of death upon the doomed criminals before him!

2. Turn now to the more gracious aspects of God's economy. As there are peoples whom He destroys, so on the other hand there are those whom, while indeed He chastises, yet at the same time He preserves. He gives them shame, but not perpetual shame. He disciplines; but when discipline has worked its remedial benefits, he recompenses them for their former ignominy, and gives them honor and prosperity.

The merciful aspect of God's economy shines out in human history as clearly as His justice and judgement. The Almighty seized upon superior nations and, by mingled chastisements and blessing, gradually led them on to greatness. That this discipline of nations is carried on in the world is evident. Probation, that is, as designed to teach self-restraint, and to carry on improvement, is imposed upon them, as well as upon individuals. It is part of the history of all nations and all races; only some will not take it; seem to have no moral discernment to use it; and they, just like wilful men, are broken to pieces. Some, again, fit themselves to it, and gain all its advantages. What was the servile sojourn of the children of Israel, four hundred years, in Egypt, but a process of painful preparation for a coming of national and ecclesiastical responsibility? What, at a later period, the Babylonish captivity, but a corrective ordeal, to eliminate from them every element of idolatry? What was the feudality of Europe, but a system of training for a high and grand civilization?

Now it seems to me that these several experiments were not simply judicial and retributive. For vengeance crushes and annihilates; but chastisement, however severe, saves, and at the same time corrects and restores. We may infer, therefore, that these several providences were a mode of divine schooling, carried on by the Almighty for great ends which He wished to show in human history.

But how? In what way does God carry on His system of restorative discipline? The universal principle which regulates this feature of the Divine system is set forth very clearly in the Eighteenth Psalm; "With the merciful thou wilt shew thyself merciful; with an upright man thou wilt shew thyself upright; with the pure thou wilt shew thyself pure; and with the froward thou wilt shew thyself froward." These words show the principles by which God carried on His government. And they apply as well to the organic society as to single persons.

We have already seen that with the froward God showed Himself froward; that, those who resist Him, God resists, to their utter shame and confusion. Their miseries were not corrective or disciplinary. They were the blows of avenging justice; the thunder-bolts of final and retributive wrath! In their case, moreover, there was a constitutional fitness to destruction, brought upon them by their own immoral perverseness. So, too, on the other hand, we may see qualities which God favors, albeit He does put the peoples manifesting them to trial and endurance. He sees in them cultivated elements of character, which, when brought out and trained, are capable of raising them to superiority. He does not see merit; and it is not because of desert that He bestows His blessings. But when the Almighty sees in a nation or people latent germs of virtues, he seized upon and schools them by trial and discipline; so that by the processes of divers correctives, these virtues may bud and blossom into beautiful and healthful maturity.

Now, when the Psalmist speaks of the merciful, the upright, and the pure, he does not use these terms in an absolute sense, for in that sense no such persons exist. He speaks of men comparatively pure, upright, and merciful. Some of the nations, as I have already pointed out, were at the lowest grade of moral turpitude. On the other hand, there are and ever have been heathen peoples less gross and barbarous than others: peoples with great hardihood of soul; peoples retaining the high principle of right and justice; peoples with rude but strong virtues, clinging to the simple ideas of truth and honor; peoples who, even with a false worship, showed reluctance to part with the gleams which can, though but dimly, form the face of the one true God of heaven!

Now the providence of God intervenes for the training and preservation of such peoples. Thus we read in Genesis that, because of man's universal wickedness, "it repented the Lord that he made man"; but immediately it says that he approved "just Noah, and entered into covenant with him." So, after the deluge, God saw, amid universal degeneracy, the conspicuous piety of one man; for obedience and faith were, without doubt, original though simple elements of Abraham's character. To these germinal roots God brought the discipline of trial; and by them, through this one man, educated up a people who, despite their faults, shed forth the clearest religious light of all antiquity, and to whom were committed the oracles of God.

The ancient Greeks and Romans were rude and sanguinary Pagans; and so, too, the Germans and the Scandinavians tribes. Yet they had great, sterling virtues. The Greeks were a people severely just; the Spartans, especially, rigidly simple and religious. The Romans were unequaled for reverence for law and subjection to legitimate authority. Tacitus, himself a heathen, extols the noble and beneficent traits of German character, and celebrates their hospitality and politeness. The Saxons, even in a state of rudeness, were brave, though fierce; truthful; with strong family virtues, and great love of liberty.

Added to these peculiarities we find the following characteristics common to each and all these people—common, indeed, to all strong races; wanting in the low and degraded. The masterful nations are all, more or less, distinguished for vitality, plasticity, receptivity, imitation, family feeling, veracity, and the sentiment of devotion. These qualities may have been crude and unbalanced. They existed perchance right beside most decided and repulsive vices; but they were deeply imbedded in the constitution of these people; and served as a basis on which could be built up a character fitted to great ends.

Archbishop Trench, in his comment upon the words of the "Parable of the Sower"—that is, that "they on the good ground are they who, in an honest and good heart, having heard the word, keep it"—says, "that no heart can be said to be absolutely good; but there are conditions of heart in which the truth finds readier entrance than in others." So we maintain that there are conditions of character and of society, to which the divine purposes of grace and civilization are more especially fitted, and adapt themselves. Such, it is evident, is the explanation of the providential spread of early civilization. It passed by the more inane peoples, and fastened itself to the strong and masculine. Such, too, was the spontaneous flow of early Christianity from Jerusalem. It sought, as by a law of affinity, the strong colonies of Asia Minor, and the powerful states along the Mediterranean; and so spread abroad through the then civilized Europe.

Does God despise the weak? Nay, but the weak and miserable peoples of the earth have misused their prerogatives, and so unfitted themselves to feel after God.

And because they have thus perverted the gifts of God, and brought imbecility upon their being, they perish. The iniquity of the Amorites in Joshua's day was full—as you may see in Leviticus xviii—full of lust and incest and cruelty and other unspeakable abominations; and they were swept from the face of the earth! They perished by the sword; but the sword is not an absolute necessity to the annihilation of any corrupt and ruined people. Their sins, of themselves, eat out their life. With a touch they go. It was because of the deep and utter demoralization of Bois Gilbert that he fell before the feeble lance of Ivanhoe; for, in the world of morals, weakness and death are ofttimes correlative of baseness and infamy.

On the other hand the simplest seeds of goodness are pleasing to the Almighty, and He sends down the sunshine of His favor and the dews of His conserving care into the darkest rubbish, to nourish and vivify such seeds, and to "give them body as it pleaseth Him; and to every seed his own body." And the greatness of the grand nations has always sprung from the seeds of simple virtues which God has graciously preserved in them; which virtues have been cultured by gracious providences or expanded by Divine grace, into true holiness.

3. Let us now apply the train of thought thus presented to the history and condition of the Negro; to ascertain, if possible, whether we can draw therefrom expectation of a future for this race.

At once the question arises: Is this a race doomed to destruction? Or is it one possessed of those qualities, and so morally disciplined by trial, as to augur a vital destiny, and high moral uses, in the future?

To the first of these questions I reply that there is not a fact, pertinent to this subject, that does not give a most decisive negative. The Negro race, nowhere on the globe, is a doomed race! It is now nigh five hundred years since the breath of the civilized world touched, powerfully, for the first time, the mighty masses of the Pagan world in America, Africa, and the isles of the sea. And we see, almost everywhere, that the weak, heathen tribes of the earth have gone down before the civilized European. Nation after nation has departed before his presence, tribe after tribe! In America the catalogue of these disastrous eclipses overruns, not only dozens, but even scores of cases. Gone, never again to take rank among the tribes of men, are the Iroquois and the Mohegans, the Pequods and the Manhattans, the Algonquins and the brave Mohawks, the gentle Caribs, and the once refined Aztecs.

In the Pacific seas, islands are scattered abroad like stars in the heavens; but the sad fact remains that from many of them their population has departed, like the morning mist. In other cases, as in the Sandwich Islands, they have long since begun their funeral marches to the grave! Just the reverse with the Negro. Wave after wave of a destructive tempest has swept over his head, without impairing in the least his peculiar vitality. Indeed, the Negro, in certain localities, is a superior man, to-day, to what he was three hundred years ago. With an elasticity rarely paralleled, he has risen superior to the dread inflictions of a prolonged servitude, and stand, to-day, in all the lands of his thraldom, taller, more erect, more intelligent, and more aspiring than any of his ancestors for more than two thousand years of a previous era. And while in other lands, as in cultivated India, the native has been subjected to a foreign yoke, the Negro races of Africa still retain, for the most part, their original birthright. The soil has not passed into the possession of foreign people. Many of the native kingdoms stand this day, upon the same basis of power which they held long centuries ago. The adventurous traveler, as he passes farther and farther into the interior, sends us reports of populous cities, superior people, and vast kingdoms; given to enterprise, and engaged in manufactures, agriculture, and commerce.

Even this falls short of the full reality. For civilization, at numerous places, as well in the interior as on the coast, has displaced ancestral heathenism; and the standard of the Cross, uplifted on the banks of its great rivers, at large and important cities, and in the great seats of commercial activity, shows that the Heralds of the Cross have begun the conquest of the continent for their glorious King. Vital power, then, is a property of the Negro family.

But has this race any of those other qualities, and such a number of them, as warrants the expectation of superiority? Are plasticity, receptivity, and assimilation among his constitutional elements of character?

So far as the first of these is concerned there can be no doubt. The flexibility of the Negro character is not only universally admitted; it is often formulated into a slur. The race is possessed of a nature more easily moulded than any other class of men. Unlike the stolid Indian, the Negro yields to circumstances, and flows with the current of events. Hence the most terrible afflictions have failed to crush him. His facile nature wards them off, or else, through the inspiration of hope, neutralises their influence. Hence, likewise, the pliancy with which, and without losing his distinctiveness, he runs into the character of other people; and thus bends adverse circumstances to his own convenience; thus, also, in a measurable degree, linking the fortunes of his superiors to his own fate and destiny.

These peculiarities imply another prime quality, anticipating future superiority; I mean imitation. This is also universally conceded with however, a contemptuous fling, as though it were an evidence of inferiority. But Burke tells us that "imitation is the second passion belonging to society; and this passion," he says, "arises from much the same cause as sympathy." This forms our manners, our opinions, our lives. It is one of the strongest links of society. Indeed, all civilization is carried down from generation to generation, or handed over from the superior to the inferior, by the means of this principle. A people devoid of imitation are incapable if improvement, and must go down; for stagnation of necessity brings with it decay and ruin.

On the other hand, the Negro, with a mobile and plastic nature, with a strong receptive faculty, seizes upon and makes over to himself, by imitation, the better qualities of others. First of all, observe that, by a strong assimilative tendency he reduplicates himself, by attaining both the likeness of an affinity to the race with which he dwells; and then, while retaining his characteristic peculiarities, he glides more or less into the traits of his neighbors. Among Frenchmen, he becomes somewhat the lively Frenchman; among Americans, the keen, enterprising American; among Spaniards, the stately solemn Spaniard; among Englishmen, the solid, phlegmatic Englishman.

This peculiarity of the Negro is often sneered at. It is decried as the simulation of a well-known and grotesque animal. But the traducers of the Negro forget that "the entire Grecian civilization is stratified with the elements of imitation; and that Roman culture is but a copy of a foreign and alien civilization." These great nations laid the whole world under contribution to gain superiority. They seized upon all the spoils of time. They became cosmopolitan thieves. They stole from every quarter. They pounced, with eagle eye, upon excellence wherever discovered, and seized upon it with rapacity. In the Negro character resides, though crudely, precisely the same eclectic quality which characterized those two great, classic nations; and he is thus found in the very best company. The ridicule which visits him goes back directly to them. The advantage, however, is his own. Give him time and opportunity, and in all imitative art he will rival both of them.

This quality of imitation has been the grand preservative of the Negro in all the lands of his thraldom. Its bearing upon his future distinction in Art is not germane to this discussion; but one can clearly see that this quality of imitation, allied to the receptivity of the race, gives promise of great fitness for Christian training, and for the higher processes of civilization.

But observe, again, that the imitative disposition of the Negro race leads to aspiration. Its tendency runs to the higher and the nobler qualities presented to observation. Placed in juxtaposition with both the Indian and the Caucasian, as in Brazil and in this land, the race turns away from the downward, unprogressive Indian, and reaches forth for all the acquisitions of the Caucasian or the Spaniard. And hence wherever the Negro family has been in a servile position, however severe may have been their condition, without one single exception their native capacity has always

    —glinted forth
    Amid the storm;

preserving the captive exiles of Africa from annihilation; stimulating them to enterprise and aspiration; and, in every case, producing men who have shown respectable talent as mechanics and artisans; as soldiers, in armies; as citizens of great commonwealths; not unfrequently as artists; not seldom as scholars; frequently as ministers of the Gospel; and at times as scientific men, and men of letters.

I referred, at the beginning, and as one of the conditions of a Divine and merciful preservation of a people—for future uses, to the probation of discipline and trial, for the cultivation of definite moral qualities. Is there any such large fact in the history of this race? What else, I ask, can be the significance of the African slave-trade? What is the meaning of our deep thraldom since 1620? Terrible as it has been, it has not been the deadly hurricane portending death. During its long periods, although great cruelty and wide-spread death have been large features in the history of the Negro, nevertheless they have been overshadowed by the merciful facts of great natural increase, much intellectual progress, the gravitation of an unexampled and world-wide philanthropy to the race, singular religious susceptibility and progress, and generous, wholesale emancipations, inclusive of millions of men, women, and children.

This history, then, does not signify retribution; does not forecast extinction. It is most plainly disciplinary and preparative. It is the education which comes from trial and endurance; for with it has been allied, more or less, the grand moral training of the religious tendencies of the race.

Here, then are the several conditions, the characteristic marks which, in all history, have served to indicate the permanency and the progress of races. In all other cases they have been taken as forecasting greatness. Is there any reason for rejecting their teachings, and refusing their encouragements and inspirations, when discovered in the Negro?

I feel fortified, moreover, in the principles I have to-day set forth, by the opinions of great, scrutinizing thinkers. In his treatise on Emancipation, written in 1880, Dr. Channing says: "The Negro is one of the best races of the human family. He is among the mildest and gentlest of men. He is singularly susceptible of improvement."

Alexander Kinmont, in his "Lectures on Man," declares that "the sweet graces of the Christian religion appear almost too tropical and tender plants to grow in the soil of the Caucasian mind; they require a character of human nature of which you can see the rude lineaments in the Ethiopian, to be implanted in, and grow naturally and beautifully withal." Adamson, the traveler who visited Senegal, in 1754, said: "The Negroes are sociable, humane, obliging, and hospitable; and they have generally preserved an estimable simplicity of domestic manners. They are distinguished by their tenderness for their parents, and great respect for the aged—a patriarchal virtue which, in our day, is too little known." Dr. Raleigh, also, at a recent meeting in London, said: "There is in these people a hitherto undiscovered mine of love, the development of which will be for the amazing welfare of the world ... Greece gave us beauty; Rome gave us power; the Anglo-Saxon race unites and mingles these; but in the African people there is the great, gushing wealth of love which will develop wonders for the world."

1. We have seen, to-day, the great truth, that when God does not destroy a people, but, on the contrary, trains and disciplines it, it is an indication that He intends to make something of them, and to do something for them. It signifies that He is graciously interested in such a people. In a sense, not equal, indeed, to the case of the Jews, but parallel, in a lower degree, such a people are a "chosen people" of the Lord. There is, so to speak, a covenant relation which God had established between Himself and them;

dim and partial, at first, in its manifestations; but which is sure to come to the sight of men and angels, clear, distinct, and luminous. You may take it as a sure and undoubted fact that God presides, with sovereign care, over such a people; and will surely preserve, educate, and build them up.

2. The discussion of this morning teaches us that the Negro race, of which we are a part, and which, as yet, in great simplicity and with vast difficulties, is struggling for place and position in this land, discovers, most exactly, in its history, the principle I have stated. And we have in this fact the assurance that the Almighty is interested in all the great problems of civilization and of grace carrying on among us. All this is God's work. He has brought this race through a wilderness of disasters; and at last put them in the large, open place of liberty; but not, you may be assured, for eventual decline and final ruin. You need not entertain the shadow of a doubt that the work which God has begun and is now carrying on, is for the elevation and success of the Negro. This is the significance and the worth of all effort and all achievement, of every signal providence, in this cause; or, otherwise, all the labors of men and all the mightiness of God is vanity! Nothing, believe me, on earth; nothing brought from perdition, can keep back this destined advance of the Negro race. No conspiracies of men nor of devils! The slave trade could not crush them out. Slavery, dread, direful, and malignant, could only stay it for a time. But now it is coming, coming, I grant, through dark and trying events, but surely coming. The Negro—black curly-headed, despised, repulsed, sneered at—is, nevertheless, a vital being, and irrepressible. Everywhere on earth has been given him, by the Almighty, assurance, self-assertion, and influence. The rise of two Negro States within a century, feeble though they be, has a bearing upon this subject. Thus, too, the rise in the world of illustrious Negroes, as Touissant L'Ouverture, Henry Christophe, Benjamin Banneker, Eustace the Philanthropist, Stephen Allan Benson, and Bishop Crowther.

With all these providential indications in our favor, let us bless God and take courage. Casting aside everything trifling and frivolous, let us lay hold of every element of power, in the brain; in literature, art, and science; in industrial pursuits; in the soil; in cooperative association; in mechanical ingenuity; and above all, in the religion of our God; and so march on in the pathway of progress to that superiority and eminence which is our rightful heritage, and which is evidently the promise of our God!

A Resemblance and a Contrast Between the American Negro and the Children of Israel, in Egypt, or the Duty of the Negro to Contend Earnestly for His Rights Guaranteed under the Constitution[3]

Francis J. Grimké   (Exod. 1:9–10, KJV)

In this record, there is a contrast suggested between our people in this country and the children of Israel in Egypt, and also a resemblance to which I desire, for the moments that I shall occupy, to call attention.

(1) The children of Israel went down into Egypt of their own accord. Ten of the sons of Jacob first went down to buy corn, owing to a very severe famine that was raging in their own country, and in all the surrounding countries. This journey was again repeated some time afterwards, at which time, they were joined by Benjamin—the man in charge of affairs having made that a condition of their seeing his face. It was during this second visit, that Joseph was made known to his brethren, through whom an earnest invitation was sent to his father, Jacob, and all the members of the family to come and stay in the land, with the promise that all of their wants would be supplied. It was in response to this invitation that the family packed up everything which they had and went down into Egypt. They went down from choice: it was a voluntary thing on their part. They were not forced against their will.

The opposite of this was true in the case of the coming of our forefathers to this country. It was not a voluntary act on their part. They were seized by slave hunters and against their will forced from the land of their birth. Left to themselves they never would have sought these shores.

(2) The children of Israel were few in number when they went down into Egypt. There were only about seventy-off souls in all. During their sojourn, however, they greatly multiplied: so much so that at the time of the Exodus, 1491 B.C., according to the census that was taken under the divine direction, there were 603, 550 men over twenty years of age who were able to go to war. No mention is made of the male members of the population under twenty, nor of the old men who were unfit for active military service; nor of the women and female children. The whole number must have been between two and three millions. Assuming that Jacob went down in the year 1706, B.C., and that the Exodus was in 1491, this increase came about a little over two centuries.

The same fact is noticeable in the reference to our people in this country. The first installment came in 1619, and the importation of slaves was prohibited in 1808. According to the census for 1790, we numbered then 752,208. Fifty years afterwards, the number had increased to 2,873,648. In 1890, the number had gone up to 7,740,040, while the last census shows our present number to be 8,840,789. This is a very remarkable showing, when we remember the large mortality of the race, and the fact that the increase has been purely a natural one, without any accessions through immigration. It shows that we are a very prolific race, and that there is no danger of our dying out.

(3) The Egyptians were alarmed at the rapid increase of the children of Israel, and sought in one way or another to diminish their number, or to arrest their increase. The first method was to work them to death, to kill them off by hard labor, and by cruel treatment. This method failed, however; instead of decreasing they went on steadily increasing, becoming more and more numerous. Then another method was resorted to—the mid-wives were directed to strangle the male children to death at birth. This also failed.

And a third and last method was devised: a decree was issued compelling parents to expose their own children to death. Under this decree, Moses, the great law-giver, would have perished had he not been providentially rescued by Pharaoh's daughter from an untimely death.

The rapid increase of our people in this country has also been a source of disquiet, if not of positive alarm, to the white element of the population. In 1889, when the census showed an increase of over 22 percent, you will remember what an excitement it created, and what absurd predictions were made as to the possibility of the country being overrun by Negroes. In 1890, when the percentage was cut down owing to inaccuracies in the census of 1890, what a sense of relief was felt by the whites. The rapid increase of the colored population of this country is no more welcomed or relished by the white American than the rapid increase of the Jewish population was by the Egyptians. There has been no concerted action on the part of the whites to cut down our numbers, as was done in Egypt; the process of destruction, however, has gone on all the same. In the Southern section of our country, especially, the hand of violence has been laid upon our people, and hundreds and thousands of them have, in this way, been sent to untimely graves. The convict lease system, has also had its influence in diminishing our numbers. Whether this was its intention originally or not, I am not prepared to say, but the fact is, it has had that effect. Through the Convict Camps, the exodus from this world to the next has been amazingly frequent. The avarice, the cupidity of the white man, as illustrated in the grinding conditions imposed upon the colored farmer, under the crop lease system, has also done much to increase the hardships of life for us and to shorten our days.

(4) The Egyptians were afraid that the children of Israel would get up and leave the land: and this, they didn't want them to do. They wanted them to remain, not because they loved them, or because of any special interest which they felt in them as such; but from purely selfish considerations. They were valuable as laborers. From the narrative we learn that they worked in the fields, made bricks and built treasure cities for Pharaoh. It was a great thing to have at their disposal, a population of this kind, who could be pressed into service whenever they were needed. In those oriental monarchies, when great public works, like the building of the Pyramids,

were carried on by the State, and when it required an enormous number of workmen, it was of the utmost importance to the State to have constantly at hand the means of supplying this want. And this they found in the rapidly increasing Jewish population, and accordingly, were not disposed to tolerate for a moment, the idea of their departure. How strongly they felt on this matter, is evident from the reply which Pharaoh made to the demand of Moses, "Thus saith the Lord, the God of Israel, Let My people go that they may hold a feast unto me in the wilderness." And Pharaoh said, "Who is the Lord, that I should hearken unto His voice to let Israel go." The same is also evident from the fact that it was not until the land had been visited by ten great plagues, ending with the death of the first-born, that they were willing to let them go.

When the children of Israel first went down into Egypt it was with no intention of remaining there permanently. It was intended to be only a temporary sojourn, during the continuance of the famine, which drove them there. Nor was it in accordance with the divine plan that they should remain permanently, as is evident from the record, in forty-six of Genesis. "And God spake unto Israel in the vision of the night, and said, Jacob, Jacob." And he said, "Here am I." And he said, "I am God, the God of thy fathers: fear not to go down into Egypt, for I will there make of thee a great nation: I will go do down with thee into Egypt, and I will surely bring thee up again." And you will also remember what God said to Abraham, in response to the question, "Whereby shall I know that I shall inherit it," that is, the land of Canaan. "Know of a surety that thy seed shall be a stranger in a land that is not theirs, and shall serve them; and they shall afflict them four hundred years; and also that nation, whom they shall serve, will I judge: and afterwards they shall come out with great substance."

Now in both of these respects, things seem to be somewhat different with us in this country. If we may judge from the representations in the newspapers and magazines, which are made from time to time, it would appear that the white Americans would be very glad to have our people arise and get out of the land. We hear a great deal about schemes for deporting the Negro, and in certain sections of the South, and even in certain parts of Illinois, the attempt has been made to forcibly drive him out. While I do not apprehend that there will ever be any general movement to get rid of us, to forcibly deport us from the country, nevertheless, I do not believe that there would be any regrets or tears shed on the part of the whites, if such a things should occur. I think the great majority would be glad to get rid of us. With the Negro out of the country, what a love feast there would be between the North and the South; how they would rush into each others arms, and fondly embrace each other, and rejoice over the fact that at last the great barrier which has stood between them for so many years had been removed. With the Negro out of the country, what a bright prospect there would be of building up a respectable White Republican Party in the South; so we are told by some Republican fools, who lose sight of the fact that the glory of the Republican Party does not depend upon its getting rid of the Negro, but on the contrary, whatever of glory there is attached to it has come from its connection with the Negro. Why is it called the grand old party? What is it that has given it its pre-eminence; that has rendered it immortal; that has covered it with imperishable glory? Is it not the noble stand which it took for human rights; the magnificent fight which it made against slavery and rebellion, out of which came the great amendments to the Constitution, the Thirteenth, Fourteenth, and Fifteenth? It was the enactment of these great amendments that has given it its chief claim to distinction, and that will ever constitute its crowning glory. Yes, even the Republican party, I believe, would be glad to see us go. In two Southern States already, two Republican conventions have declined to receive or admit colored delegates. If some Moses would rise up today, as of old, and say to this nation, as was said to Pharaoh, "Let my people go," it would not be necessary to send any plagues in order to have the demand enforced. I believe from every part of the land—North, South, East and West, there would be but one voice, and that would be, Let them go.

The children of Israel wanted to go, while the Egyptians didn't want them to go; the reverse of that, I believe, is true in our case in this land. The white Americans would be glad to have us to, but there is no desire or disposition on our part to go. So far as I have been able to ascertain the sentiments of our people, it is our purpose to remain here. We have never known any other home, and don't expect, as a people, ever to know any other. Here and there an individual may go, but the masses of our people will remain where we are. Things are not exactly as we would like to have them; no, they are very far from being so, or from what we hope some time they will be, but bad as they are, we are nevertheless disposed to remain where we are. Besides, it would be cowardly to run away. Wherever we go we will have to struggle. Life is real, life is earnest everywhere. And since we are in the struggle here, we had just as well fight it out here as anywhere else. And that is what we are going to do. We are not going to retreat a single inch. We are not going to expatriate ourselves, out of deference to a Negro-hating public sentiment.

It was the divine plan that Israel's stay in Egypt should be only temporary; God's purpose was ultimately to lead them back to the land of Canaan, from which they had come. And it has been intimated, from certain quarters, that this is to be true of us; that God had providentially permitted us to be brought to this land, in order that we might be trained for future usefulness in the land of our forefathers. This is the view that has been taken by some white men, and also by some colored men. It may be so; but I confess, so far, I have not been able to discover any evidences of such a purpose. In the case of the Jews, the record showed what the purposes of God were in regard to that people; but we have no such revelation touching ourselves. God spoke to Abraham, and God spoke to Jacob, and showed them what was to be; but where are the Abrahams and Jacobs among us to whom he has spoken? There are those who are ready to speculate, but speculation amounts to nothing. What the divine purposes are touching this race no one knows. And therefore in the absence of any definite and positive information, we will assume, that this purpose is that we remain just where we are. Until we have very clear evidence to the contrary, we are not likely to take any steps to go elsewhere.

(5) The Egyptians were afraid that the children of Israel, in case of war with a foreign power, would join their enemies and fight against them. And well might they have feared. In the first place, the whole world at that time was in a state of war. It was might that made right. Wars of conquest were constantly going on. One nation or state felt perfectly justified in making war against another, if it was deemed to its interest to do so. As a matter of fact there was always liability of an invasion from some foreign power. This was a possibility, which Egypt, as well as every other country, had to take into consideration, and to provide against. At any moment the enemy might be seen approaching; at any moment their safety might be imperilled.

In the second place, with this possibility staring them in the face, their treatment of the Jews, in case of an invasion, would very naturally have led them to feel that the sympathy of the Jews would be with the invaders instead of with them. The reason assigned in the narrative, however, for this fear is, lest through such an alliance with a foreign power, they succeed in getting out of the land. This shows conclusively that the Jews evidently wanted to get out of the land and had possibly intimated that. The Egyptians didn't want them to go; and yet, strange to say, instead of setting themselves to work to make it so pleasant and agreeable for them that they would not want to go, the very opposite policy is pursued—the policy of oppression, of injustice, of violence. Instead of seeking to win them by acts of kindness, they inaugurated a reign of terror, sought to intimidate them, to crush out of them every spark of manhood, to reduce them to the level of dumb, driven cattle. What a strange thing human nature is; how short-sighted, how blind, how utterly stupid men often are, and men from whom we might naturally expect better things. If the Jews were to remain in Egypt, as the Egyptians desired to have them do, wasn't it a great deal better to have their love than their hatred, their friendship than their enmity? And even if they were going out, was it not better to have their good will than their ill will? For it was just possible, that some time in the future, they might need the help even of the descendants of Jacob, little and insignificant as they were at that time in their estimation. It was the day of small things with them; but there was no telling what their future might bring forth. As a matter of fact, we know that they did become a great and powerful nation.

It is just possible that the absurd and ruinous policy pursued by the Egyptians was due also to a sense of race superiority, and the assumption that if they were in any way civil, if they treated the Jews with the common courtesies that one human being owes to another, it might create within them a desire for social equality. It is possible that the fear of being overrun by an inferior race may also have fired their imagination, blinding their vision, and blunting their moral sensibilities. Whatever the reason may have been, the fact remains that the policy inaugurated by them was an utterly heartless and brutal one; and this policy they continued to pursue until it was reversed by the divine interposition, until God's righteous indignation was excited, and the angel of death was sent forth and smote the first-born throughout the land, and overthrew the tyrants in the Red Sea. It is only a matter of time when all such oppressors the world over will meet a similar fate. God is not dead—nor is he an indifferent onlooker at what is going on in this world. One day He will make requisition for blood; He will call the oppressors to account. Justice may sleep, but it never dies. The individual, race, or nation which does wrong, which sets at defiance God's great law, especially God's great law of love, of brotherhood, will be sure, sooner or later, to pay the penalty. We reap as we sow. With what measure we mete, it shall be measured to us again.

The absurdity of pursuing such a policy is evident from the disastrous consequences which followed. The voice of lamentation that was heard throughout the land of Egypt, the pall of death that hung over every home, and the appalling catastrophe at the Red Sea, which was the culmination of a series of terrible judgments, all came out of it. It was a policy which brought upon them only wretchedness and misery from which they did not derive a single advantage or reap a single benefit.

The policy pursued by them, not only did not benefit them, but did not in the least interfere with the divine purposes concerning the Jews. In spite of their policy of oppression, of injustice, bitter hatred, God let the children of Israel out all the same and safely conducted them to the Promised Land. The race that puts its trust in God, and is willing to be led by God, is safe. The heathen may rage and the people imagine a vain thing, but they will be powerless to stay its progress. They may worry and vex it for a while, but they will not be able to do it any permanent injury, or seriously to interfere with its development, with its onward and upward march. The race that puts its trust in God has always, under all circumstances, more for it than against it. There is never therefore any reason for fear, or for becoming discouraged as long as it maintains its grip upon the Almighty, as long as its attitude is one of simple child-like dependence.

This is not the point, however, that I had in view in referring to this aspect of the subject, which we are considering under this fifth general head. We were speaking under this head of the fear entertained by the Egyptians of the children of Israel joining their enemies, in case of an invasion, and fighting against them. And what I want to say, in this connection is, that there is no just ground for any such fear in regard to our people in this country. Whatever else may be said of the black man, the charge of disloyalty cannot be truthfully made against him. From the very beginning he had been loyal to the flag and has always been willing to lay down his life in its defense. In the War of the Revolution; in the War of 1812; in the Mexican War; in the great Civil War; and in the War with Spain, he stood side by side with other citizens of the Republic facing the enemy; and in all of our national cemeteries may be found evidences of his patriotism and valor. It is only necessary to mention Milliken's Bend, Port Hudson, Fort Wagner, Olustee, during the great Civil War, and San Juan Hill, during the Spanish War, as evidences of his valor and patriotism. Joseph T. Wilson, who was himself a gallant soldier in the 54th Massachusetts, has written a book, entitled, *The Black Phalanx*, in which he traces the history of the Negro soldiers of the United States, from the earliest period through the great war of the Rebellion. It is a glorious record, and one that puts the patriotism of the Negro beyond all question. Whenever the call of danger has been sounded he has always been ready to respond, to bare his bosom to the bullets of the enemy.

This is all the more remarkable when we remember what his treatment has been in this country. Buffeted, spit upon, his most sacred rights trampled upon, without redress, discriminated against in hotels, restaurants, in common carriers, deprived of his political rights, shot down by lawless ruffians, every possible indignity heaped upon him, while the State and Nation look on, the one justifying the outrages, or at least doing nothing to prevent them, and the other protesting its inability to protect its own citizens from violence and injustice. Such treatment is not calculated to inspire one's patriotism, to kindle one's love for a government that permits such injustice and oppression to go on without, at least, the attempt to check them. And yet in spite of these monstrous wrongs that have gone on and are still going on, unrestrained by State or Federal authority, the record of the Negro for patriotism will compare with any other class of citizens. He has been just as constant, just as unswerving in his devotion to the Republic as the most favored class. Oppressed, down-trodden, discriminated against, denied even the common civilities of life, and yet, in the hour of danger, always ready to stretch forth his strong black arm in defense of the Nation. How to explain this, I do not know, nor is it necessary. It is with the fact alone that I am concerned. There it is, and it is true of no other element of the population. There is no other class of citizens, which, if treated as we have been and are still being treated, would evince any such patriotism, would show any such willingness to lay down their lives at the nation's call, as we have. The fear of the Egyptians cannot therefore be the fear of the white citizens of this country. The Negro has never shown any disposition to fight against the Republic, or to ally himself with a foreign foe. His sympathies have always been with the stars and stripes.

In our city we are now having what is known as the annual encampment of the Grand Army of the Republic. This army is an organization made up of the surviving veterans of the great Civil War. It is called the Grand Army. Mr. Gladstone used to be called the Grand Old Man, because he summed up in himself many great qualities. He was a matchless orator, a profound thinker, a great scholar, a man of encyclopedic information. The Republican Party is sometimes called the Grand Old Party, and the name is not inappropriately applied to it. There are many things connected with its history that justify that title. It has done some grand things, and it has had associated with it some of the bravest, truest, noblest, and brainiest men that this country has produced—men, who were not afraid to do right; who felt, as Lowell has expressed it:

> Though we break our fathers' promise,
>   we have nobler duties first;
> The traitor to Humanity
>   is the traitor most accursed;
> Man is more than Constitutions;
>   better rot beneath the sod,
> Than be true to Church and State
>   while we are doubly false to God.

A party with such men, as it had in it years ago, may well be called "The Grand Old Party." I take the term, grand, to apply to the old party—the party as its used to be, not the party as it is today, with its petty little program of a White Republican Party in the South; the elimination of Negro office-holders in the South, out of deference to white southern sentiment; white supremacy in the Philippines and Puerto Rico; and the undue prominence that is given to material things; while it is indifferent to the rights of its citizens of color—caring more for dollars and cents, for material prosperity, than for righteousness, for simple, even-handed justice, which alone exalts a nation. It used to be the Grand Old Party. It is no longer such. There isn't a single thing about it, either in what it is at present doing, or in its purposes with reference to the future, to which the term "grand" can be truthfully applied. It has lost its fine sense of righteousness. It no longer gives evidence of those higher instincts, those nobler sentiments, that make nations and parties truly great. It grovels in the dust. Its aims and purposes are of the earth earthly. It is in the interest of commerce and trade and material development that it is bending its energies, and taxing its resources—forgetful of the fact, that it is true of a nation as of an individual, that its real true life does not consist in the abundance of the good things which it possesseth. Lowell, in his Ode on France, after describing the overthrow of the French tyrant during the great revolution, gives utterance to these significant words:

> What though
> The yellow blood of trade meanwhile should pour
> Along its arteries a shrunken flow,
> And the idle canvas droop around the shore?
> These do not make a state,
>   nor keep it great;
> I think God made
> The earth for man, not trade;
> And where each humblest human creature
> Can stand, no more suspicious or afraid
> Erect and kingly in his right of nature,

To heaven and earth knit with harmonious ties,—
Where I behold the exaltation
Of manhood glowing in those eyes
That had been dark for ages,
Or only lit with bestial loves and rages,
There I behold a Nation;
The France which lies
Between the Pyrenees and the Rhine
Is the least part of France;
Burns through the craftsman's grimy countenance
In the energy divine
Of toil's enfranchised glance.

Unfortunately neither Republicans nor Democrats in this country seem to recognize the great fact enunciated in these lines, but it is true nevertheless; and no party is entitled to the designation "Grand," which does not accept it and act in the light of it.

It is not of the Republican party that I started to speak, however, but of the Grand Army of the Republic. The term "Grand," as applied to this army, is a fitting tribute to the great services which it has rendered in the Republic. It was this army, the remnant of which is in our city today, that saved the life of the Republic; that put down rebellion; and that gave efficacy to Lincoln's great Proclamation of Emancipation. Had he not had back of him this Army, his proclamation would have been unavailing. An army that has to its credit these great achievements may well be called Grand. It is the Grand Army of the Republic. There have been other armies of the Republic—the army of the Revolution, the army of 1812, the army of the war with Mexico, and of the Spanish-American war, but the Army of the Republic, both as to numbers and as to the importance of its achievements, is the Army that put down that Rebellion, and with it the accursed system of slavery, which was like a millstone about the neck of both races. All honor to these brave men. Too much cannot be said in praise of their valor and patriotism. As the years go by, as their numbers decrease, as one by one they go to join their comrades on the other side, the more and more should we honor those who still remain among us. I am glad of this annual encampment; glad of the parade connected with it, glad to look in the face, and to have others look into the faces of the brave men who stood by their guns and stood watch over the nation, when Rebellion sought to dissolve the union and to rivet more firmly the fetters upon four million of bondmen. And, I am especially glad to know that in these parades of the veterans who saved the nation, are to be found not only white men, but black men as well. I hope that these representatives of our race will always attend these annual gatherings, even though it may entail some sacrifice on their part to do so. It is a splendid object lesson to the whole nation; and it is a fitting rebuke to those recant white Americans who say, "This is a white man's country." If it is a white man's country, what are these black heroes doing in these annual parades? If it is a white man's country, why is it that in all our national cemeteries are the graves of Negroes? Why is it that in every war since the beginning of the Republic, on sea and land, the blood of the Negro has spurted in its behalf? Why is it that on the pension roll of the nation today are widows and orphans and battle-scarred heroes of this race? If this is a white man's country, why are Negroes ever called upon to take up arms in its defense? I am glad of these annual encampments, I say, and glad of the share which we have in them. Let every Negro veteran who can, always make it a point to be present at these gatherings, and always get into the ranks and march with the procession, in order that the multitudes who gather from all parts of the country may look on and take knowledge of the fact that the Negro is a man, and that he can do a man's part, and that he may be relied upon to do his part as a citizen of the Republic. It is a grand object lesson, I say, to the nation, to see these colored men in line under such circumstances. And so far as we are concerned, we should never by our absence permit that lesson to be lost.

In thinking of this Grand Army of the Republic I am painfully reminded of the fact that though the War of the Rebellion is over, and has been over for more than thirty-five years; and though the great amendments to the Constitution have been enacted, making us freemen and citizens, and giving us the right of the ballot, we have not yet been put in possession of these rights. We are still discriminated against and treated as if we had no rights which white men were bound to respect. And I have called attention to this condition of things, in this connection, to remind us of the fact that, though the Civil War is over, the battle for our rights in this country is not yet over. The great amendments are a part of the law of the land, but the same treasonable and Negro-hating spirit that sought to perpetuate our bondage, and to keep us in a state of hopeless inferiority, is still endeavoring to accomplish its purpose by seeking to nullify them. There is a spirit abroad in this land, which is determined that we shall never be accorded the rights of American citizens. And that spirit you have got to meet, and I have got to meet, and we have all got to meet. And it is from these old battle-scarred survivors of the Civil War, that we may learn how to meet it—with courage, with invincible determination, with the earnest purpose never to be surrendered. Be assured that these wrongs, from which we are suffering, will never be righted if we sit idly by and take no interest in the matter. If we are indifferent even those who might be disposed to assist us will also become indifferent. We must show the proper appreciation, the proper interest in ourselves. We must agitate, and agitate, and agitate, and go on agitating. By and by, our very importunity will make itself felt. The people, in the midst of whom we are living, if not from a sense of justice, or right, or fair play, will on the principle of the unjust judge, who cared neither for God nor man, but who said, "I will right the widow's wrong, lest by her continual coming she weary me," be constrained to right our wrongs.

In the struggle which we are making in this country for the recognition of our rights as men and citizens, there is another thing which I want to say. There is little or nothing to be expected from those members of our race, whether in politics or out of it, who value their little petty personal interests above the interest of their race; whose first and last and only thought is, What is there in the struggle for me, what can I get out of it? And who, when they have gotten their little out of it, are perfectly willing to sacrifice the race, to turn it over to the tender mercies of its enemies; to stand by and see it despoiled of its rights without one word of protest. It is rather from the men who are willing to make sacrifices, and to suffer, if need be, for principle; who cannot be satisfied, and cannot permit themselves to be silent in the presence of wrong, in order to ingratiate themselves into the favor of the dominant race, or that they might hold on to some petty office or position. If we are to succeed; if we are to make the proper kind of a fight in this country for our rights, we have got to develop a class of men who cannot be won over by a few offices or by being patted on the shoulder; men, who, like John the Baptist, are willing to be clothed in camel's hair, and to subsist on locusts and wild honey, to wear the coarsest clothing, and be content with the plainest food, in order that they might be free to follow the dictates of their own conscience that they might be unhampered in the fight which they are making for their rights, and for the rights of their race. The men whose policy is to look out for self first, and to concern themselves about the race only so far as professing interest in it may be a help to them in working out their selfish ends and purposes, are men that are unworthy of our confidence. The men that we should honor, and that we may safely follow, are those who are willing to lose themselves, to subordinate their selfish interests in order that the race may find itself, may come into the full enjoyment of all its rights. That was the spirit exhibited by Garrison, though he was battling for the rights, not of white men, but of black men.

> In a small chamber, friendless and unseen,
> Toiled o'er his types one poor, unlearned young man;
> The place was dark, unfurnitured, and mean;
> Yet there the freedom of a race began.
> Help came but slowly; surely no man yet
> Put lever to the heavy world with less.

What a picture is that! We can see it all! The dingy little room, dark, unfurnitured, and mean; and we can understand how difficult it must have been for him to keep soul and body together; and yet he was willing to endure all, to suffer all, for the sake of the cause to which he had dedicated his life. That was a white man suffering for black men! What ought not black men to be willing to suffer, to endure, for themselves? If we are to succeed, I say, in the struggle through which we are passing, we have got to develop within the race itself more of the spirit which Garrison possessed—the willingness to be found, if necessary, in a small chamber, dark, unfurnitured and mean, and to be friendless, in the struggle which we are making for the new emancipation from the fetters of caste prejudice, and from the injustice and oppression through which we are at present subjected. We are still dragging the chain; and we will go on dragging it until the race itself wakes up and sets itself earnestly to work to break it. We are not sufficiently in earnest; we are too easily lulled to sleep; we are too easily satisfied; we are not sufficiently impressed with the gravity of the situation—with the true inwardness of the motive which is leading our enemies on, enemies within the race as well as without it, in the assaults which they are making upon our rights. Edwin Markham, in a little poem entitled "Thoughts for Independence Day," asks the question:

> What need we, then, to guard and keep us whole?
> What do we need to prop the State?

And the answer which he makes among others is:

> We need the Cromwell fire to make us feel
> The public honor or the public trust
> To be a thing as sacred and August
> As some white altar where the angels kneel.

And that is what we need, "the Cromwell fire," to make us feel that the rights guaranteed to us under the Constitution, are

> as sacred and August
> As some white altar where the angels kneel.

If we felt that way, we would not lightly surrender these rights, as too many are disposed to do.

At this Grand Army Encampment, when the issues of the great Civil War are brought vividly before us, it is a good time to look into each other's faces; to give each other the pass-word; and to pledge ourselves anew to stand by our colors. Mr. Webster, in his eulogy on Adams and Jefferson, represents John Adams saying, on the question of independence, "Sink, or swim; live, or die; survive, or perish," we pledge our hands and hearts to each other, never to give up the struggle. Stanley is represented, while in Africa, as saying, "Nothing except the Bible gave me such comfort and inspiration as these lines from Browning":

> What on earth had I to do
> With the slothful, with the mawkish, the unmanly?
> Being—who? one who never turned his back, but marched
>   breast forward,
> Never doubted clouds would break,
> Never dreamed, though right were worsted, wrong would
>   triumph,
> Held, we fall to rise, are baffled to fight better,
> Sleep to wake.

And this is what we must do, "March breast forward"; that is the kind of men that we must be—the kind of men that we must seek more and more to develop among us—men of courage, of faith, of steady purpose, of uncompromising fidelity to principle. Douglass was a man of that type. A majestic figure! A leader, who never turned his back; and who never compromised his race; a leader, who was always true; and who, down to the very last, stood panoplied in its defense. It is the Douglass-type of leaders that we want—leaders who respect themselves, and to whom the interests of their race are above price. Long may the memory of this illustrious man linger with us, to stimulate our ambition; to arouse our slumbering energies; and to put within us the earnest purpose to continue the fight for equal civil and political rights in this land which we have helped to develop and to save.

At the battle of Copenhagen, 1801, Nelson was vice-admiral and led the attack against the Danish fleet. By accident one-fourth of the fleet were unable to participate, and the battle was very destructive. Admiral Parker, a conservative and aged officer, seeing how little progress was made after three hours' conflict, signaled the fleet to discontinue the engagement. That signal was No. 39. Nelson continued to walk the deck, without appearing to notice the signal. "Shall I repeat it?" said the lieutenant. "No; acknowledge it." He turned to the Captain: "You know, Forley, I have only one eye. I can't see it," putting his glass to his blind eye. "Nail my signal for close action to the mast," cried Nelson. That was his order to continue the fight. And the fight was continued, and the battle was won. And so, when signals come to us, as they have come and are coming, from within the race, as well as from without it, bidding us give up the struggle; telling us to cease to agitate, to protest, to stand up for our rights; telling us not to trouble ourselves; that it doesn't do any good; that we had better let things go, which means, go the way our enemies want them to go; that all this agitation tends only to make things worse, to engender hard feelings— to all such signals let us, like the intrepid Nelson, turn our blind eye towards them; let us not see them; and go right on fighting the battles of the race. If we are true to ourselves and to God the victory will be ours. It may be slow in coming, but come it will. Nothing is to be gained by withdrawing from the contest. Our duty is to remain firm; to plant ourselves squarely and uncompromisingly upon the rights guaranteed to us under the constitution, and to hold our ground. No backward step, should be our motto.

> Today is the day of battle,
> The brunt is hard to bear;
> Stand back, all ye who falter,
> Make room for those who dare.

Thank God there have always been among us men of this stamp; men who have realized the necessity of fighting, and who have been willing to go forward, regardless of personal consequences—brave men, true men, unselfish men.

Let us hope that the number of those who falter, who are disposed to stand back, to meekly surrender their rights, may be steadily on the decrease; and that the number of those who dare, who are resolved to go forward, to stand firmly for the right, may go on steadily increasing, until there shall not be left one lukewarm, indifferent, half-hearted, non-self-respecting member of the race; until all shall be aroused, and shall be equally interested in a cause that ought to be dearer to us than life itself.

Let us be men; and let us stand up for our rights as men, and as American citizens.

> Be strong!
> It matters not how deep entrenched the wrong,
> How hard the battle goes, the day, how long.
> Faint not, Fight on! To-morrow comes the song.

The Roosevelt-Washington Episode, or Race Prejudice

Francis J. Grimké   (Acts 11:2–3, KJV)

Of the three great representative races of antiquity, the most exclusive, the most arrogant, the most inflated with pride, were the Jews. They looked down upon all other races; held them in the greatest contempt. They felt that they were the special favorites of heaven. And this was due partly to their education. When God appeared unto Abraham, and said unto him, "Get thee out of thy country, and from thy kindred, and from thy father's house into a land that I will show thee," it was with the purpose of separating unto himself a peculiar people zealous of good works and thus to prepare the way for the coming of the seed of the woman, which was to bruise the serpent's head.

After the fall wickedness grew very rapidly or the earth. The statement is, "The whole earth became corrupted." Then came the flood, and a new beginning was made in the family of Noah; but it was not very long before evil had again over-spread everything. Then it was that God took this man Abraham from his home and led him down into the land of Canaan, and began the work of building up a nation in which the knowledge of the true God would be preserved, and among whom the Messiah might appear and set up his kingdom.

In order to do this, certain things were necessary. (1) That they be separate from all other races and peoples. And (2) that they be specially trained. To this end, God entered into a covenant with Abraham, and after his death the covenant was renewed with his son Isaac, and after Isaac's death with Jacob. Then came the period of expansion, of growth, of development. In the providence of God, the family of Jacob goes down into Egypt, and while there multiplies so rapidly that the Egyptians became afraid and begin to oppress them. Then Moses comes upon the scene, and through him, under the divine direction, after working many signs and wonders, they are led out of Egypt across the Red Sea to Horeb, the mount of God, and there amid mighty thunderings and lightnings, the law was given unto them—the moral law and the ceremonial law—and the process of education and of separation begins. For forty years they wandered in the wilderness, during which time God fed them. Then he brought them to the promised land and settled them in that land.

It is impossible to read their laws without realizing that one object was to keep them to themselves, separate and apart from others. Thus, they were forbidden to enter into a covenant with other nations, to marry among them, or to follow their practices, or to worship their gods. And according to the statements in John and the Acts, they were to have no intercourse whatever with strangers, no social contact in any way with them. The reason for this was because the surrounding nations were very corrupt; and one purpose which God had in view in training them was to make them strong in character, pure, upright in heart and life.

So it is impossible to read their history without realizing that they were wonderfully blessed. They were exalted to heaven in point of privilege. As Moses expresses it, "For what great nation is there that hath a god so right unto them, as the Lord our God is whensoever we call upon him. And what great nation is there, that hath statutes and judgments so righteous as all this law, which I set before you this day?" And in the 105th psalm we have this record, "They went about from nation to nation, from one kingdom to another people. He suffered no man to do them wrong; yes, they reproved kings for their sakes; saying, touch not mine anointed ones and do my prophets no harm." All these great blessings that came to them were intended to bring them nearer to God; to purify their hearts, and to fit them to do the work which he had mapped out for them, namely, to become his chosen instruments, in the fullness of time, when Shiloh should come, to carry the blessings of the true religion unto the ends of the earth. The promise made to Abraham was: "in thy seed shall all the families of the earth be blessed." And again we have the statement, "Ask of me and I will give of thee the heathen for thine inheritance, and the uttermost parts of the earth for thy possession." Hence the great commission given by Christ to his disciples: "Go ye into all the world and preach the gospel unto every creature." That was the purpose which God had in view in the training of the Jewish nation, to use them for the dissemination of the gospel among all peoples. Instead of this, however, it had the very opposite effect upon them. The fact that they were so highly favored, that they had enjoyed so many privileges, filled them with pride, puffed them up, gave them an overweening sense of their own importance; led them to despise others, to hold themselves aloof from them; to feel that these blessings were for them only. This feeling was general among the Jews. They shrank away from contact with others as they would from a thing unclean. Peter himself was not free from it. When God wanted to use him and send him on a mission to a certain Gentile he had actually to work a miracle in order to prepare him for it. You remember the record in the tenth chapter of the Acts: "About noon Peter went on the housetop to pray, and became hungry and had a vision. He saw the heavens open and beheld a certain vessel descending, as it were a great sheet, let down by the four corners upon the earth; wherein were all manner of four-footed beasts and creeping things of the earth and fowls of heaven. And there came a voice to him, "Rise Peter; kill and eat." But Peter said, "Not so, Lord; for I have never eaten anything that is common and unclean." And a voice came unto him again the second time, "What God hath cleansed, make not thou uncommon." And this was done thrice, and straightway the vessel was received up into heaven.

"Now while Peter was much perplexed in himself what the vision might mean," the narrative goes on to say, "behold the men that were sent by Cornelius, having made inquiry for Simon's house, stood before the gate, and called and asked whether Simon, which was surnamed Peter, were lodging there. And while Peter thought on the vision, the Spirit said unto him, Behold, three men seek thee. But arise, and get thee down, and go with them, nothing doubting; for I have sent them.

It was under such pressure as this; it was only because of this message direct from heaven that Peter was induced to go down to Caesarea. And even then he had to explain to Cornelius that he was doing an unusual thing. "Ye yourselves know," he said to him and his friends who were present, "how that it is an unlawful thing for a man who is a Jew to join himself or come unto one of another nation." He justifies himself, however, by the statement, "And yet unto me hath God showed that I should not call any man common or unclean."

In order still further to strengthen Peter in what he had done, in the position which he had taken, to make assurance doubly sure that he had the approval of God in what he had done, the Holy Spirit was poured out upon Cornelius and his friends, just as he had been poured out upon the apostles and those who were with them in the upper chamber on the day of Pentecost. The same manifestation of the Spirit's presence was visible; they spoke with other tongues, the same as they had done.

Cornelius, grateful for what had been done, for the wonderful blessings which had come to him and his household, through Peter, very naturally was desirous of showing him some attention, of expressing in some way his gratitude, and so pressed him very earnestly to spend a while with them, and he accepted, so we are led to infer from the narrative. He became his guest.

Peter doubtless felt very happy over what had occurred. He had had a wonderful experience and had seen what he had never expected to see. And in this frame of mind he returned to Jerusalem, full of the subject and anxious to break the good tiding to the brethren. But he found that the news had preceded him, and that the most important part of the transaction had been entirely overlooked, the descent of the Holy Spirit upon the Gentiles, and that the only thing that was remembered and commented upon was the fact that he had gone in unto men who were uncircumcised and had eaten with them. For this he was bitterly denounced. We can imagine how they must have frowned upon him, and how they must have sought to make him feel that he had belittled himself and had brought dishonor upon the whole Jewish race by his unseemly conduct.

It is interesting to see who this man was with whom Peter ate, on whose account such a tremendous hubbub was raised. It was Cornelius. And who was Cornelius?

1. He was a Roman citizen, a member of the Latin race, then the dominant race of the world, a race that had produced a Julius Caesar, a Cicero, a Seneca, a Virgil, and other illustrious names.

2. He was a man who held an honorable position. He was an officer in the Roman army.

3. He was a man of wealth, he had an abundance of this world's good. He was able therefore to surround himself with all the comforts of this life.

4. He was a man of high social standing. This is clear from his position and from his possessions.

5. He was a man of high character. He stood well in the community, was respected by all who knew him.

6. He was a religious man, a man who feared God, who believed in prayer, and who sought to regulate his household according to the teachings of religion. There are two descriptions given of him in this tenth chapter. The first is in the second verse, "A devout man, and one that feared God with all his house who gave much alms to the people, and prayed to God always." The second is in the twenty-second verse, where he is said to be, "A righteous man and one that feareth God, and well reported of by all the nation of Jews."

From the account which we have of him, it is evident that he was an exceptionally fine man, a man of high ideals and noble aspirations, a man who would have been a credit to any community, and whose friendship any one might feel honored in possessing, but unfortunately, he happened to belong to another race, to the Gentiles, to the uncircumcised, and that fact rendered all of his splendid and noble qualities of no avail. He must be discriminated against; no Jew must enter his house; no Jew must eat with him. Peter is denounced for dining with such a man as Cornelius. The Lord Jesus Christ was censured, severely criticized for eating with publicans and sinners; but in the case of Peter it is for enjoying a social repast with one of the very finest gentlemen presented to us in the New Testament, a man very different in character from publicans and sinners. The ground of objection against him was not his character, but his race.

It is interesting also to note who these people were who attempted to frown Peter down and to criticize him.

(1) They were members of the church; they were professed Christians; but they were in the dark; they failed to catch the spirit of Christ, and to enter into the great purpose for which he had come, which was to break down the middle wall of separation between Jew and Gentile, and to make all one; they failed utterly to understand that in Christ Jesus there was to be neither Greek nor Jew, barbarian, Scythian, bond, nor free, but that all were to stand on precisely the same level.

(2) They were men who were socially inferior to Cornelius. The members of the early church were gatherd, not from the upper and aristocratic classes among the Jews, but from the common people, from what are called among us the laboring classes. The fact that they were Jews, however, led them to feel that they were superior to any Gentile, whatever might be his attainments or position. It shows the nature of prejudice, how blind and stupid it is, how unreasonable, how utterly devoid of common sense.

Sometimes it is impossible to avoid feeling contempt for it, and yet, I suppose, it deserves our pity rather than our contempt.

But I must hasten on. Poor Peter is not the only one who has been criticized for eating with a member of a supposed inferior race. Our good President is just now passing through a similar experience for inviting Booker T. Washington to dine with him. What a howl has gone up all over the South, and why? Because the President has seen fit to entertain at his table a colored gentleman, the head of a great institution, a man of national reputation, and a man, by the way, who has been more lauded by the South than any Negro who has ever lived in this country. Booker T. Washington has always been the ideal Negro in the eyes of the Southern whites; and it is the entertainment of this man that has provoked all this criticism, that has brought down the wrath of the Southern people upon the head of our worthy and honored President. These people who are criticizing the President, do not deny that Booker T. Washington is a gentleman, that he is a man of high character, of unblemished reputation. They do not deny that he is a man of some attainments, that he is a thinker, and that he knows how to express himself; they themselves rank him with the foremost orators of the country. They do not deny that he has done a great work in building up Tuskegee, one of the greatest industrial schools in the country. They do not deny that his influence has been far reaching. According to their own estimate of him he knows more about the Negro problem, the greatest problem today before the American people, and had done more than anyone else to bring about a proper understanding between the races. If the eulogies pronounced upon this man by the Southern press and by Southern men were gathered together they would fill a volume. Everywhere his praise has been sounded throughout the Southland; everywhere he has been held up and lauded to the skies.

Why then all this howl about his dining with the President? What is the trouble? A physician in this city told me once of an experience which he had, which will perhaps throw a little light on the subject. He was making a call on one of his patients, and while he was sitting by her bedside a member of the Salvation Army came in. Her first words to him, after looking him over, were: "Do you know the Lord Jesus?" His reply was, "Yes, I know him very well." "What do you know about him?" she asked. His reply was, "I know him to be a very nice colored gentleman." At which she threw her hands up in holy horror and cried out: "Blasphemy, blasphemy." "What do you mean?" said he, "do you mean to say he is not a gentleman?" "No, I don't mean that," she answered. "You said he was a colored gentleman!" It was blasphemy in the estimation of this member of the Salvation Army even to think of Jesus Christ as a colored gentleman. And that is the secret of all this hue and cry that has been going up all over the South, in regard to the Washington episode; it is because Prof. Washington happens to be identified with the despised Negro race in this country. If he had belonged to any other race under the sun it would have made no difference. He has worked his way up from chattel slavery; from the log cabin to the position which he today occupies in the public estimation, which in a Grant or a Lincoln would have made him an honored guest in any home, even the proudest in the land, but because of his race affiliation, in spite of his remarkable career, he is, in the estimation of the Southern whites, an outcast, unfit to receive any social recognition from them. It is because of his color that these fools are uttering their impotent rage. "He that sitteth in the heavens will laugh. He will have them in derision."

I for one am glad that this thing has occurred; that Booker Washington has had the opportunity of dining as a guest at the White House. I am glad, for several reasons: (1) because it shows that we have at last in the White House one who is every inch a man; one who has convictions, and convictions in the right direction, and who has the courage of his convictions. It is a great thing to be a man, to have the fear of God so implanted in the soul, and to have the love of right so strongly developed in us, that we will not be turned away from the path of duty though confronted by all the powers of darkness. You see that kind of manhood in Garrison; you get a glimpse into his soul and see what kind of moral fiber he was made of, in those magnificent words of his, "I am in earnest. I will not equivocate, I will not excuse, I will not retreat a single inch, and I will be heard." And in those burningly eloquent words of Patrick Henry, "Give me liberty, or give me death," there was the purpose to stand for the right, though death ensued.

There are some men who are so only in name. They are mere apologies for men. They are weaklings; they have no stamina, no backbone. They are putty men, easily moulded, mere tools in the hands of others. They are moral cowards; they are afraid of their own shadow. They never dare to act without finding out first which way the wind is blowing. They are afraid of doing the unpopular thing. For such men we can't help feeling contempt. Manhood is the thing that commends itself to us always, whether we agree with it or not. Give me a manly man, a man who dares to do right, who dares to follow his convictions, who dares to do the unpopular thing because it commands itself to his conscience. Such a man I believe is the present occupant of the White House, Theodore Roosevelt. Everything indicates it. A short while ago I read in the *Times* of this city the following: "I am going," he is quoted as saying, "to select the very best men for public positions. Men appointed to high public places must be high in morals and in every other respect. If the American people care to show their approval of my course as President during the three years and a half that I have to serve, by placing me at the head of the Republican ticket in 1904, I should feel deeply grateful. It would be an honor that it would be difficult for any man to decline. But if I have to pander to any cliques, combinations or movements, for their approval, I would not give a snap of my fingers for it or a nomination under such circumstances."

It has been a long time since we have heard any such manly utterance from any high official in this country.

Again, in the appointment of ex-Governor Jones, of Alabama, he said distinctly: "One reason why I have appointed him is because of his attitude on the subject of lynching." There is no dodging the question, no beating about the bush. He defines his position on the subject, and in a way not to be misunderstood. In his official capacity, in the exercise of his appointing power, he puts the seal of his disapprobation upon that phase of Southern barbarism.

And still again, in his invitation to Professor Washington to dine with him, the moral fiber of the man is also clearly seen, for he was not ignorant of Southern public sentiment in regard to the step which he was about to take. He knew that all Negroes in the South are regarded as social pariahs; but he was not deterred thereby. He wanted the professor to dine with him, and he had him, and will have him again when he wants to, Southern sentiment to the contrary, notwithstanding. Theodore Roosevelt is no reed shaken by the wind. He is not a man to be deterred from the course which he has mapped out for himself by the clamor of the multitude, by adverse criticism, or by the prating of fools.

For the first time in the history of the country a colored American citizen has dined at the White House as the guest of the President of the United States. It is a shame that it has not occurred before. For twenty-five years there lived in this city the most eminent representative that this race has yet produced, the immortal Douglass, a man of whom Theodore Tilton said:

> In the paths of men
> There never walked a grander man than he!
> He was a peer of princes—yea a King!
> Crowned in the shambles and the prison-pen,
> the noblest slave that ever God set free.

He was Marshal of the District, he was Recorder of Deeds, he was the American Minister to Port-au-Prince, he was, as the papers said at the time of his death, the most famous citizen of Washington.

The *Philadelphia Recorder* said at the time: "No other Washingtonian, white or black, has the world-wide reputation that he had. Indeed, when we think of it, it would be difficult to name any other man, white or black, in the whole country who would be as well known in every corner of the globe as is Frederick Douglass. Lincoln and Grant were such men, but I cannot think of any one now except President Cleveland and ex-President Harrison, who are, ex-officio, so to speak, our world-wide celebrities. Dr. Holmes was the last of our men of letters who had this world-wide fame, and no other class of men or women seems to have produced an international character in our time. Our great lawyers are perhaps known by lawyers the world over; our great physicians by physicians; clergymen by clergymen; journalists by journalists; business men by business men, but where is the man or woman who is known in all countries by people of all classes." And yet, during his entire sojourn in this capital city of the nation, there wasn't a man in the White House big enough and brave enough and sufficiently free from his prejudices and from the fear of offending public sentiment to invite him to dine with him. It is, to say the least, highly improbable that a man of his eminence and of his wide acquaintance with public men in high official positions of any other race could have lived here as long as he did without being honored with such an invitation, but he was not; and it was simply because of his color, because of his race affiliation. That fact, I say, is a disgrace to the country, and it reflects seriously upon the men who have occupied the Executive Mansion. Why shouldn't a colored man dine there, if he is sufficiently eminent and is of the right stamp? Is he not an American citizen? Is he not a part of this great Republic? Why should he alone be shut out and all others admitted?

Thank God there has come at last into power a man who by this act has said, Whatever others may have done, so far as I am concerned, I shall know no man by the color of his skin. What I accord to white men I will accord to black men, I shall treat all citizens alike. That is the kind of President to have; that is the only kind of a man that ought ever to be entrusted with power in a democratic republic.

(2) I am glad that this episode has occurred, because it has brought out in clearer light than anything which has ever happened before the real feeling of the South toward the Negro. It doesn't make any difference what he becomes, what his achievements are, however pure his character, however cultivated his mind, he is always to be treated as an inferior, to be kept in his place. Every Negro in the South may become a Booker T. Washington, and yet the brand of inferiority is to be stamped upon him. He is still to be forced to live apart by himself, to ride in Jim Crow Cars, to sit in dirty, filthy waiting rooms, to be denied all the common courtesies and civilities of life. That is what this incident teaches, and it makes it so plain that the wayfaring man, though a fool, need not err. The Negro can never be anything but an inferior, that is what the South believes; that is what it has been teaching; that is what this howl that has been going up about the entertainment of Professor Washington means. And I am glad that this fact has at last come out in the way it has. Let us hope that it will have the effect of undeceiving hundreds and thousands of professed friends of the Negro, who have become converts to the pernicious doctrine which has been steadily growing in favor in the North, that the South knows best how to deal with the Negro. That is true, assuming that the Negro is hopelessly inferior, but if he is a man, and ought to have a man's chance in the race of life, is it true that the South knows best how to deal with him? Is it safe to leave him in the hands of the South, entertaining the low view of him that it does? Is that according to reason? Is it according to common sense? There is but one ground upon which the North can or ought to accede to any such proposition, and that is that in its judgment the Southern white man is more kindly disposed toward the Negro; the Southern white man has a larger sense of justice in dealing with the Negro; and that the Negro left to the South will have a better chance of growing up into the full measure of the stature of a man and of a citizen. There isn't a man in the North who has given the subject any serious thought, or who has kept himself posted as to what is actually going on in the South, who believes anything of the kind. The whole past record is against any such assumption.

It is not true that the Southern white man is more kindly disposed towards the Negro. He is toward a certain kind of Negro, the Negro who knows his place, who is content to be an underling, and who believes in political self-effacement. But the manly Negro, the Negro who respects himself, who knows what his rights are, and who stands up for them, he hates, he wants nothing to do with him, he would be glad to see every one of that description driven out of the South.

It is not true that the Southern white man has a larger sense of justice in dealing with the Negro. The very reverse of that is true. What rights has a Negro that a Southern white man feels bound to respect? What is it that he hasn't done to despoil the Negro of his rights? His attitude toward him has been one of constant aggression. The Southern white man has never accepted the Fourteenth and Fifteenth Amendments to the Constitution. He has ignored the Negro's citizenship, has robbed him of his vote at the polls, and has given him scarcely the ghost of a chance in the courts of law.

It is not true that the prospects of the Negro's growing up into the full measure of a man and of a citizen are more favorable, if he is left entirely in the hands of the South. It needs no argument to prove this. It is patent on the face of it. What hope is there for the Negro, left to be dealt with by men who object to Booker T. Washington dining with the President of the United States, and who denounce the President's conduct in inviting him as an "outrage"?

Now these facts are well known all over the North. The North hasn't been asleep all these years. It has had its eyes and ears wide open; it knows perfectly well what is going on. It knows just how the Negro has been treated and how he is still being treated. And yet it has been largely won over to the let-alone policy, partly because it doesn't want to offend the South. It wants to bridge over the bloody chasm. It wasn't to bring about a spirit of fraternity between the Southern white man and the Northern white man, which is all very well; far be it for me to say a word against it; but is it right to sacrifice the Negro in so doing? When the Southern white men took up arms to destroy the Union, it was the Negro who bared his bosom to the bullets of the enemy in order to preserve it. It is well for the North to remember that. And it has also taken this position partly because of indolence, because it has become weary in well-doing, because it has grown tired of the struggle. It wants peace, but it seems to forget that permanent peace can never be won by yielding to evil. This so-called Negro question will not down, it will come up and continue to come up until it is settled, and settled right. The men of this generation in the North may adopt the let-alone policy and permit things to go on as the South dictates, but they are simply laying up trouble for their children and their children's children. As the poet has expressed it:

> They enslave their children's children
> Who make compromise with sin.

(3) I am glad of this episode because it will also have the effect of opening the eyes of Professor Washington himself, who has taken a rather rose-colored view of things in the South and of the Southern people. Now the scales will fall from his eyes and he will see things as they really are; he will see just what the Southern white men think of him in spite of all the praise which they have lavished upon him, and of the race with which he is identified. They value him simply because they believe that he accepts their view of the race problem, because they believe that he is laboring simply to make the Negro a laborer, a hewer of wood and a drawer of water. After his address before the great missionary conference held at New Orleans, a Texas editor, in speaking of him said: "He is most assuredly a man

raised up of God to do a great work among the Negroes of the South. And as long as he holds to his present theory and practice of industrial education, he is certainly entitled to the support and cooperation of the Southern people. He is doing a work second to no man of this century. And such is his consecration to his purpose and aim that, so far as we are able to judge, the money and attention bestowed upon him and his work by the people and press of the North have in no wise lifted him into the airs of conceit or unbecoming egotism. With all the prominence given to him and with his rare gifts of oratory, he is a man of commendable humility and stupendous common sense. Therefore the people of the South, regardless of race distinction, can well afford to extend all needed encouragement to Booker T. Washington in his laudable efforts to bring his people into higher attainments in the knowledge and practice of the mechanical arts and useful industry." That is to be the limit of the Negro's aspiration, "the practice of the mechanical arts and useful industry." And as long as they believe that Professor Washington believes in thus limiting the aspirations and the activities of the race, and in political self-effacement, he will be tolerated. This man distinctly says so, "As long as he holds to his present theory and practice of industrial education he is entitled to the support and co-operation of the South." If he dares to entertain any other theory or ventures to step out in any other direction, the South must withdraw all sympathy from him and relegate him to the class of undesirable Negroes, Negroes who think themselves as good as white men. Whatever may have been Mr. Washington's views in the past, he cannot fail now to see that the possibilities of the Negro in the South, unless there is a very decided change in public sentiment, are not such as a free American citizen ought to be satisfied with.

In the (4) and last place I am glad of this episode because it has brought to view the fact that we still have some friends left. The North had become so apathetic, so indifferent to the Negro, that we began to feel that our friends were becoming fewer and fewer. Men who were once identified with the cause of freedom we found fellowshiping with the man who a few years ago, in referring to the incident at the White House said,: "The action of President Roosevelt in entertaining that nigger will necessitate our killing a thousand niggers in the South before they will learn their place again." But the splendid showing of the Northern press has come like a gleam of sunshine in the darkness. They have spoken out in a way to cheer our hearts. All honor to them. May they continue to speak in the same lofty strain. What we need in the editor's chair as well as in the pulpit are men, God-fearing men—men who love righteousness and hate iniquity. And just in proportion as such men come to the front will public sentiment be moulded in the interest of justice and humanity.

Let us not be discouraged. God reigns and the right will ultimately triumph. The noble words of Norman Macleod may well close these remarks:

> Courage, brother! do not stumble,
>   Though the path is dark as night;
> There's a star to guide the humble;
>   Trust in God and do the right.

Let the road be long and dreary,
  And its ending out of sight,
Foot it bravely, strong or weary,
  Trust in God and do the right.

Perish policy and cunning,
  Perish all that fears the light,
Whether losing, whether winning,
  Trust in God and do the right.

Some will hate thee, some will love thee,
  Some will flatter, some will slight;
Cease from men, and look above thee,
  Trust in God and do the right.

Welcome to the Ransomed

Daniel Alexander Payne   (1 Tim. 2:1–4, KJV)

St. Paul addressed the Epistles to Timothy, the young bishop of Ephesus, for the purpose of giving him instruction touching the false doctrines inculcated by certain false teachers, as well as instructions respecting the qualification of the Christian ministry, their duties to themselves, to God, and the flock committed by the Holy Spirit to their special guidance.

But foremost of all the duties which he enjoined upon the Ephesian ministry and laity were those of making "supplications, prayers, intercessions, and giving of thanks for all men." For men in general, embracing the whole family of Adam, in all their varieties as nations, tribes, communities, peoples.

This is God-like, because the Eternal loves all, and manifests the infinity of this nature, by his universal care for all mankind. In this, He also demonstrates His universal Fatherhood, and thereby establishes the brotherhood of man.

But guided by the benevolence of unerring wisdom, the Apostle descends from a general to a particular statement of the case, and command us to single out from among the nations of earth their chieftains—kings and authorities—for whom we are to make special "supplications, prayers, intercessions, and giving of thanks."

To the cheerful and fervent performance of this gracious work, he presses several motives upon us—"that we may live a quiet and peaceable life in all godliness and honesty"—because "it is good and acceptable in the sight of God our Savior—because God "will have all men to be saved and to come unto the knowledge of the truth." Let us briefly trace out this line of thought.

To supplicate is to implore God submissively. To pray to God is to adore Him for His glorious perfection, to confess our sins to Him, and to beseech Him for mercy and pardon. To intercede with God is to entreat Him by the fervent, effectual prayer of faith, to be reconciled to offending man. This we may do as well for our enemies as for our friends.

We are gathered to celebrate the emancipation, yea, rather, the Redemption of the enslaved people of the District of Columbia, the exact number of whom we have no means of ascertaining, because, since the benevolent intention of Congress became manifest, many have been removed by their owners beyond the reach of this beneficent act.

Our pleasing task then is to welcome to the Churches, the homesteads, and circles of free colored Americans, those who remain to enjoy the boon of holy freedom.

Brethren, sisters, friends, we say welcome to our churches, welcome to our homesteads, welcome to our social circles.

Enter the great family of Holy Freedom; not to lounge in sinful indolence, not to degrade yourselves by vice, nor to corrupt society by licentiousness, neither to offend the laws by crime, but to the enjoyment of a well-regulated liberty, the offspring of generous laws; of law as just as generous, as righteous as just—a liberty to the perpetuated by equitable law, and sanctioned by the divine; for law is never equitable, righteous, just, until it harmonized with the will of Him who is "King of kings, and Lord of lords," and who commanded Israel to have but one law for the home-born and the stranger.

We repeat ourselves, welcome then ye ransomed ones; welcome not to indolence, to vice, licentiousness, and crime, but to a well-regulated liberty, sanctioned by the Divine, maintained by the Human law.

Welcome to habits of industry and thrift—to duties of religion and piety—to obligations of law, order, government—of government divine, of government human: these two, though not one, are inseparable. The man who refuses to obey divine law, will never obey human laws. The divine first, the human next. The latter is the consequence of the former, and follows it as light does the rising sun.

We invite you to our Churches, because we desire you to be religious; to be more than religious; we urge you to be godly. We entreat you to never be content until you are emancipated from sin, from sin without, and from sin within you. But this kind of freedom is attained only through the faith of Jesus, love for Jesus, obedience to Jesus. As certain as the American Congress has ransomed you, so certain, yea, more certainly has Jesus redeemed you from the guilt and power of sin by his own precious blood.

As you are now free in body, so now seek to be free in soul and spirit, from sin and Satan. The noblest freeman is he whom Christ makes free.

We invite you to our homesteads, in order that we may aid you as well by the power of good examples as by the beauty of holy precept, in raising up intelligent, virtuous, pious, happy families. We invite you to our social circles, in order that you may have none of those inducements which grow out of a mere love of society, to frequent the gambling halls, and grog-geries, which gradually lead their votaries to infamy and the pit that is bottomless.

Permit us, also, to advise you to seek every opportunity for the cultivation of your minds. To the adults we say, enter the Sunday Schools and the Night Schools, so opportunely opened by Dr. Pierson, in behalf of the American Tract Society. In the latter you can very soon learn to read the precious word of God, even before you shall have a familiar knowledge of the letters which constitute the alphabet.

Rest not till you have learned to read the Bible. 'Tis the greatest, the best of books. In it is contained the divine law. O! meditate therein by day and by night, for "the law of the Lord is perfect, converting the soul; the testimony of the Lord is sure, making wise the simple; the statutes of the Lord are right, rejoicing the heart; the commandment of the Lord is pure, enlightening the eyes—more to be desired are they than gold, yea, than much fine gold; sweeter also than honey and the honeycomb." "In keeping of them there is great reward." Yield uniform implicit obedience to their teachings. They will purify your hearts and make them the abodes of the Ever-Blessed Trinity.

When you shall have reached this point, you will be morally prepared to recognize and respond to all the relations of civilized and christianized life.

But of the children take special care. Heaven has entrusted them to you for a special purpose. What is that purpose? Not merely to eat and to drink, still less to gormandize. Not merely to dress finely in broadcloths, silks, satins, jewelry, nor to dance to the sound of the tambourine and fiddle; but to learn them how to live and how to die—to train them for great usefulness on earth—to prepare them for greater glory in heaven.

Keep your children in the schools, even if you have to eat less, drink less, and wear coarser raiments; though you eat but two meals a day, purchase but one change of garment during the year, and relinquish all the luxuries of which we are so fond, but which are as injurious to health and life as they are pleasing to the taste.

Let the education of your children penetrate the heart. That education which forgets, or purposely omits, the culture of the heart, is better adapted to devilish than manhood. But the education which reaches the heart, molds it, humbles it before the Cross, is rather the work of the homestead than the common school or the college. It is given by the parents rather than the schoolmaster—by the mother rather than the father.

How important, then, that the mothers be right-minded; that our young women, of whom our mothers come, be brought up with a high sense of personal character—be taught to prefer virtue to gold, and death itself rather than a violated chastity. The women make the men; therefore the women should be greater than the men, in order that they be the mothers of great men. I mean good men, for none are great who are not good.

But this requires the transforming grace of God; requires that our mothers be women of strong faith and fervent daily prayers; requires that they live beneath the wings of the Cherubim—at the foot of the Cross—loving the God-man "whose favor is life, and whose loving kindness is better than life."

Such mothers will care for the heart education of their children, and will consequently lay continuous siege to the Throne of God in behalf of their sons and daughters, even as the Syro-Phoenician mother importuned the compassionate Jesus in behalf of her afflicted daughter, or as Queen Esther did Ahasuerus in behalf of her menaced kinsmen.

Such mothers will carefully train their children as Moses was trained by his mother, preserving him pure from the vices of a Court and the baneful examples of lordly superiors; or, like Susanna Wesley, will educate their sons, as she did John and Charles, in the atmosphere of such spiritual excellence, and with such a moral power, as will make them ministering angels of good to man and glory to God most High.

Lastly—let us advise you respecting money. Some people value it too much, others too little. Of these extremes take the medium; for money has its proper value. That value lies in its adaptedness to promote the ends of Christian enlightenment; to purchase the best medical aid and other comforts in the days of affliction; to administer to the wants of old age, and to enable us to assisting making mankind wiser and better.

But how are we to get money? Get it by diligent labor. Work, work, work! Shun no work that will bring you an honest penny. 'Tis honorable to labor with our own hands. God works, and shall man be greater than God? Fools only think labor dishonorable. Wise men feel themselves honored in following the example of God, whose works adorn and bless both heaven and earth.

But when you get the pennies save them. Then you will soon have dollars. The dollars will enable you to buy comfortable homes for yourselves and for your children.

You can save your pennies—yea, dollars—if you will run away from whiskey, rum and tobacco. A few years ago an intelligent minister said that the colored people of the District of Columbia spent ten thousand dollars a year for tobacco. What a sum for poison! Better take that money to build churches and school houses; better take it to obtain and pay thoroughly educated teachers for your pulpits and your school houses—the schoolmasters as well as the preachers.

Work for money; work everyday, work diligently, and save your money when you get it.

Ever since the first stone in the foundations of the universe was laid by God's own hand till now, he has been working, and will continue working through endless ages. Follow his glorious example. Work, work, work, for an honest penny; but when you get it, pause and think three times before you spend it; but when you spend it, be sure it will yield a permanent benefit.

That the hearty welcome which we have given you, our ransomed kinsmen, may be rendered a blessing, and that the advice which we have tendered may be as good seed sown in good ground, we shall continue to make supplications, prayers, intercessions and thanksgiving to Him whose care reaches all, because His love embraces all.

To Him we commend you, O ye who are now as sheep without a shepherd—as exiles in the land of your nativity.

May He who led Abraham, Isaac and Jacob, as they wandered over Canaan and Egypt, guide, protect and bless you; raise up kind, influential friends to do you good; and when the purposes of his grace shall have been accomplished in you, may you be able, like Jacob, to say: "With my staff I passed over this Jordan, and now I am become two bands."

Now, if we ask, who has sent us this great deliverance? The answer shall be, the Lord; the Lord God Almighty, the god of Abraham and Isaac and Jacob.

But as He blessed the chosen seed, by the ministry of men and angels, so in our case, the angels of mercy, justice and liberty, hovering over the towering Capitol, inspired the heads and hearts of the noble men who have plead the cause of the poor, the needy and enslaved, in the Senate and House of Representatives.

For the oppressed and enslaved of all peoples, God has raised up, and will continue to raise up, his Moses and Aaron. Sometimes the hand of the Lord is so signally displayed that Moses and Aaron are not recognized. Seldom do they recognize themselves.

There was neither bow, spear, nor shield, in the hand of Israel, when the Lord led him forth from Egypt, so also, there was no weapon of offence nor defence in your hands when this ransom was brought you.

"Great and marvelous are thy works, Lord God almighty, just and true are the way, thou King of Saints. Who shall not fear thee, O Lord, and glorify thy name? We praise thee, we bless thee, we worship thee, we glorify thee, we give thanks to thee for thy great glory. O Lord God, Heavenly king, God the Father Almighty."

Thou, O Lord, and thou alone couldst have moved the heart of this Nation to have done so great a deed for this weak, despised and needy people!

We will, therefore, make supplications, prayers, intercession, and thanksgivings, for "all that are in authority."

The duty of supplications in behalf of the Government is rendered more binding upon us, when we consider the circumstances under which it is written. St. Paul lived under the reign of Nero, the bloody emperor, who had set Rome on fire, amused himself with drinking and music while the city was in flames; and afterwards, accused the Christians of the crime which he himself had committed, thereby causing many of them to be put to death in the most cruel manner.

Now, if it was the duty of the ancient Christians to pray for such monsters of wickedness, by how much more is it our duty to pray for a Christian Government.

Congress needs our supplications, they shall have them. The President and his Cabinet need our prayers, they shall possess them. The Supreme Court, that awful emblem of impartial justice, need our intercession, it shall not be forgotten.

Upon all these departments of law, authority and power, we shall beseech the God of Nations to send the spirit of wisdom, justice, liberty—of wisdom seeing the end from the beginning—of justice incorruptible—of liberty governed by righteous law.

To make supplications, prayers, intercession, and thanksgiving for these authorities, is the peculiar privilege of the Colored People in the United States.

They are not permitted, as in the days of the Revolution and the war of 1812, to take up arms in defence of the Government. Some, both among Anglo-Saxons and Anglo-Africans, complain of this prohibition. For my part, I am glad of it, because I think I see the hand of God in it.

The present war is a kind of family quarrel. Therefore, let a stranger take heed how he meddles, lest both parties unite to drive him out of the house. "Why shouldst thou meddle to thy hurt?"

But we can wield a power in behalf of the Government which neither rifled cannon, nor mortar, nor rocket-battery can assail, nor bomb-proof walls resist.

That power is the right arm of God—of God, who lifts up and casts down nations according as they obey, or disregard the principles of truth, justice, liberty.

The service of prayer which is required from us contemplates the most difficult as well as the noblest objects. It contemplates the need of the war. It contemplates legislation before and after the end.

Now, to manage this war, so as to bring permanent good to all concerned, requires more than human wisdom—more than human power. To legislate so as to make the masses see and feel that the laws are just, wise, beneficial, demand more than human learning or skill in government. To determine the sense and just application of these laws as Judges—to execute them faithfully and impartially as a Chief Magistrate, O how much of the spirit of God is needful! How much in the President! How much in the Cabinet!

Then there is the army. Let us not forget the brave men who constitute it—who have left their comfortable homes, beloved families, fond parents, affectionate sisters and brothers, for the hardships, dangers and painful deaths of the battle field.

Let us pray that, as some of them are, so all may become, soldiers of the Cross; so that such as are doomed to fall in the fight, may rise from their gory beds to obtain a crown of life; and those who may return to the peaceful pursuits of civil life, may be wiser and better men.

Now, then, although weak, few, despised and persecuted, we can aid all these departments of government by our daily supplications, prayers and intercessions.

In doing this service, we can accomplish what we could not if we were leading the van of battle; for conquering armies are preceded and succeeded by anguish, misery and death, but our service brings down nothing but blessings upon all.

They are also weapons, "not carnal, but might through God, to the pulling down of strongholds"; even the casting down of principalities and powers—the moving of heaven and earth.

Take two examples: When Israel fought against the five kings of the Amorites, Joshua prayed and the sun stood still upon Gibeon, while the moon hung over the valley of Ajalon, till Israel had conquered.

"John Knox was a man famous for his power in prayer, so that Queen Mary used to say she feared his prayers more than all the armies of Europe. And events showed she had reason to do it. He used to be in such an agony for the deliverance of his country that he could not sleep. He had a place in his garden, where he used to go to pray. One night he and several friends were praying together, and as they prayed Knox spoke and said that deliverance had come. He could not tell what had happened, but he felt that something had taken place, for God had heard their prayers. What was it? Why the next news they heard was "Queen Mary is dead!"

But the motives for all this work of mercy, faith, and love as furnished by the text are a weight as they are numerous. 1st. "That we may lead a quiet and peaceable life." Peace and quietude are some of the conditions of happiness. Dr. Adam Blucher says: "If the State be not in safety, the individual cannot be secure; self-preservation, therefore, should lead men to pray for the government under which they live. Rebellions and insurrections seldom terminate even in political good—and even where the government is radically bad, revolutions are most precarious and hazardous. They who wish such commotions would not be quiet under the most mild and benevolent government." This is true of communities and nations, as well as of individuals. We all desire it, and therefore it is our duty to labor for it by every instrument which Infinite wisdom has ordained and man can employ. And lo! How excellent the instruments! Prayers, supplications, intercession—thanksgiving. As Aaron approached the Mercy Seat, with the smoking censer, and was accepted so do we approach the throne of the Eternal with the burning incense of heaven's own making, and will be accepted. O, let us supplicate God for the peace and quiet of the whole nation.

2d. The other motive which Inspiration presents is that we may live "in all godliness and honesty." Godliness first, honesty afterwards. The latter is the fruit of the former. The godly man is he who fears God and keeps his commandments. Such a man will be honest in word as well as in deed; in matters of truth as well as in matters of property. Honesty is the only policy of godliness. Colored men, write this sentiment upon your hearts, engrave it in your memory. Let all your thoughts, words, actions, be controlled by this principle, it is always safe to be honest, as it is always safe to be godly. One has said, that "An honest man is the noblest work of God." But when comes the honest man? Does he not spring out of the godly? Most assuredly. For no man is truly honest, uniformly honest, and universally honest, but he who is godly. Therefore be godly, and you will be honest in all things, at all time, in all places.

3d. The third motive for this heavenly duty, this intercession in behalf of the Government is that "it is good and acceptable in the sight of God our Savior." Whatever God accepts and pronounces good, must be good: good in itself; good in its effects, always good; good for man, because ordained of God.

4th. The last motive we present for this godlike work is that God "will have all men to be saved, and to come unto the knowledge of the truth."

Hence, we must pray for these Authorities not as public men only, but as private individuals also—not as Chieftains of the Nation only, but as heads of families also—as husband, fathers, Christians. So that, while they think, write, speak, act for the public weal, their own souls may be brought under the saving power of the Gospel, and with all the members of their respective families be made the heirs of the grace of life.

O, that God may bring them all to the knowledge of the truth as it is in Christ Jesus! O, that every one of these Authorities may become a holy, wise, and just man! Then will the laws be enacted in righteousness and executed in the fear of the Lord.

These motives are enforced upon our considerations by the glorious example of the Lord Jesus Christ, who is the Mediator between God and Man, who ever giveth to make intercession for his foes as well as his friends, and with whom there is no respect of persons. Black men, red men, white men, are all alike before Him, and rise or fall, live or die as they please or offend Him.

To make prayers, intercession, supplications, thanksgivings, for national authorities you now clearly see is a command from heaven. Obey it, and you shall be blessed—always do it, and you shall be made a blessing to others. Whom God has blessed no man can curse. If God has blessed this nation, neither internal foes, nor foreign enemies can crush it.

But God will bless it if it will do right, administering justice to each and to all, protecting the weak as well as the strong, and throwing the broad wings of its power equally over men of every color. This is God-like, and God will bless his own image, be it in a nation or in a man. Then, O my country, "shall thy light break forth as the morning—thy health shall spring forth speedily—thy righteousness shall go before thee," and "the glory of the Lord shall by thy reward."

Then shall justice be engraved on our arms, and righteousness on our star-spangled banners; our armies shall then be led to battle by the Lord, and victory secured by the right arm of God.

The Brotherhood of Man[6]

Elias C. Morris   (Gen. 45:4, KJV)

The text and theme which we here present comes down to us from the pa-
triarchs of old. They present to us a rule and sentiment which should find
place in the hearts of every Christian, and should direct our conduct towards our fellow-man, and especially to those who are of the household of
faith wherever dispersed around the globe. The ties of blood relation are
prominent in the beautiful truths presented by the Scriptures, from which
my text is taken. They enable the speaker (Joseph) to rise above all priva-
tions and difficulties of the past and to forgive all the injuries inflicted,
even the jealous, murderous rage of angry brothers who sought his utter
destruction, and enable him to come forward and acknowledge them as his
equals, notwithstanding their impoverished condition. And to remove any
embarrassment which these guilty brothers might feel at a remembrance of
their past conduct towards him, Joseph hastily tells them that it was God's
purpose that he should be thus sent ahead of them, that he might preserve
life. We cannot always understand the purposes or plans of the All-wise
God in his dealings with his people, nor are we at all times prepared to accept willingly the orders of his Providence or the wisdom of his counsel.
But he surely knows what is best for us, for he can see the end from the
beginning, and knows of every obstacle which lies in our path, from the
cradle to the grave. One of the hymn-writers has rightfully said:

> Judge not the Lord by feeble sense,
> But trust him for his grace;
> Behind a frowning providence
> he hides a smiling face.

Joseph, who is the central figure in my text, was at an early age the
fondest hope of an aged but indulgent parent, and was the brightest gem
in a pious home, which fact was the cause of his brothers' hatred. But the
fact that his mind was susceptible of Divine revelations which you perhaps
would call dreams, added to the hatred which they had for him, and so
fierce became their rage that they plotted among themselves to kill him. But
the counsel of Reuben prevailed and they cast him into a pit, and as they
were eating they lifted up their eyes and saw a company of Ishmaelites.
They took Joseph out of the pit and sold him to these traders who were on
their way to Egypt, etc. Perhaps the darkest part of the picture which I shall
attempt to draw, is where an effort is made to deceive the aged father and
lead him to believe that Joseph had been destroyed by some wild beast, etc.
Those who traffic in human flesh lose their respect for pious, consecrated
humanity and will resort to any kind of diabolism to cover up their crimes.

Slavery has existed in some form or other in nearly all ages of the past.
But in some instances it proved to be a blessing in disguise, while in other
it formed some of the most blood-curdling, revolting scenes in the history
of the world. It has separated husband and wife, parents and children,

brother and sister, and broken the cords of affection which nature and nature's God have entwined around the hearts of a happy family. But these cruel separations do not, in all cases, last forever. Sometimes they are of short duration and work for the persecuted party "a far more exceeding and eternal weight of glory." When the God-appointed time came around that the brothers of Joseph should meet with him whom they had sold, and there be humiliated by their own conduct toward him, he brings forward all the true manhood in his great soul and says, "Now therefore be not grieved, nor angry with yourselves, that ye sold me hither; for God did send me before you to preserve life."

The theme of our discourse carries us beyond blood relationship and introduces us to an unexplored field of humanity which recognizes one common Father—God, and one common brother—man.

THE BROTHERHOOD OF MAN NOT A NEW DOCTRINE

The doctrine of the brotherhood of man is sustained both by law and by grace. But the church has apparently gone to sleep upon this great doctrine and allowed political, economical and social questions to relegate it to the background, thereby silencing one of the most effective weapons of the Christian religion. The opponents of this heaven-appointed doctrine have endeavored to create a prejudice against it by claiming that it teaches the social equality of the races and classes, and we are forced to admit that they have, in a measure, been successful. For many so-called Christians are so very reserved in their manner of worship that they refuse to come in contact with the common people, for fear that they will have to otherwise associate with them. But, my friends, this doctrine does not teach the social equality of the races nor the classes, beyond that rule given to the world by the Son of God, which says, "Therefore, all things whatsoever ye would that men should do to you, do ye even so to them." Hence, your sociality is based upon your own choice. If you do not desire the association of men of a different race or class, you are not required to associate with them. But is there not a difference between our social and religious life? Is not every man our brother who has accepted Christ Jesus as his Saviour? The Syro-Phoenician woman had no legal, social or racial rights which would warrant her in approaching the Son of God, but she had a religious right, and she contended for that right. Christ is not the Saviour of any particular race or class, but "whosoever will may take the water of life freely."

Class and race antipathy has been carried so far in this great Christian country of ours, that it has almost destroyed the feeling of that common brotherhood, which should permeate the soul of every Christian believer, and has shorn the Christian Church of that power and influence which it would otherwise have, if it had not repudiated this doctrine. The Apostle Peter is a notable example of those who believed that racial lines should direct in the conduct of the preaching of the Gospel of Jesus Christ. But when God had convinced him by suspending a great vessel from heaven which enclosed all manner of four-footed beasts, creeping things and fowls of the air, he at once confessed his ignorance and went with the men who sought him. And when they had come to the house of Cornelius, Peter said, "Ye know how that it is an unlawful thing for a man that is a Jew to keep company, or come unto one of another nation; but God hath shewed me that I should not call any man common or unclean," etc., etc. Cornelius tells Peter for what purpose he calls him, etc. Peter answers and says, "Of a truth I perceive that God is no respecter of persons." While Paul waited at Athens for Silas and Timotheus, whom he had sent for, and, seeing the idolatry of the city, it caused his very soul to yearn for an opportunity to declare unto the people the Gospel of Jesus Christ. His earnest and fearless presentation of the truths of the Gospel brought out certain philosophers of the Epicureans and of the Stoics, who said to Paul what such persons will say today when the truth is given without compromise or apology, "May we know what this new doctrine, whereof thou speaketh, is?" After Paul's mild rebuke of their ignorant or misguided worship of the unknown God, he proceeds to tell them that God "hath made of one blood all nations of men for to dwell on all the face of the earth." The whole world is to-day indebted to Paul for the prominence he gave to this all-important doctrine at Mars Hill. We know that the doctrine is not a popular one and that none can accept and practice it, except such as are truly regenerated. But the man who has been brought into the new and living way by the birth which is from above, by contrasting his own depraved and sinful nature with the pure, immaculate character of the Son of God after mediating what that matchless Prince underwent for him, can get inspiration and courage to acknowledge every man his brother who has enlisted under the banner of the Cross, and accepted the same Christ as his Saviour.

For nearly nineteen hundred years the church has been upon the field, and has been opposed by all the powers that the adversary could marshal. No opportunity has been or is overlooked, or passed, by those who are opposed to the principles of Christianity, but all are brought into play to weaken it, even to the equality of the races and the classes. But, sad to say, many church members have too often sided with the world, and especially so when this doctrine of the fatherhood of God and the brotherhood of man is presented. In the beginning only two classes were considered, Jews and Gentiles.

But with the multiplicity of religions has come a multiplicity of races and classes, and so prominent have the lines of caste been, that many Christians of the same faith cannot worship at the same altar; that God, who is no respecter of persons, is not pleased with the service which his chosen ambassadors are rendering, and he will not always chide. The commission which he gives is without regard to race, color or condition, but is that the Gospel be preached to every creature, not over the telephone or through the medium of the phonograph, but by the human voice, coming in direct contact with the people, all the people. If they are low, take their hands and lift them up. If too high, call them down. "Christ Jesus came into the world to save sinners," not white sinners, nor black sinners, nor red sinners, but sinners. The wise man Solomon who doubtless had an eye single to the division and opinions of men, where class is arrayed against class, and race against race, looked beyond the active scenes of life back to Mother Earth from whence we all were taken, and back to which we all must go, and says, "The rich and the poor meet together; the Lord is the maker of them all."

But let us not despair: the church will make to righteousness and put on her beautiful garments and her ministers will, ere long, declare that there be no North, no South, no East and no West; no black and no white, but we shall be one in Christ Jesus. And the complete fulfillment of that prophecy concerning Israel will be made manifest in his redeemed, which says, "After those days, saith the Lord, I will put my law in their inward parts, and write it in their hearts; and will be their God, and they shall be my people. And they shall teach no more every man his neighbor, and every man his brother, saying, Know the Lord: for they shall all know me, from the least of them unto the greatest of them."

When the Christians at Galatia were divided over this perplexing question, Paul said to them, "For as many of you as have been baptized into Christ have put on Christ," and again, "There is neither Jew nor Greek, there is neither bond nor free, there is neither male nor female: for ye all are one in Christ Jesus."

WHAT THE CHURCH WILL DO IN THE TWENTIETH CENTURY

Already the great evangelical churches are lining up for more effectual work in the coming century. And this means to me that the white man, the black man, the red man, the yellow man, all who enlist under the banner of the Cross, will form one mighty army to go mightily against the power of darkness and with the great battering ram of the Gospel pitched, as it were, upon the universal brotherhood of man, break down the strong tower of Satan until this government, as well as all the other kingdoms of the world, shall become the kingdoms of our God and his Christ, and he shall reign forever.

What Makes You So Strong?[7]

Jeremiah A. Wright, Jr.   (Judges 16:4–31, KJV)

What makes you so strong, black man? How is it that 370 years of slavery, segregation, racism, Jim Crow laws, and second-class citizenship cannot wipe out the memory of Imhotep, Aesop, Akhenaten and Thutmose II? What makes you so strong, black man?

How is it that after all this country has done to you, you can still produce a Paul Robeson, a Thurgood Marshall, a Malcolm X (el-Hajj Malik el-Shabazz), a Martin King, and a Ron McNair? What makes you so strong, black man?

This country has tried castration and lynching, miseducation and brainwashing. They have taught you to hate yourself and to look at yourself through the awfully tainted eyeglasses of white Eurocentric lies, and yet you keep breaking out of the prisons they put you in. You break out in a W. E. B. DuBois and a Booker T. Washington; you break out in a Louis Farrakhan and a Mickey Leland; you break out in a Judge Thurgood Marshall and a Pops Staples; you break out in a Luther Vandross, Magic Johnson, Michael Jordan, Harold Washington, or a Doug Wilder. What makes you so strong, black man?

I don't care what field we pick, you produce a giant in that field. What makes you so strong? The world tried the poisons of self-hatred, of distorted history, of false standards of beauty. They taught you that you were ugly and stupid, slow and retarded, dim-witted and dull-witted, good only for stud service and getting high, and yet you keep on turning out a Sterling Brown and Vincent Harding, a Jim Forbes and Kwame Nkrumah, an Allan Boesak and William Gray, a Steve Biko and Bill Cosby, a Dave Dinkins and Doug Wilder. What makes you so strong, black man?...

And what makes you so strong, black woman? How could you produce a Queen Hatshepsut whose reign was one of the most outstanding in the Eighteenth Dynasty of Egypt. This African queen ruled powerfully, masterfully, and with dignity fifteen hundred years before our Lord Jesus Christ was born. How could you produce the warrior queens of Ethiopia and Nubia and the five fine queens known as Candace who opposed the southward movement of the armies of Alexander the Great and changed the whole course of Greek history? What makes you so strong, black woman?

How is it that 370 years of being used as a breeder and a toy for the master, and being used as a punching bag for Willie Lee, and being messed on and messed over, walked on and walked out on—how is it that 370 years of that does not kill the spirit of Queen Ann Nzinga; Cleopatra; Nefertiti; Makeda, the Queen of Sheba; Mary, the mother of Jesus; and Hadassah, the rebel queen who defiantly said, "If I perish, I perish"? What makes you so strong, black woman?

How is it that after all this world has done to you, after all white women have done to you, after all white men have done to you, after all black men have done to you, you can still produce an Angela Davis, a Toni Morrison, a Barbara Jordan, a Betty Shabazz, an Oprah Winfrey, and a Winnie Mandela. What makes you so strong, black woman?

This country has tried negation and degradation. They have taught you to look down on your broad hips and thick lips. They've taught you to hate your hair and to keep it at all costs from going back. Going back to what? Africa? Going back to the way God made it? To what? They have taught you that the less you look like "Miss Ann," the worse off you are. And yet you keep breaking out of the prisons they put you in. You break out in a Nannie Burroughs, a Fannie Lou Hamer, and a Jessie "Ma" Houston. You break out in a Roberta Flack, an Anita Baker, a Jackie Joyner-Kersee and a Nina Simone. I don't care what field we pick, you black women keep turning out giants in the field, even those fields they told you were reserved for men only. What makes you so strong, black woman?

They told you that you were not allowed in the field of medicine, and here you come with a black M.D. graduating from medical school in the 1800s. What makes you so strong, black woman? They told you that no black women were allowed in the field of ministry, and here you come with the Reverends Jini Moore, Gwenn Pierre, Barbara Williams, Lola Nelson, Devanah Johns, Lana Reese, LaVerne Harris, Mickey Moseley, the Reverend Joan Campbell, and Bishop Barbara Harris. What makes you so strong, black woman? They told you no women were allowed in the male-dominated field of TV journalism, and here you come with a Melanie Lawson and an Oprah Winfrey. They tried the poison of low self-esteem; they tried the poison of low expectations; they tried the poison of lesbianism; they tried the poison of despair. They told you the numbers aren't there— the brothers are in prison, on dope, unemployed. And what do you do? You refuse to give up. You keep on turning out Zora Neale Hurstons and Mari Evanses, Maryse Condes and Gladys Knights. You keep on turning out Winnie Mandelas and the mothers of Zimbabwe, the mothers of Soweto, the mothers of Angola, the mothers of Namibia, the mothers of Mississippi. What makes you so strong, black woman?

What makes you so strong, black people? No other race was brought to this country in chains. No other race had laws passed making it a crime to teach them how to read. No other race had skin color as the determining factor of their servitude and their employability. No other race was hounded and haunted when they wanted to be free. No other race was physically mutilated to identify them as property, not people. No other race was lied to and lied on like the African race. No other race had its names taken away in addition to its language and music. No other race was denied more and deprived of more, treated as badly and treated as less than human. No other race was treated like the Africans were treated, and yet no other race has done so much after starting out with so little, defying all of the odds and breaking all of the records. What makes you so strong, black people? How were you able to do what? Jimmy the Greek wants to know. Tom Brokaw wants to know. Ted Koppel wants to know. Geraldo wants to know. I have a feeling that Oprah Winfrey already knows. What makes you so strong, black people?

How were you able to build the great pyramids of Cheops? How were you able to build the grand lodge of Maat? How were you able to build the first universities in the world? How were you able to survive the horrors of slavery, to survive the loss of two hundred million in the Atlantic Ocean, to survive the hatred of Europeans, to survive a holocaust five times worse than Hitler's holocaust, and to then take a Jesse Owens over on Hitler's turf and stick it in Hitler's ear? How were you able to do that? What makes you so strong, black people? Is it something in your African blood? Is it something in your African psyche? Is it something in your African soul? Is it something in your African spirit? What makes you so strong, black people?

Samson's Weakness

How is it that you keep coming? You see, that was Delilah's question. And one of Samson's problems was that he answered her question. If you read this whole biography of Samson, you discover that Samson had several problems. He never did get that love thing straight. Samson was reared in a God-fearing home. His mother and father were together. He had a strong male role model, but he never could pull off that right combination in terms of a committed relationship. Dr. Jawanze Kunjufu of our church would say that his focus was on the outside, the external, and not on the inside, the internal.

Samson ruled Israel for twenty years, and he ruled during some tough times. His people were under oppression. His people were constantly under attack. They were assaulted by the twin demons of assimilation and segregation. Though Samson ruled successfully for twenty years politically, he never was quite able to put it all together in his personal life. He kept being attracted to girls of another race. (It's in the book.) And he kept acting on those attractions as if they were love. First, he had his mother and daddy set up a marriage with somebody he didn't even know. Why would you do that, Samson? "Cause she looked good and makes me feel good." Then he tried sex without commitment. He went to bed with a prostitute.

He was able to judge disputes between conflicting parties; he was able to judge lawsuits—civil suits and criminal suits. He was able to administer the office of judge with prudence and integrity. He had twenty years of service on the bench with no bribes, no deals, no tarnish on his integrity. He was a judge of Israel for two decades in an oppressive and hostile situation. He judged a people who sometimes turned on each other rather than turning to each other. He judged a people whom sociologists would say were a permanent underclass, with no chance for survival or success. He was brilliant in his political life, but he bombed out in his personal life. He was absolutely no judge of character and a complete failure when it came to judging the opposite sex or choosing relationships with them.

After a marriage that did not work out and after a hooker who set him up, he saw another fine woman with a body by Fisher, and he was hooked. Everyone has got a certain weakness in life. Well, good looks and good sex just happened to be Samson's weaknesses. Not once does the Scripture say that Delilah cared anything at all about him. She had men waiting in another room. But he didn't care; he loved her. She looked good and she made him feel good—a transient reality. Not only did she not feel the same way, she made it plain that money meant more to her than a man. But even after she tricked him three times, Samson kept right on going back. Love wouldn't let him wait, and love wouldn't let him think. Then again, Samson did not know the difference between love and lust, between looking good and feeling good. You see, love is internal; looks and lust are external.

Contract or Covenant

Samson had some problems, but his biggest problem was that he answered Delilah's question. He told somebody who didn't care anything about him, and who had made that obvious, that which was of ultimate importance in his life. The King James Version of that passage says, "he told her all his heart" (Judges 16:17). The Hebrew word is *leb*, connoting feeling, will, intellect, the center of everything. Dr. John Kinney, Dean and Associate Professor of Theological Studies at Virginia Union School of Theology said, "Can't nobody but God keep your whole heart. You don't give your whole heart to nobody but God." And Kinney was just echoing what Jesus said: "Thou shalt love the Lord thy God with all thy heart" (Matthew 22:37, KJV).

You see, nobody can keep your heart like God can. Oh, a person can tug at your heart strings and make your heart heavy or happy. A person can hurt your heart or break your heart. He can make your heart skip a beat; she can make your heart glad or sad, but nobody can keep your whole heart. Nobody can handle it. Only God has hands big enough to handle your whole heart.

What makes you so strong, Samson? How can you say you love me if you won't tell me what makes you so strong? How can you say you love me if you won't go to bed with me? How can you say you love me if you won't try this cocaine with me? How can you say say you love me if you won't buy this thing for me? How can you say you love me if you won't do like I ask? Watch those if clauses. If you get an *if* clause in the relationship, that's a contract, and love isn't a contract; love is a covenant.

Dr. Jawanza Kunjufu said his grandmama put it this way: "I make sure I give 110 percent every day. It ain't about what he gives; I got to make sure I give all I got every day." You see, that's a covenant. It's not *if … then*; it's *nevertheless, in spite of, anyhow.* There's a book called *The Dance-Away Lover* that talks about the three stages in relationships. There is the romance stage in all relationships, and we like that. There's the problem stage; then there's the commitment stage. To reach the commitment stage, you have to move from romance through problems, down to commitment.

But what do we do? We enjoy the romance stage, and then as soon as we run into problems we dance away and find ourselves another lover.

A covenant is moving past romance through problems. That's commitment. I'm committed *nevertheless*; I'm committed *in spite of*; I'm committed *anyhow*. I'm not going anywhere because I'm going to have problems everywhere. Why? Because I'm going there and I'm taking some problems with me. That's commitment and covenant.

Second, that same person who lights up your life and starts the juices flowing is the one who is going to get on your last nerve. The same person does both. Samson didn't know that. He was only a good judge of matters of the head. He didn't know too much about matters of the heart. Maybe his Nazirite vow kept him from nurturing those relationships that would have taught him about the heart. So when Delilah pulled that *if ... then* trick on him, she had him. How can you say you love me if you won't tell me what makes you so strong? She vexed him, the King James Version says, until he told her his whole heart, that which was of ultimate importance in life. He told her what my mama used to call the God's honest truth!

Guard God's Will for Your Life

Samson revealed his secret to his enemy (to this one who cared nothing about him). He told her about his special relationship with God. He allowed his desire for her to take precedence over his devotion to God. Watch out! Don't let what somebody can do to you or do for you become more important than what God wants to do *in* you and *through* you. You see, God had set the terms for Samson's life and his labors long before Samson was born. God had set up the relationship between his servant and himself before Samson drew his first breath. God had a work to do in and through Samson. That's why he sent the angel to announce what he had on his mind.

You see, God has a work that he wants to do through African Americans—a people who have known hatred, yet who still have the strength to love; a people who have known degradation, yet who still have the strength to stand tall and produce giant after giant in field after field; a people who have known belittlement and humiliation, yet who have maintained their integrity and kept their souls intact; a people who have been lied to, lied on, and lied about, yet who still have the strength to forgive and to build strong families, regardless of those families' configuration. God has a work of redemption and healing to do through African Americans. God will do through you individually, not only corporately. Don't you know that God only made one of you, and that God pulled off a miracle when he put you together and then threw away the pattern? Watch out for what somebody can do *to* you and *for* you. Don't let that become more important than what our God wants to do *in* you and *through* you. Samson allowed a relationship that he wanted to have but could not have get in the way of the relationship that he already had with God.

They'll Put You in Chains

Samson revealed his secret to his enemy; he told Delilah about his relationship with God. Then he shared with her that which symbolized his special relationship with God. See what happens when you reveal your whole heart to others? First, they put you in chains. You give them your heart; they chain your body and then your mind. As Dr. Carter G. Woodson and Dr. Bobby Wright would both say: They can take the chains off your bodies and have absolutely nothing to fear from your mind.

Dr. Woodson said it this way: "If you tell a person to go to the back door over and over again, then one day you say, 'You no longer have to go to the back door,' do you know what that person will do? He will not only go to the back door, but if there is not one back there, he'll cut one in."

Bobby Wright was a little more earthy in saying it this way: "If they can put the chains on your mind, your behind will follow." They can chain your mind and have nothing to fear from your body. They put you in chains philosophically and psychologically. They tell you, "You ain't nothing. You ain't done nothing. Your daddy before you wasn't nothing, and your mama ain't nothing. You ain't come from nothing; you got nothing to offer, and you ain't never gonna amount to nothing."

They'll trap you in vocational training, half teaching you a skill that you can never use. They'll put you in chains sociologically, giving you the poorest schools and the worst equipment. They'll give you the worst housing at the highest cost. You'll get the lowest paying jobs, but the most whiskey, drugs and guns so you can kill each other and save them the trouble.

They'll put you in chains theologically and have you worship their god, *Dagon*. Only we don't call him Dagon anymore; we call him "Dough-sky" (Prosperity). "All that God has you can get. Come on. Just send me five dollars and I'll send you a blessed cloth. You can have it! You can have it!" They'll put you in chains theologically and have you worshiping an alien theology.

They'll Blind You

Keep reading this passage. They'll put your eyes out so you can't even see what's happening to you. You can't see the psychological chains, the physiological chains, the economic chains, the educational chains, the sociological chains, or even the drug addiction chains they've put you through. Do you know what happens when you can't see? You, the victims, become the staunchest supporters of a sick system of perpetual slavery because you can't see what the enemy has done and keeps on doing to you. Sterling Brown wrote about that half a century ago when he said, "They bought off some of your leaders, and you stumbled as blind men will."

They put chains on you. They put your eyes out. Then look at verses 24 and 25. They led Samson out and paraded him in front of the nation to make fun of him. They'll parade you on television documentaries and news shows. They'll parade you as the primary example of pathology in

America. They'll parade you as the user and the victim of the drugs that they brought into the country in the first place. Why is it that with a drug czar and the millions of dollars that we spend to fight drugs, we can't stop drugs from coming into the country? But they parade you as the primary victims. They shout, "Bring him out. Let him entertain us. You know his kind always make the best entertainers."

They made fun of Samson because of what they had done to him. They made fun of him because he used to be so strong, and now, because of his desire for one of their women, he was reduced to a nothing and a nobody. You think that's only in the Bible? Look at what they did to Senator Brooke. They made fun of Samson because he couldn't see where he was, couldn't see what was happening to him, and couldn't see where he was going. He had to be led around by a little boy. It might be that the little black children will be the ones to get us blind old folks out of this mess we've gotten ourselves into. They made fun of Samson because they had in chains the one who used to whip them. He was a part of their prison system, and they weren't about to let him go. "Call Samson out and make him entertain us!"

The Symbol Is Not the Source

But the thing that Delilah missed, and that his enemy missed, was the whole answer to what made him so strong. You see, they mistook the symbol of his strength for the source of his strength. They didn't listen to his whole answer. His hair was the symbol, not the source. Look at his whole answer. He said, "My hair has never been cut." That's a symbol. Why? "Because I have been dedicated to God as a Nazirite from the time I was born." Now that's the source of his strength. The last verse of chapter 13 says, "The LORD's power began to strengthen him." But the Hebrew says the *ruah*, the Spirit of the Lord, began to move him.

In chapter 14, when a lion attacked (v. 6), it says again the *ruah*, the Spirit of the Lord, came upon him. In chapter 15, when he grabbed that jawbone of an ass, verse 14 says the *ruah*, the Spirit of the Lord, came mightily upon him. The source of his strength was God, and the *ruah*, the Spirit of God. So he prayed (16:28) after his hair, the symbol of strength, began to grow back, "Lord, try me one more time. I know I let you down before, but try me just one more time. Give me my strength just this one more time." What he's asking for is God's Spirit, the *ruah*, God's strength, not his own.

What makes us so strong? God's strength. David answered the question: "God is our refuge and strength." What makes us so strong? Isaiah answered the question: "He giveth power to the faint; and to them that have no might he increaseth strength." God is the source of our strength.

What makes us so strong? The same thing that empowered Martin King. Not the school in Boston, but God's Spirit; not what he learned at Crozer, but God's Spirit; not what he learned in seminary, but God's Spirit. Martin was the man he was because of the Spirit of God.

What makes us so strong? God is the joy and strength of my life. When I don't have any strength, I call on him who is my strength. When I can't make it on my own, I call on the one who can make a way out of no way. *Father, I stretch my hands to thee. No other help I know. If thou withdraw thyself from me, whither shall I go?*

The Lord is my strength and my salvation. This applies to preachers, too. People have their preferences when it comes to preachers. Some people like preachers with manuscripts; others like preachers without manuscripts. Some like preachers who can "tune" a little while, and all of that kind of stuff. But let me tell you something: this preaching business isn't as easy as it looks. Sometimes I don't feel like preaching. Sometimes my spirit is too impoverished to preach. I've been in some churches in this country where the folk are so cold they kill my spirit. Sometimes they do it with the music. And so I've had, on occasion, to disrupt a service. Once I stood up in a prestigious university chapel and began to spontaneously sing the way my grandmama used to sing, "Guide my feet, Lord, while I run this race, 'cause I don't want to run this race in vain." Folks started looking at their programs trying to figure out where this came in. While I was singing my grandmama's song, I could feel my grandmama's spirit (she used to sing that song while she rocked me on her knee) getting all into my spirit. I could feel her hooking up with the Holy Ghost and passing him down to me.

Our strength comes from the Spirit of God. This same Spirit of God will empower you as he empowered our Lord, Jesus Christ. Jesus promised that he would give the Spirit to you. He has never failed on any of his promises. This is what makes us so strong.

Unexpected Blessings[8]

Jeremiah A. Wright, Jr.   (Mark 1:21–31, KJV)

Have you ever been engaged in your normal routine when all of a sudden the Lord stepped in and blessed that situation beyond your wildest dreams? I like to call those instances the times of unexpected blessings.

The biblical record is replete with instances of unexpected blessings. In Genesis 21, Abraham and Sarah, who were way past the childbearing years (she was ninety, and he was one hundred), experienced one of God's unexpected blessings: a child. Sarah said, "God has brought me joy and laughter."

In Exodus 3, an African prince who was guilty of murder and was a fugitive from justice lived in exile far away from the scene of the crime and way out of the jurisdiction of the court, with arrest warrants out on him and the statute of limitations passed in another time, in another country, in another life. With a new identity, Moses was happily married to a raven-black beauty and had several children. One day as he was tending his father-in-law's sheep on the back side of a mountain in Midian, he ran into one of God's unexpected blessings: a bush on fire and not on fire all at the same time. A voice unlike any other voice ever heard, coming from a God with a name as mysterious as the voice, was compelling him to lead his people—an unexpected blessing.

In 1 Samuel 1, a woman named Hannah prayed boldly for a child, but not just any child "as long as it's healthy." Instead, she was bold in her praying and told God she wanted a son. The prayer was answered, but far beyond her expectations. The boy she was given was to become the last of Israel's great judges. The boy who was born became the bridge between a judge named Samson and a king named Saul. The boy who was born (Samuel was his name) was the one called by God in Eli's house. Samuel was the one chosen by God to anoint and ordain the first two monarchs of the United Kingdom of Israel. Samuel was the one for whom all of Israel mourned for twenty-five years. Samuel was more than Hannah expected. He was an unexpected blessing.

The biblical record is replete with instances of unexpected blessings. Solomon prayed for wisdom, and God surprised him with unexpected blessings: more wealth, more treasure, and more fame than any king before him or after him. (See 2 Chronicles 1.)

A preacher named Isaiah, who was just doing his job up at the church house in the year that King Uzziah died, became the recipient of an unexpected blessing. You expect to be near God when you come into God's holy temple. You expect to feel God's presence when you cross over into holy precincts. That's because he promised that "where two or three are gathered in my name, I am there …"[9] But Isaiah was blessed by the unexpected. He saw the Lord, high and lifted up, sitting on his throne with his train filling the temple. Isaiah saw the seraphim on fire with six wings—two covering his face, two covering his body, and two keeping it hovering in flight. He heard them hollering "Holy, holy, holy" back and forth with voices that shook the foundation, and he felt a hot burning coal taken from the altar and placed on his lips—cleansing, but not burning. Isaiah on an ordinary day up in the Lord's house was met in an extraordinary way and blessed with unexpected blessings beyond his wildest dreams.

The biblical record is replete with instances of unexpected blessings—folks following their normal routine, doing what it is they usually do, when all of a sudden the Lord steps in and blesses in ways that could not have been imagined. Therefore, it comes as no surprise that in the first chapter of Mark's Gospel there is one more instance of the Lord stopping by with unexpected blessings.

First, the passage says, "They went to Capernaum," the prophet Nahum's village, and the place where Jesus made his home away from home. He was originally, you'll remember, from Nazareth. But the folks in Nazareth were like the folks in our hometowns: they knew Jesus *when*. Because they knew Jesus *when*, they would not let him be what God wanted him to be. Not in their town. So he moved to Capernaum. His roots were in Nazareth, but he made his home in Capernaum. We find him in this passage on the Lord's day in the Lord's house. And I like that. Jesus went to church. A man—all man—in church.

Jesus Demonstrates the Importance of Worshiping at Church

Jesus went to church to worship God. In verse 35 of this chapter he is out all by himself, alone and praying. But this passage begins with him in the church. In fact, verse 39 says that wherever he went, whatever town he was in, the Lord's day found him in the Lord's house.

And when you read all of the biographies of Martin Luther King, that's one thing they omit. They talk about his training in Boston, his training at Crozer, his training at Morehouse. But King was a preacher. He went to church.

If Jesus went to church, don't you know a whole lot of people are on their way to hell believing that "you don't have to go to church." That's only half right. Let me give you the other half. You can worship God away from the church. You can worship God wherever you are. But you don't do one to the exclusion of the other. It is not either/or; it is both/and. You worship God both in the church and when you are away from the church. You don't stay away from the church and call yourself a follower of him who, wherever he was, went to church. No. It doesn't work like that. If Jesus went to church, who, in the name of all that is holy, do you think you are? Are you better than Jesus?

So we find Jesus in Capernaum, in the Lord's house, on the Lord's day—Jesus in church. And then look at what happened. A man with an evil spirit came into the church.

The Devil Comes to Church, Too

The devil comes to church, too. I tell the folks at my church all the time, "The devil ain't got no other way of getting to church except we bring him." He came with this man in verse 23. Don't you know the devil will ride in your BMW, ride in your Mercedes Benz, get on public transportation right along with you, and when you get inside of the church, he'll break out all over the congregation. And you'll be wondering, "How did the devil get in the church?" He came with y'all. That's how.

Dr. Martin Marty, one of my mentors at the University of Chicago, told of a young white pastor and one of his old black female parishioners (the pastor pastored in a black community). On some Sundays this old woman would say, "Reverend, you sure did *teach* today. Umph, umph, umph!" Then on other Sundays she'd say, "You sure did *preach* today. Umph, umph!" One day this young pastor asked her, "Sister, what do you mean when you say I *teach*, and how is that different from when you say I *preach*?" The old woman said, "Well, Pastor, when you teach, God has given you something that you give me and I can use it for that day and later on in the week, and get through the week—when you *teach*." She said, "When you *preach*, I can just feel God's presence, and he's hugging you real tight and he's pleased. You don't necessarily give me nothin' I can use, but I can feel God hugging you, and through you I can feel God hugging me. That's when you *preach*."

Then Marty said one Sunday when this pastor was severely upset by some political situation, he came and vented his spleen in what he thought was an excellently articulated exposition of God's will for that particular existential moment. At the door, this old woman said, "Reverend, I could feel God hugging you real close today, but I don't think he was pleased. In fact, it felt like he was crying while he was holding you tight." That's another way of saying the devil does come to church, sometimes with the parishioners and sometimes with the preacher. However the devil comes, he does come.

You see, the church is the primary recruiting station for the devil (a lot of church folks don't understand this). The devil does not need to go to a cocaine party. He's got those folks. He doesn't have to go there! Here's where folks are in danger of slipping away, so the devil comes to church and gets real busy.

"Just then," the Scripture says, "while Jesus was teaching," giving folks something to hold onto, something they could use in their lives, something to make a difference in the way they approached each day ... while he was teaching like no one else ever taught (even the officers sent to arrest him said, "No man ever spoke like this man!"[10] just then (verse 23) a man with an evil spirit came into the church.

Oh, the devil comes to church, all right, but he is no match for Jesus. Jesus can whip the devil every time. When Jesus gets in you, and you get in Jesus, in the Spirit, on the Lord's day, what does the Bible say? "Resist the devil and he will flee from you."[11] When you get in the Spirit and the Spirit gets in you, the devil acts like he's seen a ghost. And he has. He's seen the Holy Ghost. The devil is no match for the Spirit of Christ Jesus. The church folks say this man has authority to give orders to evil spirits and they obey him. The devil may come to church, but he's no match for the one who is Lord of the church, the one who said, "Upon this rock I will build my church; and the gates of hell shall not prevail against it."[12]

Taking Jesus Home

Immediately after church Jesus, his disciples, including James and John, left the church and went straight to Peter's and Andrew's house. Can you imagine taking Jesus home with you after church? There's some good news here in this passage for the married folks and the single folks. A lot of us like that part about being in the Spirit on the Lord's day, in the Lord's house, but at benediction time, too often for us, it's "Later on, Jesus. Catch you next Sunday." This passage suggests something new for some of us to try: taking Jesus home after church. Are you married like Peter? Take Jesus home to where you live—up close with somebody who knows all your warts and flaws and to where being a Christian ain't all that easy. Or are you single like Andrew? Take Jesus home to see those private places that we keep so well hidden from the probing public. Can you imagine what it would be like to take Jesus home with you tonight? Would you have to straighten up the place? Or would you have to straighten up your life?

Imagine Jesus sitting at the table with you, watching you serve roasted preacher and warmed-over gossip. Imagine Jesus browsing through your books and your magazines, even the ones that you keep hidden. Imagine Jesus turning on your VCR to see what it is you watch when the children are asleep. Jesus standing in the kitchen, listening to you talking on the phone; Jesus hearing all you say and seeing all you do. Not up here, where you've got all your holy hats on, shouting "Praise the Lord," but at home, when your hair is down and your shoes are off, and the real you is just hanging all out.

Peter and Andrew took the Lord home, and what they experienced was an unexpected blessing. Peter had a wife. After all, you can't have a mother-in-law unless you have a wife. And here is Jesus all up in the midst of Peter's marriage. I've often thought that one of the reasons Peter wept so bitterly, as it is recorded in the denial scenes,[13] was perhaps because of his memories about Jesus' impact on his marriage and family life. It may be that Peter remembered a loving relationship with his wife who, like a good friend, understood his compelling imperative to leave home for a period of time and follow Jesus; he may have had that kind of love in his marriage.

Memories will bring tears to your eyes—memories of the kind of love that can only come when two people who are in love and, who because of that love, make a home together and grow from what each gives to the other. Those kinds of memories will bring tears to your eyes—memories of a love so deep that one of the African tribes has no word for it. They call this type of love a "hurting in the heart." This hurt in the heart is so profound that just talking to the person on the phone starts you smiling, grinning, and acting silly. And ain't nobody in the room but you. Memories will bring tears to your eyes—memories of a shared moment of silence, perhaps in an embrace when nobody says a word, and just a hot tear of joy from cheek to chest says it all; memories of how life has taught you that love does not consist of gazing at each other, but in looking outward together in the same direction.

To have a reservoir of memories to fall back on when disaster hits is to be fortified against defeatism and despair. And to have Jesus as an integral part of your marriage, in your home, in your prayer life, in your private life, in your plan making and your lovemaking ... Lord have mercy! No wonder Peter broke down.

Peter had a good thing, and the Lord was the center of his life and ministry. He took the Lord home and experienced an unexpected blessing.

It is not recorded anywhere that Andrew had a wife. But neither is it recorded anywhere that Andrew was defective or disadvantaged. First, he was the one who brought Peter to the Lord; and second, Jesus in this passage is in his home just as much as he is in Peter's home. Peter and Andrew, married and single, took the Lord home, and what they experienced was an unexpected blessing.

When they got home, Scripture says, Peter's mother-in-law was sick. No doubt she had been sick that morning when the others left for church. But they went to church anyhow. They had seen the Lord work in a marvelous way up at the church house, as the Lord will do every now and then. But then after church, they were going home and, if anything, the home situation had gotten worse. And isn't that how it is with us? Sometimes we leave home on Sundays, and things are in a turmoil. We meet the Lord at the Lord's house, and the Lord works in a mighty way in our souls, and we feel good; we feel great. Sometimes it feels like we've seen the seraphim that Isaiah saw. When we leave church, we can just feel the Lord hugging us and holding us, but when we get back home, things are no longer in a turmoil. They're in an uproar. Sometimes we hate to go home, because we know what's waiting for us there. But when you take Jesus home with you expect the unexpected.

The Lord Can Do Anything, Anywhere

When the churchgoers got home, Peter's mother-in-law was in bed with a fever. Somebody told Jesus about the situation. James Rowe composed a hymn about telling Jesus your problems. He wrote:

> Just tell Jesus, tell him all.
> Trials great and trials small.
> He will share them, freely bear them.
> Just tell Jesus, tell him all.

Elisha Hoffman put it another way in his hymn:

> I must tell Jesus all of my trials,
> I cannot bear these burdens alone;
> In my distress He kindly will help me,
> He ever loves and cares for His own.

When they took Jesus home and somebody told him about the situation he went straight to Peter's mother-in-law, touched her, took her by the hand, and helped her up. One touch and the fever was gone.

Now this passage says at least two things that I want to impress upon you. First, it says the Lord works in your own house just like he works in the church house. If you meet the Lord here (in church) and take him there, he is as anxious to be with you there as he is to meet you here, and he will bless you unexpectedly.

The second thing this passage says is that Jesus is good for whatever ails you. The Bible does not say what the ailment was that had Peter's mother-in-law down. It doesn't say what the condition was that gave her a fever, and I'm glad it doesn't because in not saying, what it is saying is that Jesus can relieve any kind of suffering.

If you're sick, Jesus can make you well. Even if you're dying, Jesus can make up your dying bed. If you're depressed, Jesus can get you up. If you're down, Jesus can pick you up. If you've fallen, Jesus can hold you up. If you're in sin, Jesus can fix you up. Tempted and tried? Jesus can give you the victory. Where you're weak and defeated, his grace is still sufficient. Stained from sin? His blood can still wash you. In need of a savior? He still saves from the guttermost to the uttermost. He is good for whatever ails you. It does not make any difference what your situation is. If Jesus touches you, he'll bless you in really unexpected ways. He'll get you up from wherever you are and fix you up in ways you never imagined.

Praise Yields Unexpected Blessings

But the key to God's using and giving unexpected blessings is lost when we let problems get in the way of praise. Think about how problems in your life cause you to say, "I don't want to pray. Lord, just leave me alone." But when you praise God in spite of problems, it is precious, and it is priceless, and God will bless you unexpectedly. Peter and Andrew went to church anyhow and praised the Lord, and the Lord blessed them. They had a problem at home, but they went to the church to praise.

Dr. Charles Walker[14] tells a story that illustrates this for me. He was holding a revival in New England and the man who was assigned to take him back and forth every night to the hotel was a man who could not speak the king's English. He spoke good African American English, but he couldn't speak the king's English. He never did say "revival" the whole week. He said "vavibal." He said, "Rev., that 'vavibal' blessed me." The last night, as they headed to the airport Charles remarked that though the man didn't speak the king's English, he had "money's mammy." He was driving a Lincoln that was so high that Charles said he couldn't even read those roman numerals. He wore a three-carat diamond pinky ring, Brooks Brothers shoes, and a three-hundred-dollar suit. The man said, "Rev., you don't understand how I got this. I got it by putting the Lord first in my life and praising God in spite of problems."

Charles looked at him and the man continued, "See, folks see a car, they to go get a car. They see a suit and a house, they try to get that. You know the Word says, Rev., 'Seek ye first the kingdom of God and his righteousness, and all these here things will be added unto you.'" The man said, "Let me tell you how I know that's true. Me and my wife been married over forty years. And during the depression I lost my job and we spent all of our life savings." And he said, "One Saturday night (both of us wanted to go to church the next morning and our church were eight miles away from where we lived, the bus fare were ten cents, and we only had fifteen cents to our names), my wife said, 'Honey, tell you what you do. What you do is you walk to church in the morning, and when you get to church you put a nickel in, and when you leave, you'll have a dime to ride back, 'cause it only cost a dime to ride in those days.

"And I got up, and I walked to church. I were tired, but it were a beautiful day, and as I were walking, I just felt blessed because I thought about people who didn't have no legs to walk. When I got to church, as soon as I stepped inside the sanctuary the Holy Ghost said, 'Put the whole fifteen cents in.' And I started arguing with the Lord. I said, 'No, no. No, no. "Seek ye first" don't mean that. I done walked all the way here.'"

The man continued, "The choir started singing the processional. They were singing, 'How I got over. My soul looks back and wonders ...' But all I could hear them singing was, 'Put the whole fifteen cents in.' I stood there arguing with him. We read the responsive Scripture and the Word said, 'O give thanks unto the Lord for he is good.' But all I could see on that page was, 'Put the whole fifteen cents in.' When it came time for the offering, I lost the argument. I was rubbing my dime and my nickel together, and like a drum beating in my head, it kept beating over and over again, 'Put the whole fifteen cents in.' I put it in; I watched that offering plate take our last money in the world further and further away from me.

"But don't you know the Lord blessed me through the Word. The sermon that Sunday were, 'They that wait upon the LORD shall renew their strength; they shall mount up with wings as eagles.'[15] When I left church I felt like one of them eagles. I was feeling good. I were ready to walk that eight miles back home.

"I got one block from the church and a strange lady stopped me. She said, 'Mister, I don't know you, and I don't know if you need work or not, but, here, take this address, and if you do need work they're hiring there tomorrow.' And I said, 'Thank you, Jesus.' I walked another block, and the Spirit of the Lord said, 'Look down.' When I looked down I seen a dime, and I said, 'Thank you, Jesus.'"

He concluded his story: "As soon as I picked the dime up, a bus were coming, and I said, 'Thank you, Jesus.' I got up on the bus, I put my dime in, and the bus driver give me back fifteen cents change. I said, 'Mister, I ain't give you no quarter; I give you a dime.' The bus driver said, 'Shut up, man, and sit down.' I said, 'Thank you, Jesus.'

"I got back home on the Lord's day, blessed by the Lord's Word, blessed by the Lord's work, blessed by the Lord with a job, blessed by the Lord with the same fifteen cents I left home with. And that job I went to the next day to interview, boy, I held that job for thirty-three years. Thank you, Jesus."

God will fix it for you. Won't he fix it? He's a good God!
I thank you, Jesus,
I thank you, Jesus,
I thank you Lord.
Oh, you brought me from a mighty long way
A mighty long way.
I thank you, Jesus.
I thank you, Jesus.
I thank you, Jesus, I thank you Lord.
You brought me from a mighty,
A mighty long way.[16]

To Tell the Truth[27]

Katie G. Cannon   (1 Kings 22:1–38, NRSV)

Our story from 1 Kings 22 is one that deals with the price of honesty at all costs. It begins with King Ahab and King Jehoshaphat coming together to form a treaty. Now, King Ahab, the king of the ten tribes of the north, wanted back his land that had been taken by the king of Aram. So King Ahab asked King Jehoshaphat, the king of the two southern tribes, to join with him in a united front against Aram in order to take back his land. But before King Jehoshaphat would agree to join in King Ahab's war, he demanded that they check out the situation by discovering what God wanted them to do. In other words, King Jehoshaphat said to King Ahab, "Before I am as you are, before my people become your people, before my horses become as your horses, let us first inquire for the word of God" (1 Kings 22:4–5, paraphrased).

King Ahab agreed that it was fitting and proper to find out if God would be on their side in battle. So Ahab, the king of the north, called forth about four hundred prophets into his court, and all four hundred prophets lied to the king. They told King Ahab that there was no doubt he would win the war with a landslide! They assured the king that God was on his side and that he should go up and take back his land. The prophets started chanting, "Go up! Go up to Ramoth-gilead because God will put the land in your hand, O King." King Ahab was quite satisfied with this prophecy because he believed that four hundred prophets, all saying the same thing, could not be wrong.

King Jehoshaphat, though, was still not satisfied, so he asked King Ahab, "Is there not another prophet of God? Isn't there another prophet in your court besides those four hundred, all of whom agreed that you will win against Aram?" King Ahab threw up his hands and said, "Yes, there is yet one man who is a prophet. His name is Micaiah, son of Imlah, but he never prophesies anything good for me; only disaster."

King Ahab sent for Micaiah, the prophet. While the kings waited for Micaiah to arrive, the four hundred other prophets continued to dance and chant, "Go up! Go up, O king, to Ramoth-gilead, because God will put the land in your hand." Meanwhile, the messenger found the prophet Micaiah and told him, "If you value your life, you will agree with the four hundred other prophets and speak favorably by telling King Ahab that he will win in war." But Micaiah said, without fear or trembling, "Whatever God wants me to say, that I will say. Whatever God lays on my heart of hearts to tell the king, that is what I will tell him."

When Micaiah appeared before the kings, Ahab said to him, "Micaiah, shall we go to battle in Ramoth-gilead, or shall we not?" Sarcastically, Micaiah answered King Ahab, "Yeah, go on up and triumph." When the king sensed that Micaiah was playing with him, he said, "How many times must I tell you to say nothing but the truth?" Micaiah replied, "O King, if you go to war, you will be defeated, for I saw all Israel scattered upon the mountains of Gilead, as sheep that have no shepherd. An enticing, lying spirit is in the mouths of the other prophets. If you go to war, God has decreed disaster for you." King Ahab was full of anger. He ordered his guard to throw Micaiah into prison and feed him only reduced rations of bread and water until the battle was won and the king returned, a victor.

King Ahab and King Jehoshaphat prepared their armies to go to war. They went to Ramoth-gilead and waged an all-day battle against the Arameans. About sunset, a cry went up, "King Ahab is dead! King Ahab is dead! Everyone to his own city; everyone to his own country!" The body of King Ahab was brought back to Samaria and buried. And so, the words of the prophet Micaiah came to pass.

The title of our sermon is "To Tell the Truth." Most of us hate liars. Some of us hold resentment against people who will not tell the truth. Others of us have utmost suspicion for folk who tell one fib or another.

There used to be a popular television program called *To Tell the Truth*. And down in my neck of the woods, whenever this game show came on, people would gather around the television and listen to the affidavit so that we could judge for ourselves who was the real person and who were the two impostors. Everyone in the household had her or his own gimmicks for distinguishing the real person from the phonies.

One group said you can always tell the real persons because they look straight at the camera while the liars have shifty eyes. Another group argued that you can tell the genuine characters by their posture because those not telling the truth are jittery, shifting from one foot to the other. A few folks even went so far as to say that they knew who was real and who was fake based on their gut feelings or inner vibrations.

So many of us live out our days as impostors. Even though we never appear on a game show like *To Tell the Truth*, far too many of us have a tendency to live our whole lives as lies, telling one lie after another, wherein we refuse to speak out the truth that God lays on our heart of hearts in times of crisis simply because we lack the courage to be true prophets of God. By this, I mean that we tend to be impostors by following the will of the majority power brokers due to our lack of moral stamina during times of tough decision making.

Sometimes God will lay something on our hearts to say to another person or to a committee or to those who control our paychecks, but instead of standing our ground and speaking the truth that is revealed to us, far too often we follow the crowd, get on the bandwagon, shrug our shoulders, and muzzle ourselves, acquiescing to the tyranny of the majority. Sisters and brothers, our concern today is that for us to be silent when God has given us a message to deliver to God's people is to be guilty of lying. To sit still with our lips sealed, to act as if the cat has gotten our tongues, not to mumble a word when God has revealed a specific truth to us that our community is in dire need of hearing, results in our living a lie. We find ourselves in situations wherein we have something to say, a message that has come to us through a prayer or a dream or a song or in daily devotions; and we take this revelation and sit on it. We refuse to share it with those who need it the most, all because we are afraid to stand alone against the maddening crowd.

For instance, in family life, how many times have we sat idly by and watched a sister or a brother, a niece or a nephew, a child or a grandchild, an aunt or an uncle, a parent or a grandparent, get a bad shake on a deal? Let us think about the times when loved ones have come to us, seeking our opinions on an issue—whether they should stay in school or accept a job opportunity, whether they should marry a particular individual or have a child at a given point in their lives, whether they should get a divorce or put their elderly relatives in a nursing home. By not giving voice to what we really believed, we went along with the multitude; like a broken record, we repeated what everybody else around us was saying.

Again, for instance, in our places of work, we often refuse to stand and speak the whole truth, nothing but the truth, so help us God. Think about it. Too often we know someone is cheating on the time clock, ripping off supplies from the office, stealing money from the kitty; yes, all kinds of conspiracies are going on. Yet, we live a lie by acting as if we are ignorant of the whole situation.

Still again, in the church, right in the house of prayer for all people, even when we are fully aware of what is right and what is wrong, we see something going obviously wrong, but we follow the crowd, silently giving our consent so that we can all keep on doing what we are doing until we can't do it anymore. In those crucial times when God has given us a message to say to the people, too many of us live life as liars by being silent simply because we lack the spiritual fortitude to speak the truth, nothing but the truth, so help us God.

The serious danger with this is that if we keep on being silent in time of speech, if we keep on living as impostors instead of authentic Christians, if we keep on living as liars instead of tellers of truth, then our lives will amount to no more than noisy gongs and clanging cymbals (see 1 Corinthians 13:1), which are "full of sound and fury, signifying nothing" (Shakespeare). Therefore, let us discover, define, and develop elements of courage that relate to telling the truth in order that we might live as true prophets in the name of our Lord and our God.

The first element of courage we must embrace related to telling the truth is that we must *discover* what the divine gift is that God has given us. What this means is that each one of us has specific talents and abilities. God created us and brought us forth to do a particular task in life. To discover our God-given talents is the first element of courage because it prevents us from trying to be a jack-of-all-trades and master at none; it keeps us from spreading ourselves too thin. Instead, we will be able to zero in on what specific truth is ours to share.

Micaiah, that prophet who served in the court of King Ahab, was fully aware of the message that God sent him to proclaim to the King. If the king went into battle, he would surely die. Without any ifs, ands, or buts, Micaiah disagreed with the four hundred other prophets and spoke the divine message from God. Telling the truth may mean that we too will be isolated, ostracized, alienated, imprisoned, and put on short rations. As the songwriter says, living a life of truth may mean there are some things we may not know; there may be some places we cannot go; but there is one thing of which we are sure. And that is, God is real, for we can feel God deeply in our souls. If we are going to be modern-day Micaiah, then we too must know in our heart of hearts what is the task that God is calling us to do, what the message is that God is commanding us to communicate, what the truth is that we must tell so that our living will not be in vain.

The second element of courage we must embrace related to telling the truth is that we must *define* the revelation God gives to us. Once we discover our God-given talents and know the stance we must take on a given dilemma, we need to let the revealed truth grow both inside us and outside us. Too often we want to select and handpick the people with whom we share the Good News. We want to voice our opinions among two or three behind closed doors. But the Bible is telling us that we must prepare ourselves to speak the truth before powers and principalities, against spiritual wickedness in high places.

If we return to Micaiah in our text, we find that even when the messenger located the prophet and wanted him to go along with the majority opinion and not to speak against the desires of the king, Micaiah responded, "Whatever God wants me to say, that is what I will say." This is the essence of defined truth—to know beyond the shadow of a doubt what message we need to share in those places where crucial decisions are being made so that our living will not be in vain.

The third and final element of courage we must embrace related to telling the truth is that we must *develop* a God consciousness. Each of us needs a direct relationship with Almighty God. Truth cannot be absolutized once and for all and squeezed into a permanent mold because truth is active and dynamic. If we want the strength and power to be truth tellers, we must stay in touch with the Creator and Sustainer morning by morning, day by day.

The text tells us the prophet Micaiah told King Ahab that God was not in favor of his going to war against the Arameans at that particular time. But we continue to read and study the Scriptures, we find that in another situation God tells the people to fight and destroy all living things in the camp of their enemies. To develop courage as tellers of truth, we must keep the lines of communication open between us and the Deity so that we can speak truth to particular situations at specific times. The sure way that we can grow as Christians is that once we have discovered truth and after we have defined the unique character of the truth being revealed to us, we continue to stay in touch with the Source of all truth so that we can put an end to the lie of silent consent and, in turn, stand forth courageously as true prophets so that our living will not be in vain.

All in all, let us discover, define, and develop our specific truth from Almighty God so that when the challenge is before us, we will stand up and declare in the presence of the majority the truth that God is laying on our heart of hearts, knowing that though they slay us, yet we will trust God. Will the real you please stand up?

How to Know You Are in the Kingdom[18]

A. Louis Patterson, Jr.   (Matt. 16:18–20, KJV)

Every head bowed and every eye closed. Gracious God, our Father, we thank you afresh for the total sufficiency of Jesus Christ and for the perfect teaching ministry of the Holy Spirit. We ask now that you will give us the right words to say. Let us say them with clarity, with boldness and with confidence. Remind us afresh that when you speak, you never stutter; that you are still saying what you mean and still meaning what you say. Teach us to function as ordered by the Divine Orderer and to experience another level of living. Teach us also that if we disobey, we suffer disastrous consequences. Choose now to release the Holy Spirit through human personality to do what He has been sent to do. And in advance, we thank you for your goodness, your grace, your guidance, your greatness and your glory through Christ our Lord, Amen.

To Dr. Green and to all of you my friends in the faith. I thank God for our fellowship together in Jesus Christ, and for our future together in the unseen realities of life. I am literally traumatized by the muscle of the mind of our previous speaker, Dr. Charles Quillan. To develop that kind of mind, he must be involved in mental aerobics of some kind. Listening to him made me feel like a mental midget. Nevertheless, we are grateful that God has navigated the circumstances of life and brought us to this appointed hour. It reminds me of Dr. Sandy Ray, a prince of preachers, who told a story about a cat show. He said that they were having a cat show at Carnegie Hall, and cats were being imported from all over the world. Cats with great pedigree from Australia, Bangladesh, Calcutta, Paris, London, South America, Canada, and from all over the world were imported for this great cat show. And one fellow came to the recognition that they were having this cat show so he ran out into the back alley and grabbed up an old alley cat and enrolled him in the show. This fellow's friends said, "Now, John, you know that an old alley cat like that will not win anything with all these sophisticated cats from all over the world." John said, "Oh, I know that, but the reason I enrolled him is because I thought the exposure would do him good." So, I asked myself, why did Dr. Green initiate the effort to extend me the invitation after knowing me all these years. I assumed that he concluded that the exposure would do me good, and I agree.

I have looked toward this moment with anticipation, and I appreciatively applaud the track record of this conference; for it is looked upon nationwide as the largest and best of its kind anywhere. So I have come today to make myself available for the perfect teaching ministry of the Holy Spirit.

If you will do three things with me, God will revolutionize our lives; and one of the first things you will do when you get to heaven is to rush up and kiss me for what the Holy Spirit will say today. Amen.

Have you heard of the lady who married four times on purpose. It was her goal from a child up to marry four different men. The first man she wanted to marry was a banker, the second one was an actor, the third one was a preacher, and the last one was an undertaker. Somebody asked her why that would be the ambition of her life. The woman responded saying that one was for the money, one was for the show, one was to get ready, and one to go.

I want to do a simple exposition of the divinely inspired written Word of God; for I have found that God's word never returns to Him void, but words always do. God has promised to bless His words, and not our words about His words. So, I would suggest that if you do three things, God will bless us today. First, step back and watch the miraculous ministry of the Holy Spirit operate in your concentric circle of contacts; and indeed, I am speaking to myself as well as to you. I want us to recognize that what I am going to say is the Word of God. It is not Johnny Carson's Late Night Show, it is not Helen Gurley Brown's magazine; it is the Word of God. Secondly, I want us to respond to the Word of God in your own heart. Don't look around and say that I wish Sister Sue were here. God has navigated the circumstances of life and brought us under the authority of His word so that He can do something in us, so that He can do something for us, and so that He can do something through us. After we recognize it as God's word, and respond to it in our own heart, the third thing I want us to do is to rush out and put it into practice. This point is critical because nothing will ever happen until we put into practice the Word of God.

When I was a younger preacher, I thought that the equation for spiritual growth was time plus knowledge. I thought if I taught people long enough and waited for a lapse of time, then people would grow. I was in error. The equation for spiritual growth is located in the Fifth Chapter and the Fourteenth Verse of the Book of Hebrews. The equation is time plus knowledge and, as the verse says, *"By reason of constant use, we leave babes in Christ and become mature saints."* The key is that without constant use of the Word of God, we remain stalled, stagnant, and stymied. So we have to rush out and put it into practice. I want to start with the basics today.

I want to talk about a verse of Scripture, and then walk around this passage from the mind of the Master in St. Mark the Twelfth Chapter and section "B" of the Thirty-fourth Verse. I'll read the verse. *"And when Jesus saw that he answered discreetly he said unto him, Thou art not far from the kingdom of God."* Not far from the kingdom. I wonder if I have ever asked myself why my situation may be as it is. The answer suggested by this text is that it may be because I am not far from the kingdom. I was on Delta Airlines yesterday in Houston, Texas, preparing to come here, and I looked out the window and there was a baggage handler who was there, and he was close to the plane. But even after we had traveled hundreds of miles, very likely he was in the same spot that I left him, and the reason is because he was close to the plane but not in the plane.

One of the first things I do whenever I sit down on a plane, in order to create an avenue to share my faith, is to ask the person sitting next to me that if he had twenty-five thousand dollars laying around how would he invest it? I have been doing this for twenty-five years just as an opener. Lo and behold, one gentleman started talking at length and made an interesting statement that I thought I would pass on to you because I have xeroxed it in my own mind and I wanted to pass out copies this morning. As Freddie K. Haynes, of Dallas, said, "To tell the truth, sir, people are going broke and people are getting rich in the same business." He said a lot depends on the person making the investment. As long as life shall last, I plan never to forget that: that in the same business some people are going broke and others are getting rich. I wonder how it is at your situation. If I were to walk out of here today and my car did not start, I ought not curse the automotive industry in Detroit because, while my car did not start, other cars are running smoothly. The thing I ought to do is check under my hood. For very likely the problem is under my hood. Are you sure that you are in the kingdom? I think theologians would suggest that the kingdom is the realm, the rule, the reign and the righteousness of God.

And Jesus said to this sophisticated academician that you are not far from the kingdom. So, I thought it would be helpful if we would submit today to a radical redefinition of reality based on the pastoral presence of Jesus Himself; for He is the one who makes this suggestion that you can be close and yet not in. What I would like to do is to examine and investigate and analyze and hopefully expiate and explicate some triumphant truths of helpful holy hints on how to make sure that we are no longer just close to the kingdom but actually in it. So if I should do violence to the homiletical structure of the integrity of this text hermeneutically, I believe you will understand because of the brevity of time and the immensity of the message and the familiarity of the text. Listen to what the contextual trend of thought suggests starting with the Twenty-eighth Verse. When we examine this text, we will find the ingredients of all of our members, and yea, even of the pulpit, who are only close and not in—those who are not far from the kingdom. What are the characteristics of a person who is not far from the kingdom? I would like to examine this text, and at the conclusion, if time does not run out on me, to actually exegete a single verse that suggests the four-fold realm of a person who is committed to the person of Jesus at the price of self-denial and for the purpose of the glory of God.

Verse twenty-eight gives us some classic insight about a person who is not far from the kingdom. One of the scribes came to Jesus. I believe all of us recognize that a scribe had a multiplicity of responsibilities. He is one who, of course, was a writer, a keeper of the records whose assigned task was to interpret the law, serve as a keeper of the law, and ultimately, to be a judge of the law. He came to Jesus and raised a question. One of the scribes came. Now, we stop there and we find the first ingredient of a person who is not far from the kingdom. The reason he is not far from the kingdom is because he came with a crowd. He came; he was wise enough to come. But just because I come to the Astrodome in Houston and see the Rockets play is no suggestion that I am a member of the team. Close and yet not in. And believe it or not, we have a lot of people who come every Sunday and have been coming for the last forty years; they are there with the crowd but are still not in. Have you ever noticed that all church fights originate with people who are "the closest up"; never from the distant spectators but always from some tricky trustee, or from some devilish deacon, or some critical choir member, or from some pitiful pew member. And the reason is because they have been coming with the crowd. And I should also suggest because of some wickedness within, because the fight can start because of wickedness within the preacher. It might well be said that all of us are close, not far from the kingdom. So, he came with the crowd; but that's not all I see in this verse. One of the scribes came with the crowd and having heard ... Now I did a primitive etymological root study of the meaning of this word "heard." This word carries the connotation of comprehending the content. The boy has intellectual integrity; he's a scribe. He's a scribe, and he wanted to hear this one who taught as one having authority. So he didn't come to go to sleep. According to the verse, he didn't come to read a newspaper or the bulletin. He did not come to look out the window while the preacher was preaching. He comprehended the content. And the reason I know this is true is because it is suggested in the text. So here is a man who is not far from the kingdom; he is one who has come with the crowd and who has comprehended the content. But he does something else here. He reasoned and perceived. That means he concluded correctly, because when Jesus spoke back to him, Jesus said to him that you have answered discreetly; or, in other words, you have thought this thing out. So this scribe, with his analytical mind, not only came with the crowd and comprehended the content, he also concluded correctly. The reason I know this boy is close is because actually it is a microcosmic scenario of ninety percent of our own members.

The next thing this scribe did in the verse is, he asked Jesus a question. This means that he communicated his concerns. Whatever else that is, it is prayer. Remember the words of Jesus, "... *ask what you will* ..." So here is a description of a person who can be sitting in the congregation where I pastor for forty years and still be not far from the kingdom. Anybody who comes with the crowd, then comprehends the content, then concludes correctly, then communicates his own concerns is not far from the kingdom. But why is it that he is still away from the kingdom even though he is not far from the kingdom? There are two reasons. When you read this text and conclude the contextual trend of thought, you will find that this man omitted two things. The first thing he omitted was that he did not confess his own condition.

The second thing he omitted was that he did not commit himself to Christ. All he did was come with the crowd, comprehend the content, conclude correctly and communicate his own concerns. But he made no commitment to Christ which is predicated upon what theologians suggest is "horologer"; the confession, the acknowledgment, the announcement, the agreement from God's point of view of his present condition. That's why he was not far from the kingdom. When was the last time you heard somebody actually confess? I find that people have a sense of self-sufficiency. I find that a person can be filled with troubles and trials and tribulations, can know nothing except fear and frustration, and fracture and fruitless failure, can be miserable underneath the skin, cynical and disillusioned, and hard to get along with, and will blame somebody else for his present pilgrimage. There is a distinct absence of confession of our own waywardness.

The Bible says that we are sinners by the consequence of the imputed sins of Adam. We are sinners by choice of our own desire to dictate the agenda, dominate the audience and demonstrate our authority; and we have a conversation that is wicked because our throats are open sepulchers. Our conduct is miserable because our feet are swift to mischief. In fact, our character is defective because there is none that doth good, no not one. And yet, we come every Sunday only to hear some new thing; and Jesus says to us "you are not far from the realm, the rule, the reign and the righteousness of the sovereignty of God." He is saying to everybody here that the reason you are yet alive is because God has a beautiful blueprint drawn up by the Divine Architect of your life. And the reason you are here is because He wants to build a super structure on the foundation of your commitment to Christ. And yet, I believe you will agree with me that some of us may be still in the valley, and there is a yearning in our hearts that says we are made for what my pastor, Dr. E. V. Hill, calls the third level in life. Some of us are down in the basement when we were made to dwell on the third floor; and yet, because we are not far from the kingdom, when the astrogate of the divine providence takes off at 650 miles per hour, 35,000 feet in the spiritual sky, we are still handling the baggage of a sickly secular society. Preacher, how can I make sure that I am in the kingdom? I want you to be able to leave here knowing once and for all whether or not you are just close or actually in the Kingdom of God. You need the principles of spiritual aerodynamics to rise above the law of sinful gravity. Sin will hold you down unless you have access to higher power. You will be able to arrive at your desired destination without stress, strain or struggle because you will be in the plane.

Listen to this. "... *And thou shalt love the Lord thy God with all thy* ..." This is His answer to the scribe who was not far from the kingdom. I ought to give a definition of love. A lot of people have love mixed up with lust; lust is a legitimate desire gone out of control seeking to be fulfilled outside of God's original design. There are only three things all of us want. We want the protection of God, the approval of others, and pleasure for self. And we try to arrive at that outside of God's design, so we lust for position or prestige or power or prominence of position. And we end up struggling because that's heavy baggage to carry. But love ... listen to this definition of love ... Love is a minimum of emotions and a maximum of evaluation of need and the meeting of that need in a spirit of self-sacrifice by doing what needs to be done, even when you don't feel like doing it. Now, that's love. Love can literally be capsulized and summarized in a single word; that word was enunciated and elucidated in the Garden of Gethsemane when Jesus said "... *nevertheless* ..." that's love.

It is not necessary that I share this experience but I am seeking your best good and the glory of the Father. I will share this scripturally authentic and attractive definition of love; all we have to do is stick it on the end of John 3:16. And if our definition does not harmonize with John 3:16, it is not "agape" love. It is not divine love; it is human love. God did not look down at me and get a queasy feeling. He did not have emotions running up and down his spine saying, "Ooooohoo, I can't stand it." What God did was, He came as Jesus incarnated in the flesh. What He did was to do what needed to be done by an act of the will, in spite of feelings. You know what has been the most revolutionary theological disclosure in all the Bible for me personally? It is this: That nowhere in the gospel does the Lord talk about feelings, and only two times in the New Testament, and only one time related to us. Hebrews, Chapter Four, talks about feeling, but it does so in terms of the high priestly ministry of Jesus, because He is not one who cannot be touched with the infirmities of our feelings.

In Ephesians, Chapter Four, when He talks about feelings, it has negative connotation when He says we are past feelings and have given ourselves over to licentiousness, failing to understand the unseen realities of life. So when I depend on feelings, I am depending on the most unproductive and unreliable phenomena on the face of the earth. Jesus says, if any man "will" ... and I want to talk about that before this week is over ... not, if any man feels. It is an act of the will. He says that He does not care how you feel, you can be in the kingdom by the commitment of your will to Christ. And so He says here in this verse, "*love ...*" (That's verse thirty.) "*Thou shall love the Lord thy God ...*" Here it is. This is what separates the boys from the men. He says you have to love God with all your heart. And do you know why Jesus started in the embryonic presentation of this triumphant truth with the heart? It is because "heart," in the Bible theologically, is the biggest word in the Bible for the unseen realities of man. Everything that makes me underneath the skin, is categorized as the heart. And that, of course, will include the mind, emotions and will. The reason I know this is true is that sometimes we say "I know it in my heart." By saying, "I know!" we suggest an intellectual capacity. That's knowledge. Other times, we say, "I feel it in my heart," and that is the emotional capacity of the unseen reality of men. But there are other times when I say, "I did it with all my heart," and that connotes physical strength.

What Jesus is saying is that you can be close to the kingdom; you can be coming with crowd, comprehending the content, concluding correctly and communicating your own concerns and never really love me in your heart. Because what you do, Al Patterson, upon the stage if rhetoric with the applause of men in the gallery, can be diametrically opposite of your practice out in the arena of your daily reality. Don't you know that just because I can preach with a beautiful moan, that's no sign that I am in the kingdom. The reason I know that's true is because I can moan without a message; I can holler without holiness; I can preach without purity. Just because a musician can tickle the instrument with flexible dexterity is no sign that he is in the kingdom because Jimmy McDuff can play an organ and

Oscar Peterson can play a piano, or at least he could. Just because I can do oratorical flights with my voice in singing and throw my voice all up in the balcony is no sign that I am filled with the Holy Ghost ... Johnny Mathis can hit the high C without the help of the Holy Ghost.

Let me tell you how to know if you are in the kingdom. I am in the kingdom when I am in private on my knees before God in my heart. What I am in private is what I am period. I honestly believe this and I don't mean any harm ... but I ought to also tell you that I have my return ticket in my pocket. Listen! Listen! Listen! I believe that what a preacher is in private on his knees before God is what he is period. The Church is supernatural in origin; it has to be supernatural in operation. And any preacher not praying is playing. And any church not praying is straying. And you don't revolutionize planet earth with a playing preacher and a straying church. That's why God navigates the circumstances of life sometimes and lets the floods of life come because He is trying to get my attention. When God lets the floods come, He is not trying to drown me; He is trying to teach me how to swim. When He lets trouble come, He is not trying to destroy me; He wants to develop me. He says that the way you get that done, Al Patterson, is to love me in your heart. How? Henry Bryant is the most noted Christian psychologist in the world today and he says that the average Christian spends less than five minutes a week on his knees before God in private. That leaves 167 hours and 55 minutes with the standards, the strength, and strategies of a sickly secular society. Love Him in your heart and you will take the first step inside the kingdom. That is not all that's in the verse. Just in case I run out of time, I will share this with you; I have not finished a sermon in the last twenty-one and a half years. So don't get restless; I simply quit because whenever I am preaching, the next verse always waves at me and says please say a word about me. I have found that the word is so pregnant with truth that it gives birth while I am yet preaching.

Love ... Verse Thirty: "*Thou shall love the Lord with all thy heart and with all thy soul ...*" There is a different theological nuance here. I don't want to get into a theological debate with academicians and sophisticated dialectical theologians over the difference between heart and soul. But I do know this, that wherever you find the word "soul" in the Bible, and I will give one example, it is always inextricably tied up with one's ambitions, attitudes and activities in terms of the mind, emotions, and will. Remember the rich fool who had a bountiful crop and didn't know where to store them and he looked up and said to his soul ... He then expressed his ambitions based on his activity of a new construction because of his attitude of me, myself, and I. And Jesus says here that whatever my ambitions are for the future, they have to include the Lord thy God and Him only. Thou shall love the Lord thy God with all your ambition, with all of your attitude and with all of your present activity. You know what God does when he gets ready to bless a person? I am going to like it here because you are always asking the right questions.

Whenever I express my ambition to God, the first thing that He looks at is my present activity. And if my present activity does not harmonize with my expressed ambition, He focuses on my attitude; because it is my attitude that gives birth to the other two. A whole lot of folks say that if they had a million dollars they would do a lot. God is more interested in the $1.25 you already have. And if I am not loving him with all of my heart and with all of my soul with what I presently have, it may be that I want the joys of the kingdom without the responsibilities of the kingdom. That's why the rich young ruler went away sorrowful; he wanted all of the joys of the kingdom but none of the responsibilities thereof. So when the Lord looked at his attitude and his activities and his ambitions, He said that you are such a lovely young man but unfortunately you are not in the kingdom. That's the verse.

Lest I hold you too long ... there is another word in Verse Thirty ... and with all of your mind. I tell our church all the time that I refuse to let anybody come on the campus of Corinth and leave his or her thinking faculties at home. My goal is not to run you up the wall emotionally and you not know why you went up there. My goal is to cause us to consider, and to think, and to meditate, and to study because everything changes when proper content produces proper character, and proper character produces proper consequences. We can never have proper consequences until proper content is dispensed. And God uses content to change character. Be ye transformed by the renewing of your mind. When Jesus called his disciples in the Fourth Chapter of the book of Matthew, the Nineteenth Verse, he said, follow me by an act of the will, I don't care how you feel. A few verses later, in the Fifth Chapter, the First Verse of Matthew, the Bible says that He taught them. And the word here is "dedache," truth, organized structure, revelation from a higher source. Nothing happens until we get people in the word—until we activate their mind with the Word of God. He said that you have got to love me with all your mind. Not only did He commence His ministry by teaching, but also, in the Twenty-fourth Chapter, the Forty-second Verse of the book of Luke, after they had crucified Him on Calvary, the Bible says He got up early one Sunday morning and the first thing He said to his men opened their eyes to the Scriptures. He said to them how important it is to get your mind operating on another level of thought. And up until the day He was taken up, He was still speaking of the things pertaining to the kingdom of God.

Pro-vi-dence[19]

Mozella Mitchell   (1 Kings 17:14, RSV)

Thus says the LORD the God of Israel, "The jar or meal shall not be spent, and the cruse of oil shall not fail until the day that the LORD sends rain upon the earth."

One of the names we call God by is Providence. That's because we know that God will provide. We're so sure God will provide for us that we have given God that name. We've added *nce* on the end of it, Providence. God is the essence of providing; God is Pro-vi-dence itself. Very often we hear people say, "I believe in divine providence," meaning, of course, that they believe in the farsighted goodness of God. That means God cares for us and looks out for us and provides for our needs.

It's a wonderful thing to be called a child of God. I'm grateful today to be able to say, "It's a wonderful thing to be a child of God." And I can say this because I know what God has done for me. And I know what God has done for other people. I wonder, what would we do without God? I have no idea how I ever made it in life before I came to believe in God. What I do know, however, when I think about it, is that God was just so good to take care of me long before I gave much thought to believing in and living for God. We all wander along in life, not really knowing what's going on, not realizing that there's a good God somewhere that's keeping us going. Sometimes we're not even aware of the many narrow escapes we come through simply because there is a God somewhere who cares about us and is preserving us because we are of great value to God. I hate to think how foolish we are when we blunder along in life unaware of God's goodness.

In the story in the seventeenth chapter of First Kings, God's goodness came to the poor widow of Phoenicia in the hour of her greatest need. We see at least two good things happening in this story. First of all, the prophet of God is following the leadership of God and ministering to the woman who is in need. And at the same time, God is providing for the needs of both the prophet and the poor widow. God has worked these two things together so well that it just amazes you.

There is a famine in the land. Ahab is king of Israel (the Northern Kingdom), and he's married to Jezebel. So the people are led to the worship of Baal, an idol god. Because of this great sin, the Lord has brought a famine upon the land. Now, we might stop and think here and wonder, if God is so good, then why is God doing this terrible thing? Why is God permitting these people to suffer so? It's not their fault that their king has chosen to worship an idol.

But God works in a mysterious way. God is good, but God will permit things to happen to us in order to bring to our awareness the source of our blessings. God is not going to stand for us enjoying this goodness while being disobedient and disrespectful. We may run along for a long time and think we're getting away with something. Eventually, however, God will remind us that God is the benefactor we've been taking for granted.

So in this text, God told Elijah to tell Ahab that God was sending a famine. Of course, there were innocent people who would suffer also.

But one of the remarkable things about this story is that it shows that even in the midst of the famine God took care of God's own children and provided for them.

Elijah's life was in danger because of the dreadful prophecies he had been announcing against the sinful king and his people. So God told him to go hide out by the brook (near the Jordan). He would drink water from the brook, and God would command the ravens to bring him bread and meat there. Now you know how ravens are. They prey on others and ordinarily wouldn't bring you anything. But God found a good use for them here. Elijah did as he was told. The ravens fed him in the morning and fed him in the evening, and he satisfied his thirst on the waters of the brook. But after a while the brook dried up, and Elijah could not last without water.

God then sent Elijah to the poor widow of Phoenicia. But this poor woman had just enough meal and oil to fix one more meager dinner for herself and her son. And this widow had lost all hope as she stood facing starvation. When Elijah asked her for a little bread, she said that she had only enough for herself and her son and was just about to go and fix so "we may eat it, and die."

But this woman didn't know to whom she was talking. She was talking to a man who had experienced the goodness of God in the midst of famine. She was talking to a man who knew that God would provide. She was talking to one who trusted in God. Elijah said to her, "Go ahead and fix me a little cake as I asked you, and I know the Lord will provide. God has sent me to tell you that the jar of meal shall not be spent, and the cruse of oil shall not fail until the day that the Lord sends rain upon the earth."

Now, this woman didn't know what was going to happen, but she did as she was asked to do. And not only did the jar of meal and cruse of oil not give out, but her son was also restored to health after a grave illness. She knew then that Elijah was a man of God.

Now, you can imagine how serious the situation was. It had been a long time—years—since it had rained. All the crops had failed, and all the rivers were drying up. The people all around the countryside were dropping dead of hunger, of thirst, and of disease. Maybe this poor widow's husband had passed away for the same reason. She and her son were left for just a little while longer before they too would perish. I imagine the widow and her son had gone on for several days now without eating, saving as long as possible that last bit of meal and oil, the only thing that stood between them and starvation. Now the time had come when they couldn't hold out any longer. They had to eat the very last morsel of food and face up to the inevitable.

Just at this critical moment entered this man who'd been sleeping out by the brook and was probably all dirty and smelly. He had been out there on that brook for many months without a change of clothes. Of course, he could have bathed and washed what he had on in the brook. But he probably didn't have any soap, so it probably hadn't done much good. At any rate, he was, no doubt, all hairy without a shave, tired and weak, and thirsty from this long walk from the brook to the city's gate.

Elijah probably spoke just above a whisper, being nearly out of breath. And the first thing he asked for was a drink of water. He said, "Give me a little to drink!" And then he remembered that he was hungry also. So he said, "Give me a little bread to eat!" And finding out that she had this one last amount of food sustenance for her and her son, he said, "Wait, don't fix it for you and your son, but fix me a little first, and then go and prepare what remains for you and your son."

The woman must have been puzzled by the audacity of this stranger. She must have stared at him long and hard. Yet, there must have been something persuasive about this man, or the spirit of God must have moved in the heart of the woman in a special way. For she went ahead and prepared the mite of meal for the man as he had asked.

Now, you can imagine what happened when she went back to the jar of meal and the cruse of oil to fix the dinner for herself and her son. She must have dipped meal from the jar and poured oil from the cruse, and—astonishingly—the contents still remained the same. And the next day she must have dipped meal and poured oil, and still no change in the contents. And the next day and the next day and on and on, the meal kept coming, and the oil kept flowing because God had his hand on the woman, on the meal and oil and on the man whom she had fed. God is so good. That's why they call God Providence.

In times like these we live in today, it gives me great joy to go back into the Scripture and to read about the eternal goodness of God. This was many centuries ago, and by this I know that God didn't just start being good yesterday, but God has always been good. And I have a right to expect the same goodness from God. God's gonna keep on being good to those who trust in God and obey God's voice.

Now, there are those who are doubtful, who would try to say that this miracle didn't really happen because God never goes against natural laws. When the meal gave out, it was out, they would say. And you can't expect God to reverse things and produce meal continually out of nowhere just so that Elijah and this woman and her household could continue to eat. God just doesn't tamper with the natural order of things.

But I say to these people, I don't need an explanation for God's action because I know that God can do anything God wants to do. If you need an explanation, look at it this way. Anything God does is natural. It may not look natural to you because you don't know all of God's natural ways. You see a few laws of nature and you conclude that that's all there are. But God has not revealed all of these laws to us. What we call miracles are a part of these laws that God has not yet given us the power to comprehend.

And I want you to know today, I believe in miracles. If it hadn't been for miracles I don't know where we would be today in this country where every possible means has been tried to keep us down and to destroy us. But still we rise, and still we survive. This is because God has performed miracles for us. Let me tell you, we have inherited a great faith in the miracles of God. Now I believe like this: if you don't believe in miracles, they won't happen for you.

We live in a messy time today. I don't need to draw a dreary picture for you of how bad things are. You see it on the TV everyday. You read about it in the newspapers, and you see it before you as you drive or walk down the street or just look out the window. It's a bad time. It's worse than a famine in this respect. With a famine you know that when the rain comes everything is going to be all right again. But today the rain doesn't help the situation. We don't know when things are gonna clear up and people can go back to work and to school and what have you.

I wish that I could say to you right now that you will have a job by a certain date and will be able to provide adequately for your family. I wish that I could say to you right now that you will be able to get the loan to buy that house or car you need so badly. I wish that I could say to you right now that the interest rates are gonna go down to an affordable level tomorrow and the inflation is gonna end in the morning and the recession and the depression are gonna go away before the week is out. But I can't say these things.

What I can say to you is that you're in the hand of a good God, and God will take care of you! Now, how God will do it, I don't know. But I do know that your jar of meal shall not be spent and your cruse of oil shall not fail if you respect God and obey. In the sixth chapter of Matthew, Jesus says don't be anxious about your life, don't have fears about what you shall eat or drink or about what you shall wear. Look at the birds of the air, the lilies of the field. If God looks after them, how much more will God care for you? And somebody said, "His eye is on the sparrow"—a seemingly worthless creature—"and I know He watches me."[20]

Finally, however, God has no hands or feet but our hands and feet. This means that we have to look out for each other and for other people. We do not know when God may send someone to us for help. Therefore, we must not turn anyone away empty. Like the poor widow of Phoenicia, we may not have enough for ourselves and our own people. But God demands that we share what we have with other people. And just as surely as we do what God says to do, our jar of meal shall not be spent and our cruse of oil shall not fail. God will surely provide for us.

Bad Black Dude on the Road[21]

Fred C. Lofton   (Acts 8:26–39, KJV)

And the angel of the Lord spake unto Philip, saying, Arise, and go toward the south unto the way that goeth down from Jerusalem unto Gaza, which is desert. And he arose and went: and behold, a man of Ethiopia, an eunuch of great authority under Candace queen of the Ethiopians, who had the charge of all her treasure, and had come to Jerusalem for to worship, was returning, and sitting in his chariot read Esaias the prophet. Then the Spirit said unto Philip, Go near, and join thyself to this chariot. And Philip ran thither to him, and heard him read the prophet Esaias, and said, Understandest thou what thou readiest? And he said, How can I, except some man should guide me? And he desired Philip that he would come up and sit with him. The place of the scripture which he read was this, He was led as a sheep to the slaughter; and like a lamb dumb before his shearer, so opened he not his mouth. In his humiliation his judgment was taken away: and who shall declare his generation? for his life is taken from the earth. And the eunuch answered Philip, and said, I pray thee, of whom speaketh the prophet this? of himself, or of some other man? Then Philip opened his mouth, and began at the same scripture, and preached unto him Jesus. And as they went on their way, they came unto a certain water: and the eunuch said, See, here is water; what doth hinder me to be baptized? And Philip said, If thou believest with all thine heart, thou mayest. And he answered and said, I believe that Jesus Christ is the Son of God. And he commanded the chariot to stand still: and they went down both into the water, both Philip and the eunuch; and he baptized him. And when they were come up out of the water, the Spirit of the Lord caught away Philip, that the eunuch saw him no more: and he went on his way rejoicing (Acts 8:26–39 KJV).

Let us look at the subject "Bad Dude on the Road." But before we begin, it is necessary, given the identity of this dude, to add a small but important word—"black"—a word to which all African-Americans can relate. In Acts 8 we meet a "Bad *Black* Dude on the Road!"

The dictionary defines a *dude* as someone who is fastidious in manners, dress, bearing, and skill. When I was a lad in North Carolina, we used to refer to someone highly skilled as a "bad dude." African-Americans still do this in the ghetto today; it is a great compliment when someone calls a man "a bad dude."

If you recall, the 1991 play-off between the Los Angeles Lakers and the Chicago Bulls was billed as a contest between two bad dudes, sometimes called the "M and M Boys," "Magic" Johnson and Michael Jordan. Magic was the worst dude on the floor, and Michael was the worst dude in the air. These were some *bad dudes!*

In the book of Acts we have another bad, black dude, a black presence from Ethiopia, from a land we call Africa today. Most of the preaching I have heard on this passage focused on Philip and he is, indeed, from one point of view, a leading character in these verses. Philip had gone to Samaria in obedience to God's command to carry the gospel to that part of the country and the uttermost parts of the earth.

But I choose to place attention on the Ethiopian, the black man receiving the good news of the gospel of Christ from Philip. Here was a man stripped of his manhood, as we African-American men are today. Black people (particularly men) are robbed of their personhood in this country today, in the courthouse, schoolhouse, White House, even sometimes the church house.

The recent case involving officers of the law in Los Angeles, California, who brutalized a defenseless black man, merely because of his color, is only one case in point. I might add that racism is on the rise as never before. I'm sure that many reading this can give personal testimonies in this regard.

The Ethiopian experienced living in hell as a result of physical castration. But the hell was both physical and psychological. In the days of Queen Candace of Ethiopia, in whose service the Ethiopian labored, it was mandatory that a man who worked in the service of the queen submit to castration. It was, in other words, both a condition of employment and a requirement of existence. This Ethiopian, like our own black men today, had to forgo his manhood as the price for his continued existence. Here was a man who lived in hell!

Physically, he existed in hell because of his obligation to those in power. He submitted to the most dehumanizing circumstance thrust upon a human being, denial of the God-given capacity of sexual and procreative expression, forming the crown of manhood. This capacity is God's gift of sharing in his continuing creation—a gift to man and the lower animals. Above all, the male values his ability to consummate a relationship with the female. I suspect that Kunta Kinte chose the mutilation of his foot rather than castration (as punishment for running away) for this very reason.

Psychologically, the Ethiopian resided in hell because from the moment of emasculation he had to live with the fact of castration, with the state of castration-conscious, always aware that he could no longer function adequately as a male. African-American males find it hard to function adequately as males because of the hell they live in. Thomas F. Pettigrew (*A Profile of the Negro American*) states, "The ubiquity of racial prejudice in the United States guarantees that virtually every Negro faces at some level the effects of discrimination, the frightening feeling of being black in what appears to be a white man's world."

America castrated black people when they brought us from Mother Africa, and we remain victimized by that crippling legacy. Many African-Americans worked jobs and never received a promotion. Others with less experience, education and know-how stepped up the ladder of success while we stood by discouraged, disappointed, disgusted, and dismayed. When I pastored a church in Columbus, Georgia, some years ago, I became acquainted with a deacon who was in that church, an African-American man with one of the most brilliant minds I've ever come across, a true natural mathematical genius. He served as treasurer of our church for over forty years. He could not go to college because he never completed high school. This black man secured employment in the Columbus post office and worked for forty-four years. He received one promotion in all those years. A white man who entered the postal service at the same time as the deacon in my church eventually rose to become postmaster...

Now, back to the eunuch in the Bible passage. His boss, Candace, the queen, had bestowed great power and authority upon him. He maintained responsibility for her financial affairs, "in charge of all her treasure" (v. 27). The eunuch had been commissioned to journey to Jerusalem to seek further knowledge of the religion of Israel. This was truly a bad, black dude.

Some of the brothers encounter problems working with sisters in authority over them, and can't deal with it. I experience no difficulty in this kind of situation. If the sister's got more—education, ability, grace, gifts, and whatever—she's just got it. And brothers, we must learn to admit it, accept the reality, and learn to work for and with her.

The man in this narrative must have been a financial wizard, someone who knew how to hold and handle the queen's money wisely. This area hits many black people negatively. Plenty of us think we can spend money on this side of town and on the other side at the same time. We think of ourselves as what the Las Vegas casino operators call "High Rollers." But let's face it—we are *"Low Rollers"* (and some are *"No*-Rollers,")* who need to put all we have in one pot, not split our money up and carry it uptown and downtown!

In my hometown, Memphis, an esteemed trustee (now deceased) in our church was president of a little bank worth about seventy million dollars. And even though it's one of the best-run banks in town, an employer of African-Americans, practically all of the checks written by black members of our churches are issued by the white banks in our half-black, half-white city. Can our situation get more ironic than this?

What is wrong with black people that we can't handle our own money? Explain for me this twisted love affair we have with white folks in the economic arena. Why take the fruits of our labor and give them to the affluent for the uplifting of their community and elevating of their people, while our own black communities plead for life and liberation? I pray that Almighty God will let me live to see a reversal of this pitiable situation someday.

Back to the eunuch—the bad, black dude described in our text. Not only was this man entrusted with the treasury of the powerful queen, but on the spiritual side, he feared God. God's Word says he came to Jerusalem to worship, and on his way back to Ethiopia he sat in his chariot reading Isaiah the prophet.

This black man sought spiritual guidance, and at this point in his life the Lord intended to reward him abundantly. Scripture promises, "He who comes to God must believe that he is, and that he is a reader of them that diligently seek him." I've discovered if you stay with God and seek him diligently, he will reward you.

> If you seek his face early in the morning,
> God will reward you.
> If you seek him at the noon hour,
> God will reward you.
> If you seek him late at night,
> God will reward you,
> For he is a God that neither slumbers nor sleeps.

I've been seeking him for a long time, and he always made a way for me. When I went to Morehouse College in Atlanta back in the fifties, I had no father to count on, nor any Merit Scholarship, Pell Grant, financial aid, or work-study program to help me. But I had a praying mother and an almighty God on my side. In answer to my mother's prayers, Dr. Mays, the college president, opened up his heart and adopted me into his home, where I lived as his son for four years of undergraduate study and two years of graduate theological study. When I entered the college, I hardly owned a dime; but with God's help, when I left the college, I didn't owe a dime. God *will* make a way, I tell you!

It is disturbing to hear young African-American males and females complaining today because of the lack of this or that—no family, no father, no "wheels," sometimes no nothing. I hasten to remind them if they possess a creative positive attitude combined with whatever other blessings that have come their way—good health, sharp minds, strong bodies—they already hold all that they need. If a young person is endowed with one or a combination of these attributes, along with a willingness to work and succeed, and a willingness to seek and serve God, "God will surely make a way!"

Notice what the eunuch engaged in while he sat in his chariot. He read. Picture him in your mind's eye—legs crossed, body relaxed, and eyes intently fastened on a curiously compelling and intriguing passage of Scripture. "He was led as a sheep to the slaughter; and like a lamb dumb before his shearer so opened not his mouth: In his humiliation his judgment was taken away: and who shall declare his generation? for his life is taken from the earth" (Acts 8: 32–33).

Imagine now his perceptive mind beginning to wonder, "Who are the sheep?" "Who's the slaughterer?" "Why? Why? Why?" These same questions continuously hound theologians, scholars, preachers, and teachers through the centuries and across the pages of time.

This is what reading God's Word will do for us. It opens up the windows of our minds so the refreshing and invigorating breezes from Heaven can enter into our parched narrow hearts, minds, and souls. Empowerment exists in reading God's Word. God says, "My word shall not come back to me void." His Holy Word will broaden your understanding, expand personal vision, and increase the depth of your love, hope, and faith. READ HIS WORD!

This fellow was no doubt reading from the Hebrew Scriptures, the Septuagint, which is the Greek version of the Old Testament—an indication that the eunuch was bilingual. This bad, black dude was a scholar as well as an economist!

Parents, help your children to develop a love of learning as young people. Expose their developing senses to great music, art, and poetry. Introduce your children to authors, composers, scientists, and artists—especially those of color. Take time away from the video movies and games. Accompany them to the planetarium, art galleries, library, museums, and the zoological and botanical gardens found in most of our cities. Life is more than Disney, Spike Lee, Robin Givens, and top rap groups, though all of these maintain their place.

The children are in our hands, malleable, marketable, vulnerable, and breakable. It is our responsibility—yours and mine—to encourage, nurture and guide them, as well as provide for their physical needs. Many mothers, grandmothers, sisters and aunts care for our children lovingly, but alone. These women need the help of bad, black dudes.

Even if you have a daughter or son on the other side of town, let them know you love them. If you do not love your own flesh and blood, you cannot claim to love the God who made you. Matthew tells us, even a sparrow shall not fall to the ground without the Father's knowledge. Men, love your sons, daughters and wives. When you love them, you show love for the Father!

On his return home from worship, somewhere between Jerusalem and Gaza, the Ethiopian was reading the book of Isaiah. Meanwhile the Holy Spirit said to Philip, "Go and join yourself to that chariot." Philip obeyed and confronted this bad, black dude with an order from on high. "Let down your chariot and let me ride. I know you're a man of prestige and power, but stop this BMW. Stop this Mercedes Benz. Stop this Lincoln Continental, this Cadillac, this Buick, this New Yorker. I've got a message that is far more powerful than you, your boss, your position, or this chariot!"

Philip asked the eunuch, "Understandest thou what thou readest?" The black man answered, "How can I, except some man should guide me?" Here, again, the intelligence of this bad, black dude is apparent. He knew he needed enlightenment and interpretation from someone wiser and more learned in the Scriptures than he. He readily admitted his ignorance in this matter. Oftentimes we read, without understanding, but something within us—stubbornness or foolish pride—keeps us from admitting our reading is not productive.

No matter how successful, prosperous, or upwardly mobile you are on the job and in society, you need somebody to interpret God's Word for you. You may be conversant with power brokers, skilled in the courtroom, adept in the halls of Congress, at home within the walls of academia, a genius in the operating room, the science lab, or the cockpit of the mighty 747—but you still need the guidance of a spirit-filled man or woman of God to help you wrestle with the life-giving, soul-sustaining, eternal, and powerful Word of God.

Then Philip opened his mouth "... and preached unto him Jesus." Therein is salvation for all of us. There it is! When Jesus is truly "preached unto us," and the message comes from the Holy Spirit, we whisper, shout, holler, or scream, "I BELIEVE THAT JESUS CHRIST IS THE SON OF GOD!" And this is what the eunuch did. And not only that, he commanded Philip to baptize him with water in the nearby stream. We see a new person, enlightened intellectually, but more importantly, spiritually enlightened. A profound change came over him. He can never be the same.

As you know, all stories, even those in the Bible, do not always end on a happy note. Today, in the real world, as we observe the stories on CNN, *General Hospital*, the *New York Times, Ebony*, and *Jet*, far too many end on a tragic note. But thanks be to God, this one ends happily. This eunuch in Candace's cabinet, this bad black dude, when he came up out of the water, "went on his way rejoicing," because he'd experienced and accepted the love and mercy of God. He now held within his heart and mind a story to tell to all he met regarding God's saving power.

I wish all of us could and would go on our way rejoicing. We must truly and sincerely believe

—That Jesus is the Son of God;
—That our blackness is a blessing and not a curse;
—That the white man can't save us—we must do it ourselves;
—That our children are precious gifts from God;
—That our women want, deserve, and need our respect;
—That crack-cocaine, AIDS, pornography, teenage pregnancy, guns, alcohol, illicit sex, and other negatives so prevalent in black communities are not going to magically disappear.

If we truly and sincerely believe God is still on the throne, sitting high and looking low, then today we too can go on our way rejoicing, singing with the bad, black dude in the book of Acts:

> Lord, I just come from the fountain,
> I'm just from the fountain, Lord!
> I've just come from the fountain,
> His name so sweet!

Yes, the eunuch went on his way rejoicing. However, the eunuch's personal salvation is not the end of the story. Tradition states his evangelistic zeal became the flame God used to start a spiritual revival in Ethiopia. He became the Paul for that section of the world. It is believed he introduced the new religion to the officials of Queen Candace's court and from there it spread to other sections of Africa.

Some historians believe this man established the Coptic Church in Ethiopia, the oldest consecutive Christian community on the continent of

Africa. One of our church fathers, Irenaeus, tells us (*Against Heresies*, iii 12:8) the eunuch became a missionary upon his return to Ethiopia.[22] William LaRue Dillard also makes this point in his book *Biblical Ancestry Voyage*: "This eunuch went back to Ethiopia and gave a full report to the queen as to his mission and shared his new-found faith in Jesus Christ. I am sure he left his position as treasurer for the queen and I am sure he became a pivotal force in spreading the Christian Gospel throughout Ethiopia."[23]

This bad black dude's conversion became the spiritual thrust that was needed to bring the Gospel to another section of the world. The penetrating light of the Lord Jesus Christ was placed in the hands of a man physically castrated by men, but (this makes a huge difference) spiritually empowered by God in and through Jesus Christ. God gave this handicapped African the glorious responsibility to "Tell the Story." Truly, those handicapped by adverse circumstances are used by a merciful God to possess in "earthen vessels" the treasure of the Word of God for the whole world.

This African searcher-after-God was thrown involuntarily into hell. Nevertheless, he rose above the awfulness of his situation to become resourceful in spite of his handicap. From his example African-American males of today can learn that handicaps are not necessarily barriers to productive living—even in hell.

If Thou Be a Great People[24]

Carolyn Ann Knight   (Josh. 17:13–18, KJV)

A change in the leadership can create a crisis in any people's movement. In the succeeding years since the deaths of Mary Mcleod Bethune, Marcus Garvey, Malcolm X, Martin Luther King, Jr., and Adam Clayton Powell, Jr., we in the African American community have been praying and searching for a personality that can galvanize the masses of people in much the same way that they did. In the twenty-first century we need a consistent voice that can capture the attention of the African American community.

Such was not the case with the people of Israel. After the death of Moses, the transfer of leadership was swift, smooth. Joshua was a fitting successor to Moses because Joshua had great courage and vision. Moses sent twelve spies to survey the land of Canaan. While ten saw only giants, Joshua and Caleb saw grapes and milk and honey. Because Joshua was able to see the invisible and believe the impossible, he inherited the role of leader. After the conquest, the children of Israel were ready to cease their wanderings in the wilderness. Joshua had the assignment of dividing the territory among the twelve tribes.

The allotment proceeded without difficulty until Joshua got to Ephraim and Manasseh. Ephraim and Manasseh were children of Joseph and Asenath, the wife that Joseph married while he was in Egypt where these children were born. Jacob adopted them and gave them a share in the inheritance with his other children. Now if I understand my geography, Egypt is in northern Africa, which means that Ephraim and Manasseh were an Afro-Asiatic people: people of color.

Upon receiving their inheritance, Ephraim and Manasseh began to grumble and complain that their share of the allotment was too small. Their assertion was based on the fact that they were a great people. Great in size and great in stature. Because of their history and family lineage coupled with a personal and abiding relationship with God Almighty, they insisted that their share of the land should be more. They said to Joshua, "We are a great people and the Lord has blessed us until now. This share of the land is too small." Joshua replied, "If you are a great people then go to the hill country and make a place for yourselves." They countered that the Perizzites and the Canaanite and giants were in the hill country with weapons of iron and chariots. Again Joshua says, "If thou be a great people go up against the Perizzites and the Canaanite and the giants."

I believe this passage is a word to this New Millennium Pastor's Conference as we prepare to face life in the twenty-first century. "If thou be a great people go up into the hill country and clear a place for yourself there!" At this uncertain point of our perilous pilgrimage upon this planet, we must recognize who we are as a people and appropriate our rightful inheritance in God and in this world. If thou be a great people ... a great preacher/pastor, a great community, a great family, a great sister, a great brother ... the challenge of the hill country awaits you.

Mind you, we are not here talking about great as a perception that is based on race or gender or class alone. I am talking about greatness as a way of harnessing and husbanding the best of our spiritual, intellectual, financial, educational, and political resources and empowering our communities and enriching this society. I am not talking about greatness as a way of exalting everything that is African and trashing everything that is European. I am talking about the greatness that the Bible says is in all of us who claim to be the people of God.

The first thing Ephraim and Manasseh had going for them was a healthy self-identity. They said of themselves, "We are a great people!" They practiced the art of self-definition. They refused to be defined by circumstances, or environment, or culture, or class, or race. We know who we are. We have a unique sense of somebodyness. We have a good memory. We know our oral tradition. We are well aware of our ancestors. Our father, Joseph, was Jacob's favorite son. Jacob, our grandfather, was a schemer, but one night by the ford of Jabbok, he wrestled with God and prevailed. Isaac, our great-grandfather, was the only son of our great-great-grandfather, Abraham, a friend of God who received the promise by faith. Oh yeah, we come from good stock.

Not only that, we have this covenant thing. God promised through Abraham and Sarah never to forsake us. That our family would be as numerous as the stars in the heavens and the sand on the seashore. Throughout history the blessing of God has been upon us. Joshua's response to all of this was, "I know that you are indeed a great people. But, if thou be a great people, you go up to the hill country and make a place for yourselves." Great people are trailblazers. Great people are visionary. Great people know how to chart a course, build a bridge, expect a miracle. Great people refuse to be victims to circumstance, color, class, or culture. Great people are not condemned by the conditions of their birth, or locked into Euro-centric thought patterns. You have enough imagination, ingenuity, intelligence, and integrity to make a place for yourselves. Do not linger on the low plains of life crying and complaining, fretting and fuming, moaning and groaning about what you cannot do or what you do not have. Be creative. Accept the challenge of the hill country.

When I think about our African American people, I know we are a great people. I submit that what we are experiencing right now—ethnic cleansing in Bosnia and Mississippi and Arkansas, bombings in New York and Oklahoma, Birmingham and Atlanta; high unemployment, no health care, poor child care, insecure social security, babies dangling from bridges, babies with bullets, children with guns, runaway teenage pregnancy, children with no hope, mothers who can't cope, fathers on dope; more black men in jail than in college; women forgotten too soon; men gone too soon, children dying too soon; sisters waiting to exhale; brothers trying to get paid; heroes becoming zeroes; many of us kept out, kicked out, knocked out, locked out, pushed out, put out, pulled out, phased out; the hopelessness and despair that pervades our communities—what we are experiencing right now is an aberration. We are wandering in a wilderness called the United States. This is not who we really are.

We are a great people. We have a great history. But you have to travel farther than the slave ship, segregation, and second-class citizenship to know who we are. We are an African American people. But more importantly, we are an African people. Many of us struggle with low self-esteem because we are more familiar with the American side of who we are than the African side. We need to get in touch with the African side of our identity. Then we will know that we come from a great family structure; where men are kings, where women are queens, where children affirm every aspect of their identity. We need to remember the great ancient cities that we built; the many contributions that we made to science and medicine, literature, the arts, religion, business. We need to get in touch with the African side to know that we are a great people.

We are a great people with a great history. We must stop reciting the failure studies that have been done on our communities. We must never forget that God has always done great things through Africans. We are formed out of adversity. From it we have fashioned our unique perspective on humanity and divinity. They gave us straw. We gave them bricks. They gave us seeds. We gave them cotton. They gave us sorrow. We wrote songs. They gave us pain. We wrote poems. They gave us trouble. We turned it into testimony. They gave us the blues. We made music. They gave us segregation. We gave them Spelman. They gave us misery. We gave them Morehouse. They gave us terror. We gave them Tuskegee. They called us failures. We gave them Fisk. They gave us burdens. We gave them Bishop. They gave us hell. We gave them Howard.

When God created beauty, God came through Cleopatra. When God created science, God came through George Washington Carver, Daniel Hale Williams, and Garrett Morgan. When God wanted music, God came through Beethoven, Duke Ellington, Marian Anderson, Paul Robeson, and Jessye Norman. When God wanted business people, God came through Madame C. J. Walker, A. G. Gaston, Earl Graves, and Reginald Lewis. When God wants athletes, God comes through Jackie Robinson, Althea Gibson, Muhammad Ali, Arthur Ashe, and Michael Jordan. When God wants to dazzle the world with dance, God comes through Judith Jamison, Alvin Ailey, Robert Mitchell, Hinton Battle, and Gregory Hines. When God wanted to give the world words, God came through Gwendolyn Brooks, Zora Neale Hurston, Langston Hughes, Maya Angelou, and Alice Walker.

Our Africanness is an instrumentality that God uses to enrich the world. God used Rosa Parks, Martin King, Adam Powell, Malcolm X, and Medgar Evers to remind the world that justice will well up like waters and righteousness like a mighty stream. God used Marcus Garvey to remind this world and us that we have one God, one aim, and one destiny. God used Randall Robinson to tell a U. S. President that your policy in Haiti is no good. God used Nelson Mandela to bring 350 years of apartheid to its knees and to tell Bill Clinton, "You run America, I run South Africa." And

God wants to use us to make a contribution to this world. You see, we are a great people. This is our day. This is our time. This is our moment. This is our season.

Joshua said to the tribes of Ephraim and Manasseh and to us, "If thou be a great people get up to the hill country and make a place for yourselves there." Stop fighting over these petty plots of land. Stop fighting over insignificant positions and titles. Stop fighting over that which is trite. Stop waiting for someone else to make or open a door. You have a great work to do: churches to build, families to save, children to nurture, men to redeem, women to empower, marriages to mend, colleges to revitalize, businesses to open, churches to revive, visions to realize, a drug epidemic to rout out, an AIDS pandemic to cure, sin to conquer, salvation to gain, songs to sing, poems to write, hell to avoid, heaven to gain. If thou be a great people, the hill country awaits you.

Mind you, it's not easy in the hill country. The Perizzites and the Canaanite are in the hill country with their vast weapons of irons and chariots. People who do not want you to be free, people who do not want you to succeed, people who do not want you to be educated, people who do not want you to make it. People who oppose God's dominion on earth. People who think that you know less than you know because you are female or male and because you are black. Establishment folk. Bound by tradition, custom, and habit. They tell you that it cannot be done. They tell you that your vision is too ambitious, that your dream is impossible. They say that we have never done it this way before. They have iron and chariots, money, methods, and means. They stand in direct opposition to your vision.

But I just stopped by to tell you that nothing can stop an idea whose time has come. Nothing can stop a people who are determined. Watch out for the opposition in the hill country. They are organized and determined. They are systematized and systemic. Sometimes it is hard to tell who they are and where they are. Sometimes they are white-collar businessmen messing with your financial institutions, health care, and social security. Sometimes it is a Democratic president who cuts the heart out of welfare and puts millions of children further into poverty. They can be neighborhood drug dealers selling drugs to your sons and daughters. Sometimes they make you think that they are for you. All of our opposition is not from people who look different than we do. There are people in our communities who do us harm. We have leaders among us who violate our trust and destroy our integrity. We must cut them down, vote them out, and replace them!

There is even opposition among churches and in the churches. There are Christians who think that their church or denomination is the only ticket in town. They build themselves up by putting you down. But this is not a day for mealymouthed ministers, poorly prepared preachers, lackadaisical laypersons, and chicken-livered Christians. This world needs a strong word from the Lord, and we have been called to speak it. As we need to put our game faces on. Step up to the plate and swing. We need to develop a

Michael Jeffrey Jordan mentality. Michael loves to be twelve points behind with six minutes left to play in the fourth quarter of game seven of the championship series. The challenge brings out the best in Michael and this third millennium will bring out the best in us. We are not going to go tripping across the threshold of the third millennium.

The late Sandy F. Ray, that great Baptist preacher from the Cornerstone Church in Brooklyn, New York, called this the challenge of the wood country.[25] If it were easy to go into the hill country, everybody would be living there. Our challenge is to conquer the hill country in our lives, in our communities, and in our nation. Now it is your turn to make a name for yourselves. We are prepared for the challenges, changes, and crises of the third millennium. We have everything that we need in the hill country. God is for us. Emmanuel is with us. The Holy Spirit empowers us. Our ancestors are rooting for us. The next generation is depending on us.

You are a great people. You have an internal mechanism to help restore our families, save our babies, empower our women, and reclaim our men. More than that, we have an Eternal Motivator who is with us. I know somebody that knows all about the hill country because he's been there. Don't get nervous. You're not going into the hill country alone. God never sends us where God has not already been. God never sends us without first preparing the way. Jesus has already met the challenge ... Jesus went into the hill country and made it a highway to heaven. He turned it into a gateway to eternity. He made it a roadway of reconciliation between God and humanity.

Jesus made a name for himself. At that name demons tremble, governments topple, blind folks can see, lame folks can walk, deaf folks can hear. At that name the dead shall live again. At that name every knee shall bow and every tongue shall confess that he is Lord to the glory of God.

Jesus Christ says to you and to me: If thou be a great people stand up, look up, get up into the hill country—not in your name, but in my name. Live your life. Realize your dreams. Let your light shine. Blow your trumpet. Sing your song. "All hail the power of Jesus' name! Let angels prostrate fall. Bring forth the royal diadem and crown Him Lord of all."[26]

NOTES

Introduction

1. Miles Jerome Jones, *Preaching Papers: The Hampton and Virginia Union Lectures* (New York: Martin Luther King Fellows Press, 1995), 39–40.
2. By marginalization is meant those who have been pushed to the periphery of culture and society; those who through a systematic effort of exclusion have been denied active participation and involvement at the center of the dominant culture. In this work marginalization refers to blacks as a class of people who have historically been denied full participation in many aspects of life by the dominant majority culture. See Lawrence Levine, *Black Culture and Black Consciousness* (New York: Oxford University Press, 1977), 138–40.
3. Cecil Cone, *The Identity Crisis in Black Theology* (Nashville: AMEC Press, 1975), 38–48.
4. Stephen Crites, "The Narrative Quality of Experience," in *Why Narrative?* ed. Stanley Hauerwas and L. Gregory Jones (Grand Rapids: Wm. B. Eerdmans Publishing Co., 1989), 69–72.
5. C. Eric Lincoln and Lawrence Mamiya, *The Black Church in the African American Experience* (Durham, N.C.: Duke University Press, 1990), 3–4.
6. David H. Kelsey, *The Uses of Scripture in Recent Theology* (Philadelphia: Fortress Press, 1975).
7. Ibid., 3–4.
8. August Meier, *Negro Thought in America, 1880–1915* (Ann Arbor, Mich.: University of Michigan Press, 1969), 130–31; Eugene Genovese, *Roll, Jordan, Roll* (New York: Vintage Books, 1976), 257; and H. Beecher Hicks, Jr., *Images of the Black Preacher* (Valley Forge, Pa.: Judson Press, 1977), 43, 155–56.
9. Throughout history some blacks have purposely chosen churches and preachers specifically to avoid any taint of the folk experience and to escape from hearing any preaching that spoke to the marginalized experience of blacks. Also, racial particularity and the preaching that grows out of probing that experience is more easily done in some denominations than others. See Albert J. Raboteau, *A Fire in the Bones* (Boston: Beacon Press, 1995), 122.
10. Major J. Jones, *The Color of God* (Macon, Ga.: Mercer University Press, 1987), 51.
11. Evans E. Crawford with Thomas H. Troeger, *The Hum: Call and Response in African American Preaching* (Nashville: Abingdon Press, 1995), 20.
12. James Cone, *God of the Oppressed* (New York: Seabury Press, 1975), 17–19.

Chapter 1: The Search for Distinctiveness in Black Preaching

1. Wardell J. Payne, ed., *Directory of African American Religious Bodies* (Washington, D.C.: Howard University Press, 1991), 21–147, 199–216; and Larry G. Murphy, J. Gordon Melton, and Gary L. Ward, eds., *Encyclo-*

pedia of African American Religions (New York: Garland Publishing, 1993), xx. The *Encyclopedia* lists some 341 black religious organizations.

2. Stephen Reid, *Experience and Tradition* (Nashville: Abingdon Press, 1990), 11; and Raboteau, *A Fire in the Bones*, 143.

3. Henry Mitchell, *Black Preaching* (New York: Harper & Row, 1970), 173.

4. Cornel West, *Prophetic Fragments* (Grand Rapids: Wm. B. Eerdmans Publishing Co., 1988), 43; Richard Lischer, *The Preacher King: Martin Luther King, Jr., and the Word That Moved America* (New York: Oxford University Press, 1995), 128–30; and Keith D. Miller, *Voice of Deliverance: The Language of Martin Luther King, Jr., and Its Sources* (New York: Free Press, 1992), 128–32.

5. Hortense J. Spillers, "Moving on Down the Line," *American Quarterly* 40 (March 1988): 84.

6. Hortense J. Spillers, "Martin Luther King and the Style of the Black Sermon," in *The Black Experience in Religion*, ed. C. Eric Lincoln (Garden City, N.Y.: Doubleday & Co., Anchor Press, 1974), 76.

7. W. E. B. DuBois, *The Souls of Black Folk* (New York: A. C. McClurg & Co., 1903; reprint, New York: Penguin Books, 1989), 155–56.

8. For a more in-depth treatment of the chanted sermon see Bruce A. Rosenberg, *Can These Bones Live?: The Art of the American Folk Preacher* (New York: Oxford University Press, 1970), 36–55. On the role of emotion in the black worship experience see Brenda Eatman Aghahowa, *Praising in Black and White: Unity and Diversity in Christian Worship* (Cleveland: United Church Press, 1996), 13–20.

9. William H. Pipes, *Say Amen, Brother!: Old-Time Negro Preaching: A Study in American Frustration* (New York: William-Frederick Press, 1951), 1–8; and Benjamin E. Mayes and Joseph W. Nicholson, *The Negro's Church* (New York: Negro Universities Press, 1969), 91–92.

10. DuBois, *The Souls of Black Folk*, 159.

11. In *Celebration and Experience in Preaching* (Nashville: Abingdon Press, 1990), Mitchell provides a systematic treatment of the importance of celebration to the black preaching event. For additional insights on the role of celebration in preaching see Frank A. Thomas, *They Like to Never Quit Praisin' God* (Cleveland: United Church Press, 1997).

12. James Earl Massey, *The Responsible Pulpit* (Anderson, Ind.: Warner Press, 1974), 101–10.

13. Gerald L. Davis, *I Got the Word in Me and I Can Sing It, You Know* (Philadelphia: University of Pennsylvania Press, 1985), xiv–xv, 46, 49–50.

14. William B. McClain, *Come Sunday: The Liturgy of Zion* (Nashville: Abingdon Press, 1990), 62–71.

15. Crawford, *The Hum*, 16–17. For additional insights on homiletical musicality in black preaching see Jon Michael Spencer, *Sacred Symphony: The Chanted Sermon of the Black Preacher* (Westport, Conn.: Greenwood Press, 1987).

16. James H. Evans, *We Have Been Believers: An African American Systematic Theology* (Minneapolis: Fortress Press, 1992), 50. Evans correctly observes that African American belief systems and practices are not learned primarily through detailed, systematic theologies, but through the spoken

word of black preachers as they reflect on scripture, tradition, and experience. The living voice (*viva vox*) continues to be the primary summons to belief.

17. Thomas Hoyt, Jr., "Interpreting Biblical Scholarship for the Black Church Tradition," in *Stony the Road We Trod*, ed. Cain Hope Felder (Minneapolis: Fortress Press, 1991), 27.

18. Evans, *We Have Been Believers*, 2.

19. Lawrence T. Jones, "Black Pentecostal," in *The Charismatic Movement*, ed. Michael P. Hamilton (Grand Rapids: Wm. B. Eerdmans Publishing Co., 1975), 145–58.

20. Robert A. Bennett, "Black Experience and the Bible," in *African American Religious Studies: An Interdisciplinary Anthology*, ed. Gayraud S. Wilmore (Durham, N. C.: Duke University Press, 1989), 130.

21. Albert J. Raboteau, *Slave Religion: The "Invisible Institution" in the Antebellum South* (New York: Oxford University Press, 1978), 318.

22. Hoyt, "Interpreting Biblical Scholarship," 29.

23. See Ephesians 6:5–9 and Colossians 3–22. Many slaves outright rejected the letter to Philemon as revelatory. See Mechal Sobel, *Trabelin' On: The Slave Journey to an Afro-Baptist Faith* (Princeton, N.J.: Princeton University Press, 1979), 154–55; and Evans, *We Have Been Believers*, 35–40.

24. J. W. C. Pennington, "A Two Years' Absence or a Farewell Sermon, Preached in the Fifth Congregational Church," Nov. 2, 1845, 22–23, Moorland-Spingarn Collection, Howard University, Washington, D.C.

25. Kelsey, *The Uses of Scripture*, 2–5.

26. Ibid., 102.

27. *Discrimen*, a Latin term defined as the act or power of distinguishing.

28. Kelsey, *The Uses of Scripture*, 160.

29. By the terms "imaginative" or "imagination," Kelsey is denoting a judgment in which some complex reality may be grasped holistically when one sees that it is like some simpler, more familiar reality. The terms "imaginative" and "imagination" are thus intended to designate the manner in which one offers metaphors and analogies. See Kelsey, *The Uses of Scripture*, 159, 178. See chapter 8, note 6.

30. When a person announces to a black congregation that he or she has been called by God to preach, one of the factors governing bodies consider in determining their fitness for ministry is the extent of their participation in "the total program of the church." By this phrase is meant whether or not the newly called preacher has received sufficient grounding in the beliefs and practices of the institutional church structure. The value of the church as an influencing factor in the lives of those who confess their call to preach is beyond measure. See William H. Myers, *The Irresistible Urge to Preach: A Collection of African American "Call" Stories* (Atlanta: Aaron Press, 1992), xxiv.

31. Lincoln and Mamiya, *The Black Church*, 399.

32. Even when one takes into consideration the very important functions of the various forms of literary texts, i.e., what the texts say and how the texts say what they say, I contend that this black biblical hermeneutic will be the primary factor in shaping how that text will be preached. Cf. Long,

Preaching and the Literary Forms of the Bible (Philadelphia: Fortress Press, 1989), 11.

33. Albert J. Raboteau, "The Black Experience in American Evangelicalism: The Meaning of Slavery," in *The Evangelical Tradition in America*, ed. Leonard I. Sweet (Macon, Ga.: Mercer University Press, 1984), 181.

34. Donald G. Mathews, *Religion in the Old South* (Chicago: University of Chicago Press), xvi–xvii.

35. Among the similarities the African converts found between their old religion and evangelical revivalism were: the conversion experience with its various forms of hysteria and ecstasy; the incantational preaching which New Light Baptists brought from New England; baptism, whether by immersion, sprinkling, or pouring; and the enthusiastic congregational singing, to which Methodists were almost fanatically devoted. See Mathews, *Religion in the Old South*, 192–94; and Sobel, *Trabelin' On*, 139–46.

36. Mark A. Noll, "Pietism," in *The Evangelical Dictionary of Theology*, ed. Walter A. Elwell (Grand Rapids: Baker Book House, 1985), 855–56; and Edward Farley, *Theologia* (Philadelphia: Fortress Press, 1983), 41.

37. The phrase "care of souls" was originally employed by the Latin Church to express a variation of meanings with respect to the care of persons. See John T. McNeill, *A History of the Cure of Souls* (New York: Harper & Brothers, 1951), vii.

38. John H. Leith, *An Introduction to the Reformed Tradition: A Way of Being the Christian Community* (Atlanta: John Knox Press, 1981), 85.

39. William A. Clebsch and Charles R. Jaekle, *Pastoral Care in Historical Perspective* (Englewood Cliffs, N.J.: Prentice-Hall, 1964), 33–56.

40. Peter J. Paris, *Black Religious Leaders: Conflict in Unity* (Louisville, Ky.: Westminster/John Knox Press, 1991), 20–21.

41. Frank A. Thomas, "The Million Man March: A Sermon for Discussion," in *Atonement: The Million Man March*, ed. Kim Martin Sadler (Cleveland: Pilgrim Press, 1996), 135–37.

42. Blacks are not quick to pull up stakes and move to a growing part of town because the spiritual and symbolic significance of location is equally important to their sense of "church."

43. For an example of a sermon whose textual applications are addressed specifically to the maintenance of the institutional church see Frank A. Thomas's sermon "Arrested by the Lord," in *Patterns of Preaching: A Sermon Sampler*, ed. Ronald J. Allen (St. Louis: Chalice Press, 1998), 43–48.

44. For an example of a corporate concerns sermon that seeks to motivate and edify blacks as a group in a positive manner see Carolyn Ann Knight's "If Thou Be a Great People," in *Patterns of Preaching*, 225–230. See also Kenneth L. Waters, Sr., *Afrocentric Sermons: The Beauty of Blackness in the Bible* (Valley Forge, Pa.: Judson Press, 1993).

45. A metaphor is defined here as a figure of speech in which one speaks of one thing in terms appropriate to another. According to G. B. Caird, a metaphor is the transference of a term from one referent with which it naturally belongs to a second referent, in order that the second may be illuminated by comparison with the first or by being "seen as" the first. See G. B. Caird, *The Language and Imagery of the Bible* (London: Gerald Duckworth & Co., 1980), 66.

46. Thomas Hoyt, Jr., "Interpreting Biblical Scholarship for the Black Church Tradition," in *Stony the Road We Trod: African American Biblical Interpretation*, ed. Cain Hope Felder (Minneapolis: Fortress Press, 1991), 21–22.

47. James H. Cone, *A Black Theology of Liberation* (Maryknoll, N. Y.: Orbis Books, 1986) 31; and Hoyt, "An Ante-bellum Sermon," 110.

48. See Delores S. Williams, *Sisters in the Wilderness* (Maryknoll, N. Y.: Orbis Books, 1993), 20–21. Williams points out that the Hagar story in the Old Testament (Gen. 16) addresses itself to matters of survival and quality of life. "The angel of Yahweh is, in this passage, no liberator God." Any attempt to put this aspect of Hagar's experience with God into a liberation metaphor stretches the text beyond what it declares.

49. C. L. Franklin, "What of the Night?" in *Give Me This Mountain*, ed. Jeff Todd Titon (Champagne, Ill.: University of Illinois Press, 1989), 166–74.

Chapter 2: The Power Motif in Nineteenth-Century African American Sermons

1. Meier, *Negro Thought in America, 1880–1915*, 130–31; and Hicks, *Images of the Black Preacher*, 43.

2. See Stephen Ward Angell, *Bishop Henry McNeal Turner and African-American Religion in the South* (Knoxville: University of Tennessee Press, 1992); Hans A. Baer and Merrill Singer, *African American Religion in the Twentieth Century: Varieties of Protest and Accommodation* (Knoxville: University of Tennessee Press, 1992); Howard N. Rabinowitz, ed., *Southern Black Leaders of the Reconstruction Era* (Chicago: University of Illinois Press, 1982); and John Hope Franklin, ed., *Black Leaders of the Twentieth Century* (Chicago: University of Illinois Press, 1982).

3. James H. Harris, *Preaching Liberation* (Minneapolis: Fortress Press, 1995), 50.

4. Mathews, *Religion in the Old South*, 217.

5. William E. Hatcher, *John Jasper: The Unmatched Negro Philosopher and Preacher* (New York: Fleming H. Revell Co., 1908), 136–37. "The Sun Do Move" was originally printed in the dialect of unlearned former slaves. I have taken the liberty of translating the sermon into plain English, which made it easier to understand, thus allowing the reader to focus on the content of the sermon and not Hatcher's attempt to put Jasper's broken dialect into writing.

6. Ibid., 137.

7. Ibid., 135–36.

8. Ibid., 141.

9. Ibid., 136.

10. Ibid., 142.

11. Ibid., 141–43.

12. Ibid., 140–41.

13. Ibid., 142.

14. Ibid., 143.

15. Ibid., 144.

16. Henry Louis Gates, Jr., "Canon-Formation, Literary History, and the Afro-American Tradition: From the Seen to the Told," in *Afro-American*

Literary Studies in the 1990s, eds. Houston A. Baker, Jr. and Patricia Redmond (Chicago: University of Chicago Press, 1989), 15.

17. Wilson Jeremiah Moses, *Alexander Crummell: A Study of Civilization and Discontent* (New York: Oxford University Press, 1989), 5.

18. Wilson Jeremiah Moses, "Civilizing Missionary: A Study of Alexander Crummell," *The Journal of Negro History* 60 (April 1975): 229.

19. Crummell said it was difficult to define with exactness the term "civilization." However, he did attempt to describe its elements: the family, the status of women, dress, culture, manners, social life, and art. See "The Greatness of Christ," in Crummell, *The Greatness of Christ and Other Sermons* (New York: Thomas Whittaker Publisher, 1882), 8–11.

20. Sandy Dwayne Martin, "Black Baptists, Foreign Missions, and African Colonization, 1814–1882," in *Black Americans and the Missionary Movement in Africa*, ed. Sylvia M. Jacobs (Westport, Conn.: Greenwood Press, 1982), 63.

21. Alexander Crummell, *The Future of Africa: Being Addresses, Sermons, Etc., Etc.*, (New York: Charles Scribner, 1862), 151–71.

22. Benjamin E. Mays, *The Negro's God* (Boston: Chapman & Grimes, 1938), 60.

23. Crummell, "Jubilate: The Shades and the Lights of a Fifty Years' Ministry," in *Destiny and Race ... Selected Writings, 1840–1898*, ed. Wilson J. Moses (Amherst, Mass.: University of Massachusetts Press, 1992), 42.

24. Ibid.

25. Ibid.

26. Ibid., 43.

27. Crummell, "The Destined Superiority of the Negro," in *The Greatness of Christ and Other Sermons* (New York: Thomas Whittaker, 1882), 332–52.

28. Miller, *Voice of Deliverance*, 20. The Lukan version of this passage—Luke 4:18–19—is also the one cited most often by James Cone and other black liberation theologians as the scriptural foundation for their own work. See also James Cone, *A Black Theology of Liberation*; J. Deotis Roberts, *Liberation and Reconciliation*; and Dwight N. Hopkins, *Black Theology USA and South Africa*.

29. Crummell, *The Greatness of Christ*, 333.

30. Ibid., 336.

31. Ibid., 332.

32. Ibid.

33. Rayford W. Logan, *The Betrayal of the Negro* (New York: Collier Books, 1954), 9–12.

34. Crummell, *The Greatness of Christ*, 336.

35. Henry Justin Ferry, "Racism and Reunion: A Black Protest by Francis James Grimké," *Journal of Presbyterian History* 50 (summer 1971): 77.

36. Louis B. Weeks, "Racism, World War I and the Christian Life: Francis J. Grimké in the Nation's Capital," in *Black Apostles*, ed. Randall K. Burkett and Richard Newman (Boston: G. K. Hall & Co., 1978), 58–59.

37. Ferry, "Patriotism and Prejudice: Francis James Grimké on World War I," *The Journal of Religious Thought* 32 (spring–summer 1975): 86.

38. Ibid., 87; and Ronald C. White, Jr., *Liberty and Justice for All: Racial Reform and the Social Gospel (1877–1925)* (New York: Harper & Row, 1990), 106–7.

39. Clifton E. Olmstead, "Francis J. Grimké: Christian Moralist and Civil Rights," in *Sons of the Prophets: Leaders in Protestantism from Princeton Seminary*, ed. Hugh T. Kerr (Princeton, N. J.: Princeton University Press, 1963), 165.

40. Francis J. Grimké, "A Resemblance and a Contrast Between the American Negro and the Children of Israel, in Egypt, or the Duty of the Negro to Contend Earnestly for his Rights Guaranteed Under the Constitution," in *The Works of Francis J. Grimké*, ed. Carter G. Woodson, vol. 1, *Addresses Mainly Personal and Racial* (Washington, D.C.: Associated Publishers, 1942), 347–64.

41. Albert J. Raboteau, "Afro-Americans, Exodus, and the American Israel" in *A Fire in the Bones: Reflections on African-American Religious History* (Boston: Beacon Press, 1995), 28–36. and Hoyt, "Interpreting Biblical Scholarship," 30.

42. Grimké, "A Resemblance and a Contrast," 348–49.

43. Ibid., 350.

44. The theory of providential design espoused the notion that God allowed blacks to be brought to America as slaves so that they might have an opportunity to hear the gospel, receive Christ and return to dark, benighted Africa to win their lost brothers and sisters to Christ. See Gayraud S. Wilmore, *Black Religion and Black Radicalism: An Interpretation of the Religious History of Afro-American People* (Maryknoll, N. Y.: Orbis Books, 1991), 119.

45. Grimké, "A Resemblance and a Contrast," 354.

46. Ibid., 363.

47. Grimké, "The Roosevelt-Washington Episode, or Race Prejudice," in *The Works of Francis J. Grimké*, ed. Carter G. Woodson, vol. 1, *Addresses Mainly Personal and Racial* (Washington, D. C.: Associated Publishers, 1942), 334–47.

48. Ibid., 334.

49. Ibid.

50. Ibid., 339.

51. Ibid., 343.

52. Ibid.

53. Ibid., 343–44.

54. Ibid., 345.

55. Ibid., 346.

56. Ibid.

57. Ibid.

58. Milton C. Sernett, ed., *Afro-American Religious History: A Documentary Witness* (Durham, N. C.: Duke University Press, 1985), 217.

59. Daniel Alexander Payne, *Recollections of Seventy Years* (Nashville: Publishing House of the A. M. E. Sunday School Union, 1888), 38.

60. Ibid., 28–29.

61. Ibid., 110.

62. Ibid., 146.

63. Ibid., 162.

64. Ibid., 289, 306–7.

65. Ibid., 324.

66. Daniel A. Payne, "Welcome to the Ransomed, or Duties of the Colored Inhabitants of the District of Columbia" (Baltimore: Bull & Tuttle, 1862), 1.
67. Sernett, *Afro-American Religious History*, 217; and Payne, *Recollections*, 146–48.
68. Clarence Walker, *A Rock in a Weary Land: The African Methodist Episcopal Church During the Civil War and Reconstruction* (Baton Rouge: Louisiana State University Press, 1982), 46–7.
69. Payne, "Welcome to the Ransomed," 11.
70. Ibid., 6.
71. Walker, *A Rock in a Weary Land*, 47.
72. Payne, "Welcome to the Ransomed," 11.
73. Ibid., 15–16.
74. Ibid., 7.
75. Ibid., 12.
76. Elias Camp Morris, *Sermons, Addresses and Reminiscences and Important Correspondence* (Nashville: Sunday School Publishing Board, 1901; reprint 1993), 177; James Melvin Washington, *Frustrated Fellowship: The Black Quest for Social Power* (Macon, Ga.: Mercer University Press, 1986), 185; and Joseph Harrison Jackson, *A Story of Christian Activism: The History of the National Baptist Convention, U.S.A., Inc.* (Nashville: Townsend Press, 1980), 63–74.
77. Rufus B. Spain, *At Ease in Zion: A Social History of Southern Baptists, 1865–1900* (Nashville: Vanderbilt University Press, 1967), 44–67.
78. Elias C. Morris, "1899 Presidential Address to the National Baptist Convention," in *Afro-American Religious History*, 283.
79. Morris, *Sermons*, 131–32.
80. Morris, "1914 Presidential Address to the National Baptist Convention," in *The President Speaks*, ed. Marvin Griffin (Austin, Texas: By the author, 1989), 66–7.
81. Morris, "1900 Presidential Address to the National Baptist Convention," in *The President Speaks*, 41–42.
82. Morris, "The Brotherhood of Man," in *Sermons* 32.
83. Ibid., 30.
84. Ibid., 31.
85. Ibid., 32.
86. Ibid., 34.
87. Ibid., 35.

Chapter 3: A Hermeneutic of Power in Contemporary African American Sermons

1. David Buttrick, *Homiletic: Moves and Structures* (Philadelphia: Fortress Press, 1987), 23.
2. Paul Scott Wilson, *The Practice of Preaching* (Nashville: Abingdon Press, 1995), 146.
3. Jeremiah A, Wright, Jr., *What Makes You So Strong?: Sermons of Joy and Strength from Jeremiah A. Wright, Jr.* (Valley Forge, Pa.: Judson Press, 1993), 147–61.
4. Ibid., 147.
5. Ibid., 150–51.

6. Ibid., 152.
7. Ibid., 152–53.
8. Ibid., 154–55.
9. Ibid., 156.
10. Ibid., 157.
11. Ibid., 158.
12. Ibid., 5–8.
13. Ibid., 9.
14. Ibid., 9–11.
15. Ibid., 9.
16. Katie G. Cannon, "To Tell the Truth," *The African American Pulpit* 1, no. 3 (summer 1998): 30.
17. Ibid.
18. Ibid., 31.
19. Ibid.
20. Ibid., 32.
21. Ibid., 33.
22. Ibid., 34.
23. Ibid.
24. Ibid., 34–35.
25. Ibid., 32.
26. Ibid., 33.
27. KJV.
28. A Louis Patterson, Jr., *Prerequisites for a Good Journey: The Hampton University Minister's Conference Sermon Series* (St. Louis: Hodale Press, 1994), 79.
29. Ibid., 82.
30. Ibid., 82–83.
31. Ibid., 83–84.
32. Ibid.
33. Ibid., 84.
34. Ibid., 87–88.
35. Mozella Mitchell, "Pro-vi-dence," in *Those Preaching Women: More Sermons by Black Women Preachers*, ed. Ella Mitchell (Valley Forge, Pa.: Judson Press, 1995), 48.
36. Ibid., 49.
37. Ibid.
38. Ibid., 50.
39. Ibid., 50–51.
40. Ibid.
41. Ibid., 53.
42. Fred C. Lofton, "Bad Black Dude on the Road," in *Living in Hell: The Dilemma of African American Survival*, ed. Mose Pleasure, Jr., and Fred C. Lofton (Grand Rapids: Zondervan Publishing House, 1995), 158–68.
43. Ibid., 159–60.
44. Ibid., 160–61.
45. Ibid., 162.
46. Ibid.
47. Ibid., 162–63.

48. Ibid., 163.
49. Ibid., 163–64.
50. Ibid., 165–66.
51. Ibid., 166.
52. Carolyn Ann Knight, "If Thou Be a Great People," 223–30.
53. Sandy F. Ray, "The Challenge of the Wood Country," in *Journeying Through a Jungle* (Nashville: Broadman Press, 1979), 75–83.
54. Knight, "If Thou Be a Great People," 224.
55. Ibid., 225.
56. Ibid.
57. Ibid., 226.
58. Ibid.
59. Ibid.
60. Ibid., 225–26.
61. Ibid., 227.
62. Ibid.
63. Ibid., 228.
64. Ibid., 229.
65. Henry Mitchell cautions against celebration that does not relate directly to the purpose of the sermon. See Mitchell, *Celebration and Experience in Preaching*, 66–7. See also Ronald J. Allen and John C. Holbert, *Holy Root, Holy Branches: Christian Preaching from the Old Testament* (Nashville: Abingdon Press, 1995), 29–31.
66. Knight, "If Thou be a Great People," 228.
67. Ibid., 225.
68. Ibid., 230.
69. See Brian Blount, *Cultural Interpretation: Reorienting New Testament Criticism* (Minneapolis: Fortress Press, 1995), 76; and Reid, *Experience and Tradition*, 22–23.

Chapter 4: The Basic Dynamics of the African American Sermon

1. Buttrick, *Homiletic*, 41.
2. Evans, *We Have Been Believers*, 67.
3. Ibid., 67–68.
4. Ibid., 69.
5. Jones, *The Color of God*, 46.
6. James Cone, *A Black Theology of Liberation*, 60.
7. Ibid., 60–61.
8. Samuel D. Proctor, *The Certain Sound of the Trumpet: Crafting a Sermon of Authority* (Valley Forge, Pa.: Judson Press, 1994), 5.
9. See James Cone, *God of the Oppressed*.
10. Evans, *We Have Been Believers*, 16–18.
11. Ibid.
12. Dwight N. Hopkins, *Black Theology USA and South Africa: Politics, Culture, and Liberation* (Maryknoll, N. Y.: Orbis Books, 1989), 2. See also James Cone, *A Black Theology of Liberation*, 1–4.
13. Paris, *Black Religious Leaders*, 287–93; and Gayraud S. Wilmore and James H. Cone, *Black Theology: A Documentary History, 1966–1979* (Maryknoll, N.Y.: Orbis Books, 1979), 260.

14. Lincoln lists the seven major historic black denominations as: the African Methodist Episcopal (A. M. E.) Church; the African Methodist Episcopal Zion (A. M. E. Z.) Church; the Christian Methodist Episcopal (C.M.E.) Church; the National Baptist Convention, U.S.A., Incorporated (NBC); the National Baptist Convention of America, Unincorporated (NBCA); the Progressive National Baptist Convention (PNBC); and the Church of God in Christ (COGIC). Cf. Lincoln and Mamiya, *The Black Church in the African American Experience*, 1.

15. James H. Harris, *Pastoral Theology: A Black-Church Perspective* (Minneapolis: Fortress Press, 1993), 55. For further discussions on bridging the gap between church practice and black theology see Dwight N. Hopkins and George Cummings, eds., *Cut Loose Your Stammering Tongue: Black Theology in the Slave Narratives* (Maryknoll, N. Y.: Orbis Books, 1991), xv; and Olin P. Moyd, *The Sacred Art: Preaching and Theology in the African American Tradition* (Valley Forge, Pa.: Judson Press, 1995), 13–32.

16. Lincoln, *The Black Church*, 178–83.

17. James Cone, *God of the Oppressed*, 17.

18. Crawford, *The Hum*, 19.

19. This dual reality of which Crawford speaks was expressed as a "felt twoness" by W. E. B. DuBois and as "biculturality" by Henry Mitchell.

20. Mathews, *Religion in the Old South*, 199.

21. Hoyt, "Interpreting Biblical Scholarship," 31.

22. Leonora Tubbs Tisdale, *Preaching as Local Theology and Folk Art* (Minneapolis: Fortress Press, 1997), 27–30.

23. Robert M. Franklin, *Another Day's Journey: Black Churches Confronting the American Crisis* (Minneapolis: Fortress Press, 1997), 33.

24. West, *Prophetic Fragments*, 274–75.

25. Ibid., 275.

26. William B. McCain, "African-American Preaching, in *The Renewal of Worship*, vol. 3, ed. Robert E. Webber (Nashville: Star Song Publishing Group, 1993), 317.

27. Harris, *Pastoral Theology*, 56.

Appendix: Sermons

1. Jasper, "The Sun Do Move," 133–49.

2. Crummell, *The Greatness of Christ*, 332–52.

3. Woodson, *The Works of Francis J. Grimke*, vol. 1, 347–63.

4. Woodson, *The Works of Francis J. Grimke*, vol. 1, 334–46.

5. Payne, "Welcome to the Ransomed, or, Duties of the Colored Inhabitants of the District of Columbia," 1–16.

6. Morris, *Sermons, Addresses, and Reminiscences*, 30–35.

7. Wright, *What Makes You So Strong?* 147–61.

8. Ibid., 1–12.

9. Matthew 18:20, RSV.

10. John 7:46, RSV.

11. James 4:7, RSV.

12. Matthew 16:18, KJV.

13. Mark 14:66–72; Matthew 26:69–75; Luke 22:1–62 (KJV).

14. Dr. Charles Walker is the pastor of the Nineteenth Street Baptist Church in Philadelphia.
15. Isaiah 40:31, KJV.
16. Traditional
17. Cannon, "To Tell the Truth," 30–35.
18. Patterson, *Prerequisites for a Good Journey*, 75–90.
19. Mitchell, "Pro-vi-dence," 48–54.
20. From the hymn "His Eye Is On The Sparrow" in *The New National Baptist Hymnal* (Nashville: National Baptist Publishing Board, 1987).
21. Lofton, "Bad Black Dude on the Road," 158–68.
22. "Bad Black Dude on the Road" is adapted from a sermon delivered at the Cornerstone Baptist Church in Brooklyn, New York.
23. William LaRue Dillard, *Biblical Ancestry Voyage* (Morristown, N.J.: Aaron Press, 1989), 223–24.
24. Knight, "If Thou Be a Great People," 223–30.
25. Ray, "The Challenge of the Wood Country," 75–84.
26. E. Perronet, "All Hail the Power of Jesus' Name!" *The New National Baptist Hymnal* (Nashville: National Baptist Publishing Board, 1987), 523.

BIBLIOGRAPHY

Aghahowa, Brenda Eatman. *Praising in Black and White: Unity and Diversity in Christian Worship.* Cleveland: United Church Press, 1996.

Allen, Ronald J., ed. *Patterns of Preaching: A Sermon Sampler.* St. Louis: Chalice Press, 1998.

Allen, Ronald J., and John C. Holbert. *Holy Root, Holy Branches: Christian Preaching from the Old Testament.* Nashville: Abingdon Press, 1995.

Angell, Stephen W. *Bishop Henry McNeal Turner and African-American Religion in the South.* Knoxville, University of Tennessee Press, 1992.

Bacote, Samuel William. *Who's Who among the Colored Baptists in the United States.* Kansas City, Mo: Franklin Hudson Publishing Co., 1913.

Baer, Hans A., and Merrill Singer. *African-American Religion in the Twentieth Century: Varieties of Protest and Accommodation.* Knoxville: University of Tennessee Press, 1992.

Baker, Houston A., Jr., and Patricia Redmond, eds. *Afro-American Literary Study in the 1990s.* Chicago: University of Chicago Press, 1989.

Benn, J. Solomon, ed. *Preaching in Ebony.* Grand Rapids: Baker Book House, 1981.

Bennett, Lerone. *Before the Mayflower: A History of Black America.* New York: Penguin Books, 1982.

Bennett, Robert A. "Black Experience and the Bible." In *African American Religious Studies: An Interdisciplinary Anthology,* edited by Gayraud S. Wilmore, 129–39. Durham, N. C.: Duke University Press, 1989.

Berlin, Ira. *Slaves without Masters: The Free Negro in the Antebellum South.* New Press, 1974.

Bevans, Stephen B. *Models of Contextual Theology.* Maryknoll, N.Y.: Orbis Books, 1992.

Blount, Brian K. *Cultural Interpretation: Reorienting New Testament Criticism.* Minneapolis: Fortress Press, 1995.

Brewer, J. Mason. *The Word on the Brazos*. Austin: University of Texas Press, 1969.

Brown, Sterling A. "Our Literary Audience." In *Speech and Power*, vol. 2, edited by Gerald Early. Hopewell, N. J.: Ecco Press, 1993.

Bruce, Calvin E., and William R. Jones. *Black Theology II: Essays on the Formation and Outreach of Contemporary Black Theology*. Lewisburg, Pa.: Bucknell University Press, 1978.

Burkett, Randall K., and Richard Newman. *Black Apostles: Afro-American Clergy Confront the Twentieth Century*. Boston: G. K. Hall & Co., 1978.

Buttrick, David. *Homiletic: Moves and Structures*. Philadelphia: Fortress Press, 1987.

Caird, G. B. *The Language and Imagery of the Bible*. London: Gerald Duckworth & Co., 1980.

Calloway-Thomas, Carolyn, and John Louis Lucaites, eds. *Martin Luther King, Jr., and the Sermonic Power of Public Discourse*. Tuscaloosa, Ala.: University of Alabama Press, 1993.

———. "A Rhetorical Analysis of the Persuasion of Francis J. Grimké." Ph.D. diss., Indiana University, 1976.

Cannon, Katie G. "To Tell the Truth." *African American Pulpit* 1, no. 3 (summer 1998): 29–35.

Carson, Clayborne, and Peter Halloran. *A Knock at Midnight: Inspiration from the Great Sermons of Reverend Martin Luther King, Jr.* New York: Warner Books, 1998.

Clark, John Franklin. *A Brief History of Negro Baptists in Arkansas: A Story of Their Progress and Development, 1867–1939*. Pine Bluff, Ark.: Arkansas Baptists, 1939.

Clebsch, William A., and Charles R. Jaekle. *Pastoral Care in Historical Perspective*. Englewood Cliffs, N.J.: Prentice-Hall, 1964.

Coan, Josephus R. "Henry McNeal Turner: A Fearless Prophet of Black Liberation." *Journal of the Interdenominational Theological Center* 1 (fall 1973): 8–20.

Coffin, Henry Sloane, ed. *The Book of Isaiah*. Nashville: Abingdon Press, 1956.

Cone, Cecil W. *The Identity Crisis in Black Theology*. Nashville: AMEC Press, 1975.

Cone, James H. *A Black Theology of Liberation*. Maryknoll, N.Y.: Orbis Press, 1986.

————. *God of the Oppressed*. New York: Seabury Press, 1975.

————. "The Meaning of God in the Black Spirituals." In *God as Father?* edited by J. Metz, 57–60. New York: Seabury Press, 1981.

————. *Speaking the Truth: Ecumenism, Liberation, and Black Theology*. Grand Rapids: Wm. B. Eerdmans Publishing Co., 1986.

Craddock, Fred B. *Preaching*. Nashville: Abingdon Press, 1985.

Crawford, Evans E., with Thomas H. Troeger. *The Hum: Call and Response in African American Preaching*. Nashville: Abingdon Press, 1995.

Crites, Stephen. "The Narrative Quality of Experience." In *Why Narrative?*, edited by Stanley Hauerwas and L. Gregory Jones, 65–88. Grand Rapids: Wm. B. Eerdmans Publishing Co., 1989.

Crummell, Alexander. *The Future of Africa: Being Addresses, Sermons, Etc., Etc., Delivered in the Republic of Liberia*. New York: Charles Scribner, 1862.

————. "The Destined Superiority of the Negro." In *The Greatness of Christ and Other Sermons*, 332–52: New York: Thomas Whittaker, 1882.

————. "Jubilate: The Shades and the Lights of a Fifty Years' Ministry." In *Destiny and Race ... Selected Writings, 1840–1898*, edited by Wilson J. Moses, 31–44. Amherst, Mass.: University of Massachusetts Press, 1992.

————. *The Greatness of Christ and Other Sermons*. New York: Thomas Whittaker, 1882.

————. *Africa and America: Addresses and Discourses*. New York: Negro Universities Press, 1969 (1891).

Davis, Gerald L. *I Got the Word in Me and I Can Sing It, You Know: A Study of the Performed African-American Sermon*. Philadelphia: University of Pennsylvania Press, 1985.

Dayton, Donald W., and Robert K. Johnson, eds. *The Variety of American Evangelicalism*. Knoxville: University of Tennessee Press, 1991.

DuBois, W. E. B. *The Souls of Black Folk*. New York: A. C. McClurg & Co., 1903.

————. *Black Reconstruction in America*. New York: Atheneum Publishers, 1935.

Dyson, Michael Eric. "Gardner Taylor: Poet Laureate of the Pulpit." *The Christian Century* 112 (January 1994): 12–16.

Earl, Riggins R., Jr. *Dark Symbols, Obscure Signs, God, Self and Community in the Slave Mind*. Maryknoll, N. Y.: Orbis Books, 1993.

Epstein, Dena J. *Sinful Tunes and Spirituals: Black Folk Music to the Civil War*. Urbana: University of Illinois Press, 1977.

Eslinger, Richard L. *A New Hearing: Living Options in Homiletic Methods*. Nashville: Abingdon Press 1987.

Evans, James H. *We Have Been Believers: An African-American Systematic Theology*. Minneapolis: Fortress Press, 1992.

Fabre, Geneviève, and Robert O'Mealley, eds. *History and Memory in African-American Culture*. New York: Oxford University Press, 1994.

Felder, Cain Hope, ed. *Stony the Road We Trod: African American Biblical Interpretation*. Minneapolis: Fortress Press, 1991.

———. *Troubling Biblical Waters: Race, Class and Family*. New York: Oxford University Press, 1994.

Ferry, Henry Justin. "Racism and Reunion: A Black Protest by Francis J. Grimké. *Journal of Presbyterian History* 50 (summer 1971): 77–88.

———. "Patriotism and Prejudice: Francis James Grimké on World War I." *The Journal of Religious Thought* 32 (spring–summer 1975): 86–94.

Fisher, Miles Mark. *A Short History of the Baptist Denomination*. Nashville: Sunday School Publishing Board, 1933.

Foner, Eric. "African Americans in Public Office During the Era of Reconstruction: A Profile." *Reconstruction* 2 1993: 20–23.

Frame, John M. Review of *The Uses of Scripture in Recent Theology*, by David A. Kelsey. *Westminster Theological Journal* 39 (1976/77): 328–30.

Franklin, C. L. "What of the Night." In *Give Me This Mountain*, edited by Jeff Todd Titon, 166–74. Urbana: University of Illinois, 1989.

Franklin, John Hope. *The Emancipation Proclamation*. New York: Vintage Books, 1963.

Franklin, Robert M. *Another Day's Journey: Black Churches Confronting the American Crisis*. Minneapolis: Fortress Press, 1997.

Frazier, E. Franklin. *The Negro Church in America*. New York: Schocken Books, 1974.

Gates, Henry Louis. "Canon-Formation, Literary History, and the Afro-American Tradition: From the Seen to the Told." In *Afro-American Literary Studies in the 1990s*, edited by Houston A. Baker, Jr., and Patricia Redmond, 14–38. Chicago: University of Chicago Press, 1989.

Genovese, Eugene. *Roll, Jordan, Roll: The World the Slaves Made*. New York: Vintage Books, 1976.

Grech, Prosper. Review of *The Uses of Scripture in Recent Theology*, by David A. Kelsey. *Biblica* 58 (1977): 278–81.

Griffin, Marvin C., ed. *The President Speaks*. Austin, Tex.: Published by the author, 1989.

Grimké, Francis J. "A Resemblance and a Contrast between the American Negro and the Children of Israel, in Egypt, or the Duty of the Negro to Contend Earnestly for His Rights Guaranteed under the Constitution." In *The Works of Francis Grimké*, edited by Carter G. Woodson. Vol. 1, *Addresses Mainly Personal and Racial*, 347–64. Washington, D.C.: Associated Publishers, 1942.

———. "The Roosevelt-Washington Episode, or Race Prejudice." In *The Works of Francis Grimké*, edited by Carter G. Woodson. Vol. 1, *Addresses Mainly Personal and Racial*, 334–46. Washington, D.C.: Associated Publishers, 1942.

Gunn, David M., and Danna Nolan Fewell. *Narrative in the Hebrew Bible*. New York: Oxford University Press, 1993.

Hamilton, Michael P., ed. *The Charismatic Movement*. Grand Rapids: Wm. B. Eerdmans Publishing Co., 1975.

Harlan, Louis R. *Booker T. Washington: The Wizard of Tuskegee, 1901–1915*. New York: Oxford University Press, 1983.

Harris, James H. *Pastoral Theology: A Black-Church Perspective*. Minneapolis: Fortress Press, 1993.

———. *Preaching Liberation*. Minneapolis: Fortress Press, 1995.

Hatcher, William E. *John Jasper: The Unmatched Negro Philosopher and Preacher*. New York: F. H. Revell Co., 1908.

Hauerwas, Stanley. "The Moral Authority of Scripture: The Politics of Remembering." *Interpretation* 34 (1980): 356–70.

Hicks, H. Beecher, Jr. *Images of the Black Preacher*. Valley Forge Pa.: Judson Press, 1977.

Hine, Darlene Clark. *The State of Afro-American History: Past, Present, and Future*. Baton Rouge: Louisiana State University Press, 1986.

Hooks, Bell, and Cornel West. *Breaking Bread: Insurgent Black Intellectual Life*. Boston: South End Press, 1991.

Hopkins, Dwight N. *Black Theology USA and South Africa: Politics, Culture, and Liberation*. Maryknoll, N.Y.: Orbis Books, 1989.

Hopkins, Dwight N., and George Cummings, eds. *Cut Loose Your Stammering Tongue: Black Theology in the Slave Narratives*. Maryknoll, N.Y.: Orbis Books, 1991.

Hoyt, Thomas J. "Interpreting Biblical Scholarship for the Black Church Tradition." In *Stony the Road We Trod*, edited by Cain Hope Felder, 17–39. Minneapolis: Fortress Press, 1991.

Hubbard, David A., and Glenn W. Barker, eds. *Isaiah: Word Biblical Commentary*. Waco, Tex.: Word Books, 1987.

Hubbard, Dolan. *The Sermon and the African American Literary Imagination*. Columbia: University of Missouri Press, 1994.

Hunter, Rodney J., ed. *Dictionary of Pastoral Care and Counseling*. Nashville: Abingdon Press, 1990.

Jackson, Joseph Harrison. *A Story of Christian Activism: The History of the National Baptist Convention, U.S.A., Inc.* Nashville: Townsend Press, 1980.

Jacobs, Sylvia M., ed. *Black Americans and the Missionary Movement in Africa*. Westport, Conn.: Greenwood Press, 1982.

Jones, Lawrence T. "Black Pentecostals." In *The Charismatic Movement*, edited by Michael P. Hamilton, 145–58. Grand Rapids: Wm. B, Eerdmans Publishing Co., 1975.

Jones, Major J. *The Color of God: The Concept of God in Afro-American Thought*. Macon, Ga.: Mercer University Press, 1987.

Jones, Miles. *Preaching Papers: The Hampton and Virginia Union Lectures*. New York: Martin Luther King Fellows Press, 1995

Kaufman, Gordon D. "Scripture and Theological Method." *Interpretation* 30 (1976): 299–303.

Kelsey, David H. *The Uses of Scripture in Recent Theology*. Philadelphia: Fortress Press, 1975.

Kennedy, George A. *Classical Rhetoric and Its Christian and Secular Tradition from Ancient to Modern Times*. Chapel Hill: University of North Carolina Press, 1980.

Kerr, Hugh T., ed. *Sons of the Prophets*. Princeton, N.J.: Princeton University Press, 1963.

Kilgore, Thomas, with Jini Kilgore Ross. *A Servant's Journey: The Life and Work of Thomas Kilgore*. Valley Forge, Pa.: Judson Press, 1998

Knight, Carolyn Ann. "If Thou be a Great People." In *Patterns of Preaching: A Sermon Sampler*, edited by Ronald J. Allen, 225–30. St. Louis: Chalice Press, 1998.

Kraus, Hans-Joachim. *Psalms 1–59: A Commentary*. Translated by Hilton C. Oswald. Minneapolis: Augsburg Publishing House, 1988.

LaRue, Cleophus J., Jr. "What Makes Black Preaching Distinctive? An Investigation Based on Selected African-American Sermons from 1865–1915 in Relation to the Hermeneutical Discussion of David Kelsey." Ph.D. diss., Princeton Theological Seminary, 1996.

Leith, John H. *Introduction to the Reformed Tradition*. Atlanta: John Knox Press, 1981.

Levine, Lawrence. *Black Culture and Black Consciousness: Afro-American Folk Thought from Slavery to Freedom*. New York: Oxford University Press, 1977.

Lincoln, C. Eric, and Lawrence Mamiya. *The Black Church in the African American Experience*. Durham, N.C.: Duke University Press, 1990.

————. ed., *The Black Experience in Religion*. Garden City, N.Y.: Doubleday & Co., Anchor Books, 1974.

Lischer, Richard. *The Preacher King: Martin Luther King, Jr. and the Word That Moved America*. New York: Oxford University Press, 1995.

————. "The Word That Moves: The Preaching of Martin Luther King, Jr." *Theology Today* 46 (July 1989): 172–82.

Lofton, Fred C., ed. *Our Help in Ages Past: Sermons from Morehouse*. Elgin, Ill.: Progressive National Baptist Convention, 1987.

Logan, Rayford W. *The Betrayal of the Negro*. New York: Collier Books, 1954.

————. *The Negro in American Life and Thought: The Nadir, 1877–1901*. New York: Dial Press, 1954.

Long, Thomas G. "The Use of Scripture in Contemporary Preaching." *Interpretation* (October 1990): 345–52.

————. *Preaching and the Literary Forms of the Bible*. Philadelphia: Fortress Press, 1989.

Lord, Albert B. *The Singer of Tales*. Cambridge, Mass.: Harvard University Press, 1964.

Lovell, John, Jr. *Black Song: The Forge and the Flame*. New York: Macmillan Co, 1972.

Luker, Ralph E. *The Social Gospel in Black and White*. Chapel Hill: University of North Carolina Press, 1991.

Marable, Manning. *W. E. B. DuBois: Black Radical Democrat*. Boston: Twayne Publishers, 1986.

Martin, Janet. "Metaphor Amongst Tropes." *Religious Studies* 17 (March 1981): 55–66.

Martin, Sandy Dwayne. "Black Baptists, Foreign Missions, and African Colonization, 1814–1882." In *Black Americans and the Missionary Movement in Africa*, edited by Sylvia M. Jacobs, 63–76. Westport, Conn.: Greenwood Press, 1982.

Massey, James Earl. *The Responsible Pulpit*. Anderson, Ind.: Warner Press, 1974.

————. *Designing the Sermon: Order and Movement in Preaching*. Nashville: Abingdon Press, 1980.

Mathews, Donald G. *Religion in the Old South*. Chicago: University of Chicago Press, 1977.

Mays, Benjamin. *The Negro's God*. Boston: Chapman & Grimes, 1938.

Mays, Benjamin and Joseph W. Nicholson. *The Negro's Church*. New York: Negro Universities Press, 1969.

McCartney, John C. *Black Power Ideologues*. Philadelphia: Temple University Press, 1992.

McCasland, S. Vernon. "Some New Testament Metonyms for God." *Journal of Biblical Literature* 68 (1949): 99–113.

McClain, William B. *Come Sunday: The Liturgy of Zion*. Nashville: Abingdon Press, 1990.

————. "African-American Preaching." In *The Renewal of Sunday Worship, Vol. 3*, edited by Robert E. Webber, 315–19. Nashville: Star Song Publishing Group, 1993.

McFague, Sally. *Metaphorical Theology*. Philadelphia: Fortress Press, 1982.

McIntyre, John. "Scripture, Authority, and Tradition." *One in Christ* 20 (1984): 320–24.

McNeill, John T. *A History of the Cure of Souls*. New York: Harper & Brothers, 1951.

Meier, August. *Negro Thought in America, 1880–1915*. Ann Arbor: University of Michigan Press, 1969.

Melloh, John A. "Publish or Perish: A Review of Preaching Literature, 1981–86." *Worship* 62 (November 1988): 498–514.

Miller, Keith D. *Voice of Deliverance: The Language of Martin Luther King, Jr. and Its Sources*. New York: Free Press, 1992.

Mitchell, Ella, ed. *Those Preaching Women: More Sermons by Black Women Preachers*. Valley Forge, Pa.: Judson Press, 1995.

Mitchell, Henry. *Black Preaching*. San Francisco: Harper & Row, 1970.

———. *Celebration and Experience in Preaching*. Nashville: Abingdon Press, 1990.

Mitchell, Mozella. "Pro-vi-dence." In *Those Preaching Women: More Sermons by Black Women Preachers*, edited by Ella Mitchell, 48–54. Valley Forge, Pa.: Judson Press, 1995.

Morris, Elias Camp, ed. *Sermons, Addresses and Reminiscences and Important Correspondence*. Nashville: National Baptist Publishing Board, 1901.

———. "1899 Presidential Address to the National Baptist Convention." In *Afro-American Religious History: A Documentary Witness*, edited by Milton C. Sernett, 272–84. Durham: Duke University Press, 1985.

———. "1900 Presidential Address to the National Baptist Convention." In *The President Speaks*, edited by Marvin C. Griffin, 29–42. Nashville: National Baptist Convention of America, 1989.

———. "1914 Presidential Address to the National Baptist Convention." In *The President Speaks*, edited by Marvin C. Griffin, 65–76. Nashville: National Baptist Convention of America, 1989.

———. "The Brotherhood of Man." In *Sermons, Addresses and Reminiscences and Important Correspondence*, edited by Elias C. Morris, 36–40. Nashville: National Baptist Publishing Board, 1901.

Moses, Wilson J. "Civilizing Missionary: A Study of Alexander Crummell." *The Journal of Negro History* 60 (April 1975): 229–43.

———. *The Golden Age of Black Nationalism, 1850–1925*. New York: Oxford University Press, 1978.

———. *Alexander Crummell: A Study of Civilization and Discontent*. New York: Oxford University Press, 1989.

———. ed. *Destiny and Race ... Selected Writings, 1840–1898*. Amherst, Mass.: University of Massachusetts Press, 1992.

Moyd, Olin P. "Elements in Black Preaching." *The Journal of Religious Thought* 30 (1975): 52–62.

———. *The Sacred Art: Preaching and Theology in the African American Tradition*. Valley Forge, Pa.: Judson Press, 1995.

Murphy, Larry G., J. Gordon Melton, and Gary L. Ward, eds. *Encyclopedia of African American Religions*. New York: Garland Publishing, 1993.

Myers, William H. *The Irresistible Urge to Preach: A Collection of African American "Call" Stories*. Atlanta: Aaron Press, 1992.

Newbold, Robert T., Jr., ed. *Black Preaching: Select Sermons in the Presbyterian Tradition*. Philadelphia: Geneva Press, 1977.

Nineham, Dennis. Review of *The Uses of Scripture in Recent Theology*, David A. Kelsey. *Journal of Theological Studies* 28 (1977): 269–72.

Noll, Mark A. "Pietism." In *The Evangelical Dictionary of Theology*, edited by Walter A. Elwell, 855–56. Grand Rapids: Baker Book House, 1985.

Olmstead, Clifton E. "Francis J. Grimké: Christian Moralist and Civil Rights." In *Sons of the Prophets: Leaders in Protestantism from Princeton Seminary*. edited by Hugh T. Kerr, 161–75. Princeton, N.J.: Princeton University Press, 1963.

Palmer, Richard E. *Hermeneutics: Interpretation Theory in Schleiermacher, Dilthey, Heidegger, and Gadamer*. Evanston, Ill. Northwestern University, 1969.

Paris, Peter J. *Black Religious Leaders: Conflict in Unity*. Louisville, Ky.: Westminster/John Knox Press, 1991.

Patterson, A. Louis, Jr. *Prerequisites for a Good Journey*. St. Louis: Hodale Press, 1994.

Payne, Daniel Alexander. *Recollections of Seventy Years*. Nashville: Publishing House of the A.M.E. Sunday School Union, 1888.

————. "Welcome to the Ransomed, or, Duties of the Colored Inhabitants of the District of Columbia," 1–16. Baltimore: Bull & Tuttle, 1862.

Payne, Wardell J., ed. *Directory of African American Religious Bodies.* Washington, D.C.: Howard University Press, 1991.

Peck, Catherine L. "Your Daughters Shall Prophesy: Women in the Afro-American Preaching Tradition." In *Diversities of Gifts: Field Studies in Southern Religion*, edited by Ruel W. Tyson, Jr., James L. Peacock, and Daniel W. Patterson, 143–56. Urbana, Ill.: University of Illinois Press, 1988.

Pelt, Owen D., and Ralph Lee Smith. *The Story of the National Baptists*. New York: Vantage Press, 1960.

Pennington, J. W. C. "A Two Years' Absence or a Farewell Sermon, Preached in the Fifth Congregational Church," 1845. The Moorland-Spingarn Collection. Howard University, Washington, D.C.

Pinckney, Alphonso. *Black Americans*. Eaglewood Cliffs, New Jersey: Prentice-Hall, 1969.

Pipes, William H. *Say Amen, Brother! Old-Time Negro Preaching: A Study in American Frustration*. New York: William-Frederick Press, 1951.

Pitts, Walter F. *Old Ship of Zion: The Afro-Baptist Ritual in the African Diaspora*. New York: Oxford University Press, 1993.

Pleasure, Mose, Jr., and Fred C. Lofton, eds. *Living in Hell: The Dilemma of African-American Survival*. Grand Rapids: Zondervan Publishing House, 1995.

Proctor, Samuel D. *Preaching about Crises in the Community*. Philadelphia: Westminister Press, 1988.

————. *The Certain Sound of the Trumpet: Crafting a Sermon of Authority*. Valley Forge, Pa.: Judson Press, 1994.

Rabinowitz, Howard N., ed. *Southern Black Leaders of the Reconstruction Era*. Urbana: University of Illinois Press, 1978.

Raboteau, Albert J. *Slave Religion: The "Invisible Institution" in the Antebellum South*. New York: Oxford University Press, 1978.

————. "The Black Experience in American Evangelicalism: The Meaning of Slavery." In *The Evangelical Tradition in America*, edited by Leonard I. Sweet, 181–97. Macon, Ga.: Mercer University Press, 1984.

————. "Black Christianity in North America." In *Encyclopedia of the American Religious Experience*, edited by Charles H. Lippy and Peter W. Williams, 635–48. Vol. 1. New York: Charles Scribner's Sons, 1988.

————. "African-Americans, Exodus, and the American Israel." In *A Fire in the Bones*, 17–36. Boston: Beacon Press, 1995.

————. *A Fire in the Bones: Reflections on African-American Religious History*. Boston: Beacon Press, 1995.

Ray, Sandy. *Journeying Through a Jungle*. Nashville: Broadman Press, 1979.

Reid, Stephen B. *Experience and Tradition: A Primer in Black Biblical Hermeneutics*. Nashville: Abingdon Press, 1990.

Rhodes, Arnold B. *The Mighty Acts of God*. Richmond: Covenant Life Curriculum Press, 1974.

Roberts, J. Deotis. *The Prophethood of Black Believers: An African-American Political Theology for Ministry*. Louisville, Ky.: Westminster/John Knox Press, 1994.

Rosenberg, Bruce A. *Can These Bones Live? The Art of the American Folk Preacher*. New York: Oxford University Press, 1970.

Sandidge, Oneal C. "The Uniqueness of Black Preaching." *The Journal of Religious Thought* 49 (summer–fall 1992): 91–97.

Scott, Manuel L. *From a Black Brother*. Nashville: Broadman Press, 1971.

————. *The Gospel for the Ghetto*. Nashville: Abingdon Press, 1973.

Sernett, Milton G., ed. *Afro-American Religious History: A Documentary Witness*. Durham, N.C.: Duke University Press, 1985.

Simmons, Charitey. "Leaders for Black Churches." *Christian Century* 112 (February 1995): 100–102.

Simmons, Martha J., ed. *Preaching on the Brink: The Future of Preaching*. Nashville: Abingdon Press, 1996.

Smith, C. S. *Sermons Delivered by Bishop Daniel A. Payne*. Nashville: Publishing House of the A.M.E. Sunday School Union, 1888.

Smith, Kelly Miller. *Social Crisis Preaching*. Macon, Ga.: Mercer University Press, 1984.

Sobel, Mechal. *Trabelin' On*. Princeton, N.J.: Princeton University Press, 1988.

———. *The World They Made Together: Black and White Values in Eighteenth-Century Virginia*. Princeton, N.J.: Princeton University Press, 1987.

Spain, Rufus B. *At Ease in Zion: A Social History of Southern Baptists, 1865–1900*. Nashville: Vanderbilt University Press, 1961.

Spencer, Jon Michael. *Sacred Symphony: The Chanted Sermon of the Black Preacher*. Westport, Conn.: Greenwood Press, 1987.

Spillers, Hortense J. "Martin Luther King and the Style of the Black Sermon." In *The Black Experience in Religion*, edited by C. Eric Lincoln, 69–94. Garden City, N.Y.: Doubleday & Co., Anchor Books, 1974.

———. "Moving on Down the Line." *American Quarterly* 40 (March 1988): 83–109.

Stewart, Carlyle Fielding. *Joy Songs, Trumpet Blasts, and Hallelujah Shouts!: Sermons in the African American Preaching Tradition*. Lima, Ohio: CSS Publishing Co., 1997.

Stewart, Warren H. *Interpreting God's Word in Black Preaching*. Valley Forge, Pa.: Judson Press, 1984.

Sweet, Leonard I., ed. *The Evangelical Tradition in America*. Macon, Ga.: Mercer University Press, 1984.

Taylor, Gardner C. *How Shall They Preach*. Elgin, Ill.: Progressive Baptist Publishing House, 1977.

TeSelle, Eugene. "The Uses of Scripture: A Logical and Some Historical Questions." *The Journal of Religion* 57 (1977): 81–85.

Thomas, Emil M. "Self-Esteem and the Black Pulpit: Preaching as the Matrix of Message and Motive in Developing Racial Pride in African-American Churches." D.Min. project, Princeton Theological Seminary, 1991.

Thomas, Frank A. "The Million Man March: A Sermon for Discussion." In *Atonement: The Million Man March*, edited by Kim Martin, 135–37. Cleveland: Pilgrim Press, 1996.

———. *They Like to Never Quit Praisin' God: The Role of Celebration in Preaching*. Cleveland: United Church Press, 1997.

———. "Arrested by the Lord." In *Patterns of Preaching: A Sermon Sampler*, edited by Ronald J. Allen, 43–48. St. Louis: Chalice Press, 1998.

Thomas, Gerald L. "African American Preaching: The Contribution of Gardner C. Taylor." Ph.D. diss., Southern Baptist Theological Seminary, 1993.

Tinney, James S. "The Miracle of Black Preaching." *Christianity Today* 20 (January 1976): 14–16.

Titon, Jeff Todd, ed. *Give Me This Mountain*. Champaign, Ill.: University of Illinois Press, 1989.

Trimiew, Darryl M., ed. *Out of Mighty Waters: Sermons by African-American Disciples*. St. Louis: Chalice Press, 1994.

Tyson, Ruel W., Jr., James L. Peacock, and Daniel W. Patterson, eds. *Diversities of Gifts: Field Studies in Southern Religion*. Urbana: University of Illinois Press, 1988.

Walker, Clarence. *A Rock in a Weary Land: The African Methodist Episcopal Church During the Civil War and Reconstruction*. Baton Rouge: Louisiana State University Press, 1982.

Walker, Wyatt Tee. *The Soul of Black Worship*. New York: Martin Luther King Fellows Press, 1984.

Washington, James Melvin. *Frustrated Fellowship: The Black Baptist Quest for Social Power*. Macon, Ga.: Mercer University Press, 1986.

———. *Conversations With God: Two Centuries of Prayers by African Americans*. New York: HarperCollins, 1994.

Washington, Joseph R. *Black Religion: The Negro and Christianity in the United States*. Lanham, Md.: University Press of America, 1984.

Waters, Kenneth L., Sr. *Afrocentric Sermons: The Beauty of Blackness in the Bible*. Valley Forge, Pa.: Judson Press, 1993.

Watts, John D. W., ed. *Isaiah 34–66*. Waco, Tex.: Word Books 1987.

West, Cornel. *Prophetic Fragments*. Grand Rapids: Wm. B. Eerdmans Publishing Co., 1988.

Weeks, Louis B. "Racism, World War I and the Christian Life: Francis J. Grimké in the Nation's Capital." In *Black Apostles: Afro-American Clergy Confront the Twentieth Century*, edited by Randall K. Burkett and Richard Newman, 58–59. Boston: G. K. Hall and Co., 1978.

Wheeler, Edward L. *Uplifting the Race: The Black Minister in the New South, 1865–1902*. Lanham, Md.: University Press of America, 1986.

White, Ronald C., Jr. *Liberty and Justice for All: Racial Reform and the Social Gospel (1877–1925)*. New York: Harper & Row, 1990.

Williams, Delores S. *Sisters in the Wilderness. The Challenge of Womanist God-talk*. Maryknoll, N.Y.: Orbis Books, 1983.

Wilmore, Gayraud, and James Cone, eds. *Black Theology: A Documentary History, 1966–1979*. Maryknoll, N. Y.: Orbis Books, 1979.

Wilmore, Gayraud S. *Black Religion and Black Radicalism: An Interpretation of the Religious History of Afro-American People*. Maryknoll, N.Y.: Orbis Books, 1983.

———. ed. *African American Religious Studies: An Interdisciplinary Anthology*. Durham, N.C.: Duke University Press, 1989.

Wilson, Paul Scott. *The Practice of Preaching*. Nashville: Abingdon Press, 1995.

Wimbush, Vincent L. "Biblical Historical Study as Liberation: Toward and Afro-Christian Hermeneutic." *The Journal of Religious Thought* 42 (1985–86): 9–14.

Woodson, Carter G. *The History of the Negro Church*. Washington, D.C.: Associated Publishers, 1921.

Woodson, Carter G., ed. *The Works of Francis J. Grimké*. Vol. 1, *Sermons*. Washington, D.C.: Associated Publishers, Inc., 1942.

Wright, G. E. *God Who Acts: Biblical Theology as Recital*. London: SCM Press, 1960.

Wright, Jeremiah A., Jr. *What Makes You So Strong?: Sermons of Joy and Strength from Jeremiah A. Wright, Jr.* Valley Forge, Pa.: Judson Press, 1993.

———. *Good News! Sermons of Hope for Today's Families*. Valley Forge, Pa.: Judson Press, 1995.

Young, Henry J., ed. *Preaching on Suffering and a God of Love*. Philadelphia: Fortress Press, 1978.

———. *Preaching the Gospel*. Philadelphia: Fortress Press, 1977.

ACKNOWLEDGMENTS
OF COPYRIGHTED MATERIAL

INDEX

3163719

Made in the USA